POLITICAL THEOLOGY TODAY

Also Available from Bloomsbury

Apocalyptic Political Theology: Hegel, Taubes and Malabou, Thomas Lynch
Unnatural Theology: Religion, Art and Media after the Death of God, Charlie Gere
Genealogies of Political Modernity, Antonio Cerella
Another Finitude: Messianic Vitalism and Philosophy, Agata Bielik-Robson
The Phenomenology of Religious Belief: Media, Philosophy, and the Arts, Michael J. Shapiro
Theological Poverty in Continental Philosophy: After Christian Theology, Colby Dickinson

POLITICAL THEOLOGY TODAY

100 Years after Carl Schmitt

Edited by
Mitchell Dean, Lotte List and
Stefan Schwarzkopf

BLOOMSBURY ACADEMIC
LONDON • NEW YORK • OXFORD • NEW DELHI • SYDNEY

BLOOMSBURY ACADEMIC
Bloomsbury Publishing Plc
50 Bedford Square, London, WC1B 3DP, UK
1385 Broadway, New York, NY 10018, USA
29 Earlsfort Terrace, Dublin 2, Ireland

BLOOMSBURY, BLOOMSBURY ACADEMIC and the Diana logo are trademarks of Bloomsbury Publishing Plc

First published in Great Britain 2023
This paperback edition published in 2024

Copyright © Mitchell Dean, Lotte List, Stefan Schwarzkopf and Contributors, 2023

Mitchell Dean, Lotte List and Stefan Schwarzkopf have asserted their right under the Copyright, Designs and Patents Act, 1988, to be identified as Editors of this work.

Series design by Charlotte Daniels
Cover image: Christ Crowning King Roger II of Sicily (1093-1154) (mosaic).
La Martorana, Palermo, Sicily, Italy (© imageBROKER / Alamy)

All rights reserved. No part of this publication may be reproduced or transmitted in any form or by any means, electronic or mechanical, including photocopying, recording, or any information storage or retrieval system, without prior permission in writing from the publishers.

Bloomsbury Publishing Plc does not have any control over, or responsibility for, any third-party websites referred to or in this book. All internet addresses given in this book were correct at the time of going to press. The author and publisher regret any inconvenience caused if addresses have changed or sites have ceased to exist, but can accept no responsibility for any such changes.

A catalogue record for this book is available from the British Library.

A catalog record for this book is available from the Library of Congress.

ISBN: HB: 978-1-3503-4451-8
PB: 978-1-3503-4450-1
ePDF: 978-1-3503-4452 5
eBook: 978-1-3503-4453-2

Typeset by Deanta Global Publishing Services, Chennai, India

To find out more about our authors and books visit www.bloomsbury.com and sign up for our newsletters.

CONTENTS

List of contributors — vii

INTRODUCTION: WHITHER POLITICAL THEOLOGY? — 1
Mitchell Dean, Lotte List and Stefan Schwarzkopf

Part 1
STATE, DEMOCRACY AND VIOLENCE

Chapter 1
WHAT'S LEFT OF CARL SCHMITT'S *POLITICAL THEOLOGY*? — 13
Mitchell Dean

Chapter 2
THE POPULIST PROMISE IN CARL SCHMITT'S POLITICAL THEOLOGY — 30
Tim Christiaens

Chapter 3
POLITICAL ATHEISM: TOWARDS A PROFANE RECONCEPTUALIZATION OF THE MODERN STATE — 45
Mikkel Flohr

Part 2
THEOLOGY, RELIGION AND THE PUBLIC SPHERE

Chapter 4
RITUALS OF TRUTH: OATH, PUBLIC DISCUSSION, ACCLAMATION — 63
Montserrat Herrero

Chapter 5
ATHEISM, POST-SECULARISM AND THE LEGITIMACY OF DEMOCRACY — 76
Miguel Vatter

Chapter 6
POLITICAL THEOLOGY, VALUES AND LGBTQ+ AS CIVIL RELIGION — 94
Stefan Schwarzkopf

Part 3
MODERNITY, HISTORY AND TIME

Chapter 7
CRISIS SOVEREIGNTY: POLITICAL METAPHYSICS IN CRISIS TIMES   111
Lotte List

Chapter 8
ONE WORLD? HISTORY AND SPACE IN SCHMITT'S POST-WAR
POLITICAL THEOLOGY   125
Nicholas Heron

Chapter 9
EXPLOSIVE PUBLICS IN THE INTERZONES OF POLITICAL THEOLOGY
AND POLITICAL MYTHOLOGY   139
Christiane Mossin

Part 4
BEYOND THE EUROPEAN GAZE

Chapter 10
TOWARDS A POLITICAL THEOLOGY OF POST-COLONIALITY   157
Kwok Pui-lan

Chapter 11
POLITICAL THEOLOGY AND UNCERTAINTY IN INTERNATIONAL
RELATIONS   171
William Bain

CODA TO PART 4: ASIA AND THE POLITICAL THEOLOGY TURN:
REVISITING AND OVERCOMING SCHMITT IN THE CENTENARY   185
Milinda Banerjee

Index   192

CONTRIBUTORS

William Bain is professor at the Department of Political Science, National University of Singapore. He is editor-in-chief of *International Relations* and the author of several books, most recently *Political Theology of International Order* (2020).

Milinda Banerjee is a lecturer at the School of History, University of St Andrews, Scotland. He is an associate editor of the journal *Political Theology* and the author of *The Mortal God: Imagining the Sovereign in Colonial India* (2018).

Tim Christiaens is assistant professor at the Department of Philosophy, Tilburg University. He has published on neoliberalism and political and economic theology and has a book on workers' autonomy in the gig economy forthcoming at Rowman & Littlefield.

Mitchell Dean is professor of public governance and head of the Department of Management, Politics and Philosophy, Copenhagen Business School. He has published on political and economic theology and is the author and editor of nine previous books, including *The Signature of Power: Sovereignty, Governmentality and Biopolitics* (2013) and, with Daniel Zamora, *The Last Man Takes LSD: Foucault and the End of Revolution* (2021).

Mikkel Flohr is a postdoctoral research fellow at the Department of Social Sciences and Business, Roskilde University. His PhD thesis examined Karl Marx's unfinished critique of political theology and he has published on Marxism and critical theory.

Nicholas Heron is a research fellow at the Institute for Advanced Studies in the Humanities, the University of Queensland. He is the author of *Liturgical Power: Between Economic and Political Theology* (2018).

Montserrat Herrero is professor of political philosophy at the University of Navarra. She is the editor-in-chief of *Anuario Filosófico* and is the author of several books, including *The Political Discourse of Carl Schmitt: A Mystic of Order* (2015).

Kwok Pui-lan is dean's professor of systematic theology at Candler School of Theology, Emory University. She is the author and editor of numerous books, most recently *Postcolonial Politics and Theology* (2021) and *The Hong Kong Protests and Political Theology* (2021).

Lotte List is a PhD fellow at the Department of Management, Politics and Philosophy, Copenhagen Business School. Her PhD thesis examines crisis theory and political metaphysics and she has published on historical materialism and political theology.

Christiane Mossin is an external lecturer at the Department of Management, Politics and Philosophy, Copenhagen Business School. Her PhD thesis examined the interzones of law and metaphysics, and she has published on law, democracy and civil society.

Stefan Schwarzkopf is associate professor at the Department of Management, Politics and Philosophy, Copenhagen Business School. He has published widely on political and economic theology and is the editor of *The Routledge Handbook of Economic Theology* (2019).

Miguel Vatter is professor in political science at the Alfred Deakin Institute for Citizenship and Globalisation, Deakin University. His most recent books are *Divine Democracy: Political Theology after Carl Schmitt* (2021) and *Living Law: Jewish Political Theology from Hermann Cohen to Hannah Arendt* (2021).

INTRODUCTION

WHITHER POLITICAL THEOLOGY?

Mitchell Dean, Lotte List and Stefan Schwarzkopf

Leaving the thorn unremoved

A hundred years have passed since German jurist and political theorist Carl Schmitt (1888–1985) published a smallish book entitled *Political Theology* (1922). In it, Schmitt defined political theology in analytical terms: 'all significant concepts of the modern theory of the state are secularized theological concepts'. This dictum led Schmitt to reformulate political theology both as a research programme for a sociology of juridical concepts and as an epistemology for a critique of a then widely shared belief in secularization. In political terms, this definition of political theology also lent itself to a much more foundational attack on liberalism, representational democracy and parliamentarianism. Schmitt argued that there existed a correlation between the metaphysical world view of an epoch and its sociopolitical structure. It was this correlation, expressed as it was in analogies between theological and constitutional concepts, that held an epoch 'together' and provided meaning and structure to its macro-political arrangements. Since liberalism had privatized religion and disavowed the relevance of theology in public life, it was unable to furnish itself with a transcendent foundation. What was left was a state that misunderstood itself as a rule-bound machinery ('ein grosser Betrieb') and a society that believed it could avoid realistic acceptance of sovereignty and of the necessity to make decisions by instead engaging in constant conversation ('ein ewiges Gespräch').

Schmitt's little book, more a brochure some eighty pages long, has remained a thorn in the side of both secular political thought and of various schools of theological thought. Hannah Arendt tellingly scribbled a note in her copy of Schmitt's *Political Theology*, in which she linked Schmitt's notion of the decision to disaster and arbitrariness (Grosser 2021: 299). For theologians, too, Schmitt's move to put the state on the one hand, and religion and church on the other hand, into an unavoidable relationship of legitimation meant that they could not hope to separate the political from the theological. Schmitt's challenge was taken up by numerous German theologians already before the end of the Second World War, and even more so during the 1960s and 1970s (Taubes 1983-7). Some of these debates enticed Schmitt to reissue his thesis about the unavoidability of the theological and the ubiquity of the political in a long afterword, which appeared in 1970 as *Political Theology II*. In it, Schmitt dealt with what he called the legend of the termination and mootness of all political theology ('Die Legende der Erledigung') and pushed his earlier identification of an inevitable mutual entanglement between theology and politics even further: the ceremonial and acclamatory character of religion creates publicness and public space in the first place (Schmitt 2008: 40–1). Against his theological critics in particular, Schmitt maintained that a church does not consist only of theologians but exists in the world, so that clear separations between two realms, the two swords of the spiritual and the earthly, were impossible to keep up: 'Then the walls tumble, and what had been separate rooms begin to permeate and beam through each other like in the labyrinths of an illuminated architecture' (Schmitt 2008: 68).

Despite Schmitt's attempt to close the debate in 1970, political theology is decidedly not a given. Doubts as to its very possibility always remained (Wiedenhofer 1975). These doubts were levelled against Schmitt even during his lifetime, and by both theologians and non-theologians. Schmitt's erstwhile friend, the church historian and theologian Erik Peterson, used patristic theology to deny the logical possibility of a political theology in the modern era. The German philosopher Hans Blumenberg, who became a late penfriend of Schmitt, attacked his take on the secularization thesis by producing an entire monograph on the legitimacy of modernity (Gereby 2008; Schmitz and Lepper 2007). As a field of academic inquiry, political theology continues to provoke and require explanation as well as justification. The very mentioning of the concept – let alone the mentioning of Schmitt's name – can create suspicions. For some, political theology remains a dangerous project that mingles transcendent demands with political affairs, a mix that is in danger of fuelling violence and divisions (Boucher 2007). In as much as modern societies both naturally assume and vitally require a separation of religion and politics, political theology is seen as something regressive, as a primordial relapse behind modern standards of rational discourse (Sajo 2008).

Yet, a number of recent publications on political theology attest to a burgeoning interest in the analytical value of the concept itself. After witnessing heated debates mostly in the German-speaking world during the 1960s and 1970s, the concept fell somewhat into oblivion. In the last two decades, however, and no doubt related to the events of 11 September 2001 and the unfolding resurgence of violent religious struggle on the stage of world politics, the concept has undergone a strong revival in the English-speaking literature. In many ways, political theology has left behind the confines of being a mere concept and has become a *field* of research in political philosophy and political theory in its own right, and even a *paradigm* within the humanities and social sciences. Studies in the theological subcurrents of politics, international relations, constitutional theory, political economy and social life continue to proliferate (Agamben 2011; Arvidsson, Brännström and Minkkinen 2015; de Vries and Sullivan 2006; Esposito 2015; Hammill and Lupton 2012; Kahn 2009; Kahn 2011; Kahn 2014; Kotsko 2018; Newman 2019; Diamantides and Schütz 2017). Since 1999, the publisher Taylor & Francis has devoted a journal to the field (*Political Theology*), and Bloomsbury Academic started its series on *Political*

Theologies in 2018. Two handbooks exist (Cavanaugh and Scott 2019; Hovey and Phillips 2015), two readers (Cavanaugh, Bailey and Hovey 2011; Phillips, Rowland and Daughton 2021) and there is even a *Guide for the Perplexed* (Phillips 2012).

The problem of Carl Schmitt

Our anthology builds on the research trend just outlined. At this moment, it is a timely publication revisiting a chronically untimely author. It would be an understatement to say that Schmitt was doubtlessly a controversial figure who wrote on controversial subjects. None of the authors in this volume underestimate the charge sheet that could be drawn up against Schmitt, and for many of us these charges are the motivation for our reconsidering his thought and legacy in relation to the emergence of political theology as a field of study.

It is well known that the charge sheet would include Schmitt's decision to join the Nazi Party, membership number 2098860, effective the first of May 1933, three months after Hitler came to power. It includes his legal and constitutional work on behalf of the regime, his public 'jurisprudential' defence of its early murderous actions and his acceptance of the office of Prussian state councillor. However, when reading his authoritative biographer Reinhard Mehring, it is difficult to imagine a more shocking intellectual and moral debasement for a jurist and political thinker than his efforts in 1936. From a position of leadership in the Association of National Socialist German Jurists, Schmitt planned and organized a conference on 'Judaism in Jurisprudence' (Mehring 2014: 341–6). The Jews were not capable of rational juristic thought, Schmitt argued, because they were without soil, state or church. In his concluding address, he suggested that the 'scientific insight of our conference' was that they were a threat to healthy *völkisch*-German thinking from two apparently antithetical directions: 'Jewish chaos and Jewish legality'; 'anarchist nihilism and positivist normativism', 'sensual materialism and abstract moralism'. He proposed that Jewish authors not be compared with others and that all their books taken out of libraries and placed in a guarded 'Judaica' section. They should only be cited with prefatory remarks about their enemy status, he concluded. The proximity of these remarks to the Nuremberg Laws on the flag, citizenship and the protection of 'German blood and honour', promulgated at the conclusion of the NSDAP rally in 1935, which he publicly defended, intensifies their abomination.

Schmitt's later defence of such actions, if we can call it that, was that he, like many in the intelligentsia, was a captive of the Nazi system and that it is impossible for an outsider to judge the meaning of his conduct. Many have pointed to his almost simultaneous denunciation by the SS in *Das Schwarze Korps* as an opportunist, warning him to cease parading as a Nazi (Schwab 2008: xxxix). Schmitt clearly feared for his physical security and for his life. In this respect, he likened himself as early as 1938 to Benito Cereno, the captive captain of the slave ship taken over by the slaves in Herman Melville's eponymous novel, whose conduct was first subject to the misjudgement of an American frigate's captain (Schmitt 2017: 22; Strong 2005). In the winter of 1945–6, while detained in an Allied camp, he would cite the Hobbesian exchange of protection for obedience, and claim, that under the conditions of civil war, he opted for what Andreas Kalyvas and Federico Finchelstein have called a 'prudential act of survival under totalitarian domination' (2017: 6). Needless to say, none of this amounts to sufficient justification, let alone redemption of Schmitt, for his absurd pseudo-scientific theorization of anti-Semitism in the context of what was then an explicitly and violently racist regime. This is why we must say that today it is Schmitt who requires prefatory remarks about his enemy status.

Nevertheless, his work does not cease to influence contemporary political thinkers from the whole range of the political spectrum, including the left (Booth and Baert 2018; Mouffe 1999; Müller 2003). Étienne Balibar has argued that we find in Schmitt 'one of the most inventive, provocative and representative bodies of thought of the twentieth century' – and to turn away from this problematic work because of its political implications would condemn us 'at best to stupidity and at worst to impotence' (2017: 38). And Jürgen Habermas, a bastion of modern rationalist thought, surprisingly dedicates the first chapter of his recent monumental history of philosophy *Auch eine Geschichte der Philosophie* to an argument against first and foremost Schmitt, along with other 'thinkers of crisis'. By the end of the book, Habermas writes, he hopes to have proven Schmitt's account of modernity wrong (2019: 70). It is telling that Habermas, in 2019, would find a 1,700 pages-long refutation of Schmitt necessary.

Our book aims at providing readers with insights into the reasons for this continued fascination as well as its possible pitfalls. As editors, we are thus not engaging in an uncritical 'anniversary' celebration, but hoping to provide a critical assessment of the intellectual afterlife and possible uses of the concept of political theology one hundred years after Schmitt's eponymous book. Centenaries of major works often cause people to reread and re-evaluate these works and their authors. Our anthology not only acts as a source and first point of reference for these debates, but also provides directions for some necessary reinterpretations of Schmitt's *Political Theology*. That these reinterpretations and perhaps even full-on intellectual assaults on his work are necessary is beyond question. Political controversy is unavoidable with an author whom some see 'as the "godfather" of political theology, and others . . . as the one of its most impeachable distorters' (Phillips 2012: 5). Schmitt once wrote of the conservative statesman Juan Donoso Cortés that his name rung in the echo of catastrophe, in the sense that he would posthumously resurface in public debate every time there was a major societal crisis. Today, the same might be said of Schmitt himself. In a time of rapidly succeeding moments of crisis – the global financial crisis, the ensuing refugee crisis in Europe and global border conflicts, followed by a viral pandemic since 2019, the violent storming of the Capitol in January 2021, the return of the Taliban in Kabul – a theory of political power through and in the state of exception is as pressing as ever. For the past two decades, cataclysmic events have reanimated conflicts over the role of the state, the power-balance between nations and inter- or transnational institutions, as well as the political power of opposing religions. As Schmitt wrote, it is not the normal situation but the exception that teaches us how our political system 'normally' works.

With this anthology, we wish to ask how the conceptual framework of political theology may serve to analyse our political conjuncture today. Has politics finally become demystified, or do we still find theological structures of thought within political institutions? And how do we make sense of the concept itself: is it merely a thesis on the parallelism of transcendent divinity and absolute sovereignty, or might we also apply the concept to address different forms of transcendence within political institutions, theological genealogies of political concepts, metaphysics of politics and the liturgies of political rituals? Is 'political theology' a theo-political programme or an analytical strategy? It is with such questions that our anthology engages. For the contributors to this volume, 'political theology' may be treated as an object of study, an analytical tool, or a field or framework of research, according to various interpretations that find support in Schmitt's own body of work. They approach political theology from a variety of perspectives, exploring these different lines of interrogation and more, expanding on the concept rather than narrowing it down to some final and unidimensional definition. Marking the centenary of Schmitt's arguably most important work, we invite readers to rediscover the notion of political theology, and to think both with and against Schmitt. Our authors assess the state of political theology today, its usefulness as a concept and its functions in national, international and global politics. Embarking on this task necessarily means to be critical with Schmitt's perspectives and their limitations. Various postcolonial, post-secular, post-liberal turns in social and political theory have all created renewed interest in Schmitt's work and in the possibility of political theology. Yet, these turns have also created sensibilities that would make any uncritical reading of Schmitt untenable.

Political theology as we know it today might have had its moment of foundation in 1922, but it needs critique and updating for a world riven by debates over race, gender and dominant institutional power structures, by a ubiquitous rejection of the previous liberal-democratic settlement and narrative and by the emergence of new forms of civil conflict, terror, war and constellations of massive power on the world stage. This book concerns the significance of political theology today. It is thus neither a question of redeeming its modern progenitor nor one of 'cancelling' Schmitt, as it is called today, which was posed recently in an august journal of international law (Weiler 2021). Rather, it is a matter of overcoming the self-cancellation of political theology Schmitt undertook when, in the address cited previously, he quoted Hitler: 'In fending off the Jew, I fight for the work of the Lord' (Mehring 2014: 345). Schmitt is thus both founder and destroyer of what we seek to explore in this volume.

The contributions

In the winter of 2020–21, the editors organized a virtual seminar series with guest speakers, out of which this anthology emerges. That particular winter was a moment of emergency from the perspective of ordinary academic work. The Covid-19 crisis had caused a total lock-down in many countries – buildings were closed, offices were inaccessible and seminars were cancelled. The only alternative to gather scholars for a conversation was online in a virtual assembly that sought to overcome the tyranny of distance and, today, the more troublesome tyranny of time-zones. As editors, we are grateful that our authors and colleagues attended the seminar series diligently and provided feedback to each other both during the virtual meetings and afterwards during the writing process. The authors included in this anthology represent a diversity of backgrounds, disciplines and academic seniority. Providing a multiplicity of voices on Schmitt and on political theology was an important criterion for us from the beginning of the project. The volume includes both established scholars as well as younger names, and it includes authors from European and North-American universities as well as from Australia and Asia. Our authors reflect a rich background from disciplines such as political philosophy, intellectual history, political theory, international politics and law, sociology and cultural studies, thus demonstrating the impressive variety that exists in the theoretical, epistemological and methodological approaches to political theology today. Each author has produced an innovative reading of the concept of political theology, while adhering to two overall structuring principles: engaging with Carl Schmitt's 1922 *Political Theology*, and assessing the relevance of the concept of political theology for our own present. The chapters are grouped under four headlines, which represent major roadways into analysing Schmitt's *Political Theology* and its relevance today.

In Part 1, entitled 'State, Democracy and Violence', chapters by Mitchell Dean, Tim Christiaens and Mikkel Flohr situate Carl Schmitt's notion of the political in general, and of political theology in particular, within current debates about a new age of post-democracy, post-liberalism, and the challenges to statecraft posed by rising tides of populism. Dean leads into the section by asking what remains of Schmitt's research programme, and what critical inspiration the Left might take from shifting its own critique of the false religiosity of politics to that of the falsity of a politics that ignores its own underlying theology. He illustrates this problem by the reappearance of public forms of confession and penitence in contemporary anti-racist politics. Christiaens' chapter uses Jan Assmann's and Peter Sloterdijk's explorations in political theology to argue that Schmitt's strategy contains the risk of disseminating violence throughout society, which is today becoming visible in right-wing populism. By developing a sustained critique of the possibilities for violence inherent in Schmitt's project of political theology, Christiaens discloses this violent potential of contemporary right-wing populism as well. Flohr aims to recover the obscured origins of Schmitt's concept of political theology in the works of Mikhail Bakunin. Flohr argues that we need not take Schmitt's concept of political theology for granted, but can (re-)invert Schmitt's political theology to develop a profane account of political theology and its entwinement with the earthly existence of the modern state.

In Part 2, on 'Theology, Religion and the Public Sphere', chapters by Montserrat Herrero, Miguel Vatter and Stefan Schwarzkopf assess the relevance of Carl Schmitt's political theology for contemporary discussions about the democratic sphere, liberal values, public discourse and acclamation. Herrero starts off this section with a chapter on the theo-politics of the oath and the role of oath-taking, public discussion and acclamation rituals in a supposedly a-religious public sphere. Using the conceptual framework of Michel Foucault, Herrero questions how oaths can be sworn in a secularized society in which the absolute witness, God, is absent. Her chapter demonstrates how political theology, as Schmitt claimed, is indispensable for understanding the oath as a central institution of contemporary politics, and how the theological-political pervades the structures of the modern state. Vatter's chapter asks provocatively whether a political theology of democracy is possible. Vatter proposes the hypothesis that the contemporary turn to 'post-secularism' can be understood as a response to Schmitt's challenge by working out a political theology of democracy that is based on radical immanence and atheism. In particular, he argues that post-secular discourse works out such a political theology in the form of a messianic discourse. Schwarzkopf's chapter argues that not only political-constitutional concepts are secularized theological concepts, but that sociocultural concepts can have such a valence, too. Drawing on Schmitt's *Political Theology* and his 1960 essay *The Tyranny of Values*, the chapter uses the LGBTQ+ movement to highlight the structure – but also the limitations – of Schmitt's idea of the immanent aggression that underpins value-oriented political philosophies.

In Part 3, entitled 'Modernity, History and Time', chapters by Lotte List, Nicholas Heron and Christiane Mossin engage with the surprisingly often overlooked historical underpinnings and the time dimensions that Schmitt's 1922 thesis relies on. In her chapter, List argues that Schmitt's theory of sovereignty implies metaphysical considerations, specifically a historico-philosophical conception of modernity as crisis temporality. The sovereign in this conception not only responds to crisis, but is itself dependent on crisis in order to legitimize sovereign power. The chapter demonstrates how Schmitt's concept of sovereignty came to be an important source for Reinhart Koselleck's concept of crisis, which itself has become one of the most important conceptualizations of crisis as a temporal structure. Herons's chapter also focuses on the role of history in Schmitt's post-war political theology, in particular his 1950 *Nomos of the Earth*. Restoring the theological backdrop to a set of ostensibly historiographical claims that Schmitt advances during the 1940s and 1950s, the chapter argues that the particular form of historicism Schmitt advocates remains an expression of his political theology. An underexplored aspect of Schmitt's enduring topicality – namely, his resistance to arguments regarding the end of history – is thereby revealed to have a political-theological basis. Mossin's chapter offers an interpretation of the foundations of Schmitt's political theology while building on his 1956 essay *Hamlet or Hecuba*. The chapter argues that the Hamlet-myth mirrors Schmitt's own myth of modernity: modernity concerns a particular kind of knowledge that resists belief, legitimacy and decision.

In Part 4, entitled 'Beyond the European Gaze', chapters by Kwok Pui-lan and William Bain take Carl Schmitt out of the familiar context of European intellectual history and constitutional politics into what is now often called 'the Global South', and the sphere of international relations. Kwok's chapter employs postcolonial theory to challenge the Eurocentric preoccupation of modern political theology that often begins with Carl Schmitt's work. She advances a postcolonial and comparative approach that addresses the realities of the majority world. Her chapter points to the need to reread Schmitt's legacy from an international framework and reimagine political theology with multiple origins and trajectories. Bain's chapter discusses the concept of 'uncertainty' in international relations. The chapter demonstrates that although Schmitt's *Political Theology* is a crucial starting point for explorations of how to apply political-theological considerations in contemporary international theory, there are ways of thinking about theological analogies other than those prescribed by Schmitt. As a coda to this section, Milinda Banerjee surveys the development of political theology, defined both in terms of the European intellectual tradition derived from Schmitt, and more broadly as the mutual nourishment of political and theological forms, in the study of South and West Asia. As his contribution and this section indicates, the future for political theology may both lie outside, and overturn, its traditional territorial and cultural boundaries.

Political theology: The next 100 years

We do not intend the book which the reader is kind enough to hold in their hands as either a compendium or a handbook. It lacks the comprehensiveness of the former or the directly pedagogical purpose of the latter. It marks two events, the publication of a small book by a then little-known jurist and political theorist a century ago and the gathering of a group of scholars who would 'meet' in extraordinary circumstances and find themselves committed to understanding the meaning of the concept, framework and problematizations posed by the idea of political theology and its relevance to key issues today. This book is definitely not a paean or a homage to a great thinker, and everyone involved in the project continues to struggle with the tension between the productive problems contained in political theology and a thinker whose moral and political choices led him into the 'Reich of the nether demons' as Ernst Niekisch put it (Mehring 2014: 285). Rather, this book should be regarded as an anthology, almost literally in the ancient Greek sense, of a gathering of flowers, of those many kinds which can bloom from such an irreconcilable tension.

For this gathering, we use Carl Schmitt it is true, but only as a starting point. In it, the reader will find an introduction to the diverse and disputed intellectual origins and multiple dimensions of the concept of political theology. More importantly, we try to make sense of political theology as an intelligible intellectual framework and analytical strategy that historians of ideas, political theorists and political scientists, social and cultural theorists and sociologists and, indeed, jurists and theologians, and others, might be able to deploy. In particular, we hope that it enables readers to dig out the presence of the sacred in what is understood as profane, the religious in what presents itself as secular and the metaphysical in a world that considers itself post-metaphysical. We seek a vantage point of understanding the liberalism, secularism and technicism that characterize the now vanishing spaces of modernity, and a point of critique of the impossibility of a pure immanence, of a networked world in which the legitimation of authority would no longer be necessary. Without any preconceived answer, and leaving it open to the judgement of the reader, we ask if political theology, as a concept, field or framework, may cast a light on the more obscure aspects of our present.

References

Agamben, G. (2011), *The Kingdom and the Glory: For a Theological Genealogy of Economy and Government*, Stanford, CA: Stanford University Press.
Arvidsson, M., L. Brännström and P. Minkkinen, eds (2015), *The Contemporary Relevance of Carl Schmitt: Law, Politics, Theology*, Abingdon: Routledge.
Baert, P. and J. Booth (2018), *The Dark Side of Podemos? Carl Schmitt and Contemporary Progressive Populism*, London: Routledge.
Balibar, É. (2017), 'Schmitt's Hobbes, Hobbes's Schmitt', in W. Montag and H. Elsayed (eds), *Balibar and the Citizen Subject*, 37–93, Edinburgh: Edinburgh University Press.
Boucher, G. (2007), 'Against Political Theology', in M. Sharpe, M. Noonan and J. Freddi (eds), *Trauma, History, Philosophy: With Feature Essays*, 267–81, Newcastle: Cambridge Scholars Publishing.
Cavanaugh, W. T., J. W. Bailey and C. Hovey, eds (2011), *An Eerdmans Reader in Contemporary Political Theology*, Grand Rapids, MI: Eerdmans.
Cavanaugh, W. T. and P. M. Scott, eds (2019), *The Wiley Blackwell Companion to Political Theology*, Oxford: Wiley Blackwell.
de Vries, H. and L. E. Sullivan, eds (2006), *Political Theologies: Public Religions in a Post-Secular World*, New York: Fordham University Press.
Diamantides, M. and A. Schütz, eds (2017), *Political Theology: Demystifying the Universal*, Edinburgh: Edinburgh University Press.
Esposito, R. (2015), *Two: The Machine of Political Theology and the Place of Thought*, New York: Fordham University Press.
Gereby, G. (2008), 'Political Theology Versus Theological Politics', *New German Critique*, 105: 7–33.
Grosser, F. (2021), 'On the Abuses and Uses of Political Theology: Schmitt, Arendt and "the Trump Moment"', in D. Finkelde and R. Klein (eds), *In Need of a Master: Politics, Theology, and Radical Democracy*, 285–303, Berlin: de Gruyter.
Habermas, J. (2019), *Auch eine Geschichte der Philosophie. I: Die okzidentale Konstellation von Glauben und Wissen*, Berlin: Suhrkamp.
Hammill, G. and J. Reinhard, eds (2012), *Political Theology and Early Modernity*, Chicago, IL: University of Chicago Press.
Hovey, C. and E. Phillips (2015), *The Cambridge Companion to Christian Political Theology*, Cambridge: Cambridge University Press.
Kahn, P. V. (2011), *Political Theology: Four New Chapters on the Concept of Sovereignty*, New York: Columbia University Press.
Kahn, V. (2009), 'Political Theology and Fiction in *The King's Two Bodies*', *Representations*, 106 (1): 77–101.
Kahn, V. (2014), *The Future of Illusion: Political Theology and Early Modern Texts*, Chicago, IL: University of Chicago Press.

Kalyvas, A. and F. Finchelstein (2017), 'Introduction', in C. Schmitt (ed.), *Ex Captivitate Salus: Experiences, 1945–7*, trans. M. Hannah, Cambridge: Polity Press.
Kotsko, A. (2018), *Neoliberalism's Demons: On the Political Theology of Late Capitalism*, Stanford, CA: Stanford University Press.
Mehring, R. (2014), *Carl Schmitt: a Biography*, trans. Daniel Seuer, Cambridge: Polity Press.
Mouffe, C., ed. (1999), *The Challenge of Carl Schmitt*, London: Verso.
Müller, J.-W. (2003), *A Dangerous Mind: Carl Schmitt in Post-War European Thought*, New Haven, CT: Yale University Press.
Newman, S. (2019), *Political Theology: A Critical Introduction*, Cambridge: Polity Press.
Phillips, E. (2012), *Political Theology: A Guide for the Perplexed*, London: Bloomsbury.
Phillips, E., A. Rowlands and A. Daughton, eds (2021), *T&T Clark Reader in Political Theology*. London: Bloomsbury.
Sajó, A. (2008), 'Preliminaries to a Concept of Constitutional Secularism', *International Journal of Constitutional Law*, 6 (3–4): 605–29.
Schmitt, C. (1922), *Politische Theologie: Vier Kapitel zur Lehre von Souveränität*, München: Duncker und Humblot.
Schmitt, C. (2008), *Politische Theologie II: Die Legende von der Erledigung jeder politischen Theologie*, Berlin: Duncker & Humblot.
Schmitt, C. (2017), *Ex Captivitate Salus: Experiences, 1945–7*, trans M. Hannah, Cambridge: Polity Press.
Schmitz, A. and M. Lepper, eds (2007), *Hans Blumenberg, Carl Schmitt: Briefwechsel 1971–8, und Weitere Materialien*, Frankfurt am Main: Suhrkamp.
Schwab, G. (2008), 'Introduction', in C. Schmitt, *The Leviathan in the State Theory of Thomas Hobbes: Meaning and Failure of a Political Symbol*, trans. G. Schwab and E. Hilfstein, Chicago: University of Chicago Press.
Strong, T. B. (2005), 'Foreword', in C. Schmitt (ed.), *Political Theology: Four Chapters on the Concept of Sovereignty*, trans. G. Schwab, Chicago, IL: University of Chicago Press.
Taubes, J., ed. (1983–7), *Religionstheorie und Politische Theologie*, 3 vols, München, Paderborn: Fink/Schöningh.
Weiler, J. (2021), 'Cancelling Carl Schmitt?'. Available online: https://www.ejiltalk.org/cancelling-carl-schmitt/ (accessed 25 August 2021).
Wiedenhofer, S. (1975), 'Politische Theologie: Entwicklung und Stand der Debatte im deutschen Sprachraum', *Didaskalia*, 5 (2): 221–54.

Part 1

STATE, DEMOCRACY AND VIOLENCE

Chapter 1

WHAT'S LEFT OF CARL SCHMITT'S *POLITICAL THEOLOGY*?

Mitchell Dean

The question 'What's left of Carl Schmitt's *Political Theology*?' raises two problems united by a homonym. First, it seeks to identify what remains today of the classic thesis of 1922 one hundred years later and in what form. Second, it asks us to identify how and to what extent political theology can be a component of critical perspectives on our societies, their present and future. The first part of the chapter then offers an inventory of the theoretical and methodological status of Schmitt's classic thesis to argue for its continued relevance; the second uses a case study, the reappearance of public forms of confession and penitence in contemporary progressive politics, to consider the normative effect of political theology. In conclusion, this chapter seeks to specify what it is that we are doing when we uncover the theological in a political practice or concept and how that can be more than a simple rejection of such a politics as theological or religious. As a prolegomenon to this investigation, we might also ask, with the help of Jan Assmann, what Schmitt did when he enunciated his thesis on political theology.

In an essay on political theology, Assmann (2005: 202) argues that Schmitt reverses a problem with a long lineage: no longer is the problem 'false religion is political', but, rather, that 'true politics is theological' because 'it knows its power comes from God'. For Schmitt, he argues, political theology 'no longer implies a critique of religion but a critique of politics. False politics is denounced by political theology as neglectful of its divine fundaments and origins' (Assmann 2005: 202). Stated less dramatically and without the supposition that Schmitt's intellectual work expresses his own faith, we could amend Assmann's formulation to say that true politics is mindful of its own theological sources and takes responsibility for their mobilization. As I argue here, then, the task of political theology is to make intelligible those sources and thus to increase the moral clarity and, hence, responsibility of styles of political thought and practice.

In ancient and early modern thought, Assmann suggests, political theology is a political term denouncing theology and religion, yet maintaining a recognition of their residual legitimacy. He provides us with a number of examples starting with a play attributed to Euripides, which offers a critique of and apology for religion

(Assmann 2005: 193). In the 'blasphemous mouth' of Sisyphos, the fear of the gods is nothing other than the invention of a shrewd man to keep the evil from doing their wicked deeds. With the historians Polybius and Diodorius Siculus, the assertion of the political function of religion again both legitimizes and criticizes. 'It legitimates religion because it argues that the belief in gods is indispensable for political order and social harmony, and it criticizes it by exposing its fictitious character' (Assmann 2005: 194). The latter would bequeath the idea that the great legislators, among them Moses, would use the strategy of 'the framing of legislation by political theology' (Assmann 2005: 195). This observation would enter early modern thought, according to Assmann, in the fifteenth century with Marsilio Ficino and his concept of ancient sages 'who conveyed to humanity both religion and the rules of social order and civilized life' (2005: 195). Following Spinoza's *Tractatus Theologico-Politicus* of 1670, many early modern thinkers (Assmann cites Toland, Ross and Warburton) use Moses as an example of the intelligent use of religion by the legislator (2005: 195–200). All these thinkers retained a notion of true religion, whether as elite (versus popular) religion, natural religion, biblical religion and esoteric (versus exoteric) religion, and contrasted it with the fictitious religion, which is a political religion or political theology.

We can note that the young Marx in his Introduction to *A Contribution to the Critique of Hegel's Philosophy of Right* (1975: 244) first retains the residual legitimacy of religion even when he coined the phrase 'opium of the people'. This is a passage that will be cited by both Ayatollah Khomeini and Michel Foucault in relation to the Iranian revolution. For Khomeini, the opium claim is introduced by the leftists in Iran to separate Iranians from one another and the Quran (Afary and Anderson 2005: 76). Foucault similarly will report that people in Iran had told him the claim was wrong, or inapplicable to their situation; he suggested that Shi'ism had played an 'undeniable role' in 'political awakening, in maintaining political consciousness, in inciting and fomenting political awareness' (Afary and Anderson 2005: 186). He would recall that Marx has also described religion in the same passage 'as a spirit of a world without spirit' and viewed the Iranian case as one of a 'political spirituality' long lost to the modern West (Afary and Anderson 2005: 266, 209).

Assmann notes that it is only with the anarchic romanticism of Bakunin that political theology 'no longer concedes religion's legitimacy and indispensability as a political fiction' (2005: 201). To Voltaire's 'if God did not exist it would be necessary to invent him', Bakunin replies, 'if God exists, he should be abolished'. Indeed, for Schmitt in *Political Theology*, it was Bakunin who, following Proudhon, wanted to disseminate Satan, and was consequently 'the theologian of the anti-theological and in practice the dictator of an antidictatorship' (Schmitt 1985: 66). As Mikkel Flohr (this volume) argues, Bakunin could be viewed as the central protagonist of *Political Theology* and an originator of the term in the text, 'The Political Theology of Mazzini' (Bakunin 1973: 214–31), a polemic against the Italian Christian republican socialist thinker published posthumously in 1871–2. Underlying its significance for Schmitt (1996: 36), he would cite this pamphlet as 'the remote symbolic skirmish of a colossal, world-historical upheaval'.

If we can put to one side Assmann's obvious anachronism here in his genealogy of the concept of political theology, we can accept the idea that criticism concerned itself, as both condemnation and affirmation, with how religion legitimized a social and political order. While the German left-Hegelians will criticize religion/theology as political, as an alienated projection of the true human essence, the anarchist tradition with Bakunin will reject religion entirely as it rejects the need for any social and political order. Bakunin in this sense destroys the affirmative element of the critique of religion.

Yet, there is a more fundamental question concerning the concept of political theology. Does Assmann's notion of a reversal capture Schmitt's position in this supposed genealogy? Is Schmitt offering an 'affirmative political theology', one that would deduce a proper politics from dogma? What dogma would be the basis of politics for Schmitt? Is his political theology simply satisfied with the act of unmasking as a critique of the pretensions and hypocrisies of the false politics of 'secularism, individualism, democracy, and free market economy, the politics of sovereign, autonomous, this-worldly man, believing himself able to negotiate the principles of truth, order and justice on a totally secular and rational basis', as he put it (Assmann 2005: 202)?

The alternative hypothesis is that Schmitt enunciated a paradigm or an analytical strategy rather than the critique or affirmation of the role of religion in politics. Rather than another twist in this long history and its multiple genealogies in Europe, Asia and beyond (Kwok, this volume), Schmitt's concept of political theology crossed an epistemological threshold in which the critique of religion in politics gave way to a framework or paradigm for thinking about and analysing politics. And, as we shall see, the essential components of this crossing are intact, with criticisms amounting to qualifications and extensions of the analytical apparatus. But even this hypothesis raises another question, or defers another question: what critical effects follow from the analysis of politics through the theological paradigm? Does the critical normativity simply lie in the demonstration offered by political theology rather than an explicit direction? Is political theology more a mode of 'problematization' of representations of the political, as we might put it today, than the positive affirmation of the very foundations of politics?

In any case, in the nineteenth century, thinkers of the 'Left' – Proudhon, Bakunin, Feuerbach, Marx – criticized religion and theology as political, while in the twentieth century and today, their descendants, Walter Benjamin and Giorgio Agamben, have criticized political and social forms, in particular capitalism, consumerism and the market, as theologies and religions. Schmitt seems to inaugurate something else: an analytical framework that problematizes the way we think about and enact politics, especially of the secular, modern, liberal kind, by calling attention to its theological sources and their transposition to the political domain. The task here is the difficult one of specifying the critical value in this move. Thus, we are led to a more fundamental question: *what are we doing when we reveal a political concept or practice to be theological*?

The classic thesis

Let's consider, then, the canonical passage at the beginning of the third chapter of George Schwab's translation of Schmitt's 1922 book:

> All significant concepts of the modern theory of the state are secularized theological concepts not only because of their historical development – in which they were transferred from theology to the theory of the state, whereby, for example, the omnipotent God became the omnipotent lawgiver – but also because of their systematic structure, the recognition of which is necessary for a sociological consideration of these concepts. The exception in jurisprudence is analogous to the miracle in theology. Only by being aware of this analogy can we appreciate the manner in which the philosophical ideas of the state developed in the last century. (Schmitt 1985: 36)

This passage could be characterized as proposing three kinds of relation between theology and politics:

a) a *vector* of movement, that of secularization, from theology to politics in early modernity and the formation of the modern concept of the state;
b) a *structural analogy* between the political and theological, with references here to a 'systematic structure' necessary for a 'sociological consideration';
c) the historical development of political concepts from theological ones, thus signalling a *conceptual political theology*. The question of how strict this generic derivation is, for instance, whether it is of form or substance, remains open, but is ultimately an empirical question that would be addressed by the tools of conceptual history or genealogy.

In the rest of this chapter, Schmitt's invocation of his relation to sociology is apparent. He speaks of 'a sociology of juristic concepts' (Schmitt 1985: 32), and 'a sociology of the concept of sovereignty' (1985: 42). Later, he adds, this sociology of concepts 'aims to discover the basic, radically systematic structure and to compare this conceptual structure with the conceptually represented social structure of a certain epoch' (Schmitt 1985: 45). In this sense, political theology is a kind of sociological method that rests on a fundamental proposition: 'The metaphysical image that a definite epoch forges of the world has the same structure as what the world immediately understands to be appropriate as a form of its political organization' (Schmitt 1985: 46).

The presence of Max Weber in these passages is clear and this is made explicit in relation to the question of causation, and the rejection of the priority of either the spiritual or material. Schmitt endorses Weber's critique of one-sidedness in history in order to suggest a parallel between two structurally connected sets of relations, one of how we understand ultimate meaning and the other of how we understand political organization. Schmitt does not have the language we have at our disposal but we could speak of a 'genealogical' model of historical derivation, and a model of relations between the metaphysical and political dispositives, that is, a 'transpositive model' (Heron 2018: 41) across domains of sacred and profane, spiritual and worldly, and so on. Each of the three kinds of relations between theology and politics – those of secularization, structural analogy and its conceptual historical derivation – has been interrogated or modified by subsequent or more recent literature, including in the last case by Schmitt himself almost immediately.

The vector of secularization

Where does the 'secularization' thesis stand? This leads us into the thorny question of the meaning of the term, of which there are at least four. First, there is a *sociological* one of the decline of religion in modern societies. Secularization in this sense is one side of an attempt to read Max Weber's account of modernity through a narrative of disenchantment and rationalization. This is the most common and widely used meaning of the term in which, as Hans Blumbenberg puts it, 'there are fewer sacred things and more profane ones' (1985: 3–4). Second, there is an *historical-political* one of the de-confessionalization or de-theologization of politics in early modern Europe after the sixteenth- and seventeenth-century period of confessional wars and the emergence of the system of territorial states. Third, there is an *economic-juridical* meaning in which it refers to the state appropriation of church property, for example in France, after the Revolution and through to the Third Republic, or, in canon law, the release of a cleric from the community and the obligations of the order (Blumenberg 1985: 19–29). Finally, we can place the transposition across domains in one direction from the theological to the political/social, as found in Schmitt's formulation given earlier, as a fourth, *analytical*, sense of the term.

Throughout Schmitt's work, one could find examples of each of these uses of the term. As we have just noted, *Political Theology* itself is interwoven with a reflection on Weber's secularization thesis. Many texts, especially *The Nomos of the Earth* (2003: 140f.) offer an account of the modern state system (the *jus publicum Europaeum*) that emphasizes the role of 'detheologization' in the formation of the modern state. However, at least in its classical forms, Schmitt's thesis is closer to the last, analytical meaning.

An initial reading of Schmitt suggests that he only understands secularization as a one-way movement between theology and politics, although this might arise from the fact that his texts tend to focus on the early modern period of the emergence of the modern state and state system, and state theory. A now established modification of the political theology programme does away with the unidirectionality in Schmitt's initial formulation (Herrero 2015: 26). Thus, Assmann's work on Egyptian doxologies and Judaism demonstrates that the transfer works in the other direction, so that 'the significant concepts of theology are theologized political concepts' (Agamben 2011: 193). Similarly, Kantorowicz's work (1946) concerning the movement of imperial acclamations to Christian liturgy confirms the possibility of movement in both directions, not only in mediaeval times, but even in the twentieth century in its final chapter on the twentieth-century revival of the *laudes* and fascist acclamations (1946: 180–5). Fascist movements, often with explicit clerical and Catholic components, in Spain in the Civil War, and Mexico and Belgium, drew upon the cry of 'Christ the King'. This acclamation was among the *laudes* reintroduced by the Church in the early part of the twentieth century and which bolstered the rise of what was called the Liturgical Movement. But there is evidence of a reverse transfer, from the fascist appropriation back to the Church itself. Thus, faced with the fascist government, Pius XI introduced a new feast of Christ the King in 1925. At the election of Pius XII fourteen years later, the crowd in Piazza San Pietro spontaneously burst into the chant of *Christus vincit, Christus regnat, Christus imperat* (Christ conquers, Christ reigns, Christ commands). The vectors of transference became so unclear that one could hear a *laudes* in Italian basilicas that bestowed 'perpetual peace, life and health' on not only the Pope and the King but also on the 'Duce Benito Mussolini the glory of the Italian nation' (Kantorowicz 1946: 186).

Furthermore, insofar as we can regard Agamben's economic theology as a political theology, the genealogy of *oikonomia* moves in both ways: from the Greek management of the household through Ciceronian rhetoric to the Pauline mystery of the Trinity to modern understandings of civil government and economy. He speaks of a 'sacralisation' as well as secularization. Acclamations, prayers and hymns are components of a 'theology of glory' that 'constitutes, in this sense, the secret point of contact through which theology and politics continuously communicate and exchange parts with one another' (Agamben 2011: 194).[1]

More broadly, can Schmitt's position be wedded to an idea of secularization in anything but a 'transpositive' sense? Hans Blumenberg reads Schmitt as 'the strongest version of the secularization theorem' (1985: 92), but surely this is not in the most common, sociological understanding of the term. Schmitt would appear to be arguing *against* the notion of secularization in the sociological sense of the word, that is, he is indicating the continuities of modernity with its theological past rather than a break. The key terms and themes of his debate with Blumenberg are all attempts to define the nature of this continuity/discontinuity. Blumenberg argues the case for a rupture, in which 'self-assertion' or 'self-empowerment' forms the legitimacy of the modern age, that is, modernity produces its own immanently generated solutions to major problems. In a response to Schmitt, he concedes some continuity of modernity with its theological past but only insofar as modern concepts merely 're-occupy' theological positions. (Blumenberg 1985: 49). Schmitt (2008: 120–1), in his scything postscript to *Political Theology II*, argues that the notion of 'self-empowerment', directed against all transcendence, is a radical form of nihilism, characterized by *tolma*, the 'audacity and joy' in the face of unfettered newness. This nihilism should be understood not as the creation out of nothingness but as 'the creation *of* nothingness as the condition for the possibility of the self-creation of an ever new worldliness' (Schmitt 2008: 129).

An alternative thesis is that the secular is not to be identified with a disenchanted modernity but a balance between distinct spheres of sacred and profane. Citing Robert A. Markus, Montserrat Herrero suggests that in Christianity, the secular is the 'sound tension' between the sacred and profane, the outer circle of that which endures until the *eschaton* (2019: 1056). The secular then becomes the field of forces that hold in relation two distinct spheres of the sacred and profane. The problem with identifying modernity with a secularized society, from this perspective, is an unsound tension in which the profane so overwhelms the sacred that the latter is denied, or only superficially acknowledged, or turned to an esoterica to be manipulated by the political cognoscenti.

Structural analogy

Several thinkers have wanted to add some qualifications and specification around the term 'analogous' in the canonical definition of political theology by Schmitt. It would seem at best a first move that gains insight and intuition, when we compare the example of the exception to the miracle, as he does. Agamben is instructive (2009: 19–20). Relying on the work of Enzo Melandri, he suggests that analogy is opposed to dichotomous logic. The analogical third is a way of living with and using, rather than resolving or overcoming, a dichotomy. Analogy thus intervenes into dichotomies not to create a dialectical resolution in a higher synthesis but 'to transform them into a force field traversed by polar tension, where . . . their substantial identities evaporate' (Agamben 2009: 20). Agamben develops this into the concept of 'signature' that marks concepts and places them in a definite field (similar to Schmitt's systematic structure) and then allows their movement across fields (2009: 40). In this context, Agamben suggests that secularization is not a concept but a signature (2011: 4).

A similar set of moves are entailed in Devin Singh's criticism of the term 'analogy', and his preference for 'homology'. For Singh, homology exceeds analogy; it involves historical relations and moments of co-emergence in different spheres (2018: 17). Similarities can be understood 'as partially the result of actual historical and conceptual interaction between the two spheres' (Singh 2018: 18), between, for example, the sovereign minting of coins for a new emperor and the Son as currency incarnating God. This seems to be helpful: without resolving the tension between a diachronic historical development – 'genealogy' in today's language – and a synchronic comparison of spheres/domains, it allows an analysis that is alert to common sources and mutual interaction, as well as movement across entire domains. In a move similar to Agamben, Singh argues that what is revealed is a 'horizon of confluence that is always receding . . . forestalling claims of origins' (2018: 18).

The terms 'signature' and 'homology' seek, then, to stress that the relation of political and theological ideas is not an occasional or metaphoric one but, as Schmitt had already emphasized, a systematic and structural one, that is, a movement of a set of consistent discursive and conceptual relations across domains. In this sense they strengthen, rather than undermine, Schmitt's initial postulates.

Beyond conceptual political theology

The classic formulation of political theology concerning its focus on the genetic derivation of concepts was quickly and fundamentally amended by Schmitt almost immediately. This occurred with the publication of what amounts to a companion volume, *Roman Catholicism and Political Form* (Schmitt 1996), from 1923. This volume announces the possibility that alongside a conceptual political theology that deals with the genesis and structure of political concepts, there is also an institutional and practical political theology of the genesis and transfer of practices and institutional forms. The thesis expressed in the title does not seek, according to G. L. Ulmen (1996: xxii), to resolve a theological dispute but to respond 'to an intellectual challenge epitomized in *The Protestant Ethic and the Spirit of Capitalism*' of Max Weber. If this is the case, three points might follow. First, insofar as Weber's thesis could be understood as an economic theology that proposes a relationship between Protestant ascetic practices and the form and conduct of life conducive to capitalism and capital accumulation, then Schmitt's political theology is a response to an economic theology. Here the Catholic Church is held to lay the juridical foundations of the public sphere that would contrast with liberalism's private sphere. Second, there can be multiple rationalizations and neutralizations, with the possibility of conflict between them. The rationalization of the political order in the modern state is itself subject to economic and ethical rationalizations that seek a neutralization of the political. Finally, confessional conflict would appear to be built into the form of the modern liberal state. The liberal critique of the state continues a form of confessional conflict conducted by other means.

The study of the social and political form of the church can be traced to Rudolf Sohm in his *Outlines of Church History* (1958), which Weber would draw upon in his account of the rationalization of charismatic authority. It also appears in Schmitt, and in the work of Schmitt's key interlocutor and critic, Erik Peterson, in his various theological writings. Peterson is particularly important because, citing *Political Theology*, in his 1935 essay 'Monotheism as a Political Problem' (2011: 234), he both announces the 'theological impossibility' of political theology in a polemical footnote and yet inadvertently gestures towards an institutional political theology focusing on liturgical action rather than theological conceptualization. The latter gesture is already contained in the brief preface to the same text, concerning that which is rendered in the recent English translation as 'political involvement' (Peterson 2011: 68) but is elsewhere translated as the 'political action' of Christians (Heron 2018: 68; Agamben 2011: 15). This political action 'can never take place except under the presumption of a triune God' (Peterson 2011: 68), and this means it can no longer be a political theology rooted in the antinomies of monotheism and polytheism, Judaism and paganism. Peterson thus views political theology as a false theology and the true political nature of the Christian church is expressed in its liturgies (in the etymological sense of 'public services'). Rather than closing political theology as he wishes, however, Peterson thus opens the pathway to an institutional political theology. Thus, he demonstrates the way in which the church takes over the public services of antiquity to constitute its own assembly (or *ekklēsia*), and leaves open the possibility that the practical or institutional action undertaken by the participants of different forms of religious organization (such as church, sects) can reappear in or be transferred to practices, institutions and domains not specifically identified as religious. In this respect,

Peterson's significance is less in his denial of the possibility of a political theology than on affirming the already political character of the Christian liturgy.

As well as examining the transfer of concepts across the different domains, political theology thus concerns what Marcel Mauss and Paul Fauconnett (2005: 10) called 'social institutions' in the sense of a 'grouping of acts and ideas already instituted which individuals find before them and which more or less imposes upon them'. Social institutions in this sense include the acclamation, avowal, confession, oath, vow and pledge, and even various musical forms that are found in both sacred and profane forms, or in contexts prior to or evading the distinction between the juridical-political and religious-theological (on the oath, see Herrero, this volume). We might also agree with Kantorowicz's observation that 'hymns are, in many respects, transcendental acclamations' (1946: 73).

It is remarkable that the basic tenets of Schmitt's 1922 *Political Theology*, and its 1923 addendum in *Roman Catholicism and Political Form*, have maintained their classic status in defining the analytical strategy of political theology. While later commentators have emphasized the possibility of movement of sacralization from the political to the theological that supplements Schmitt's emphasis on early modern and modern political forms and their theological derivation, and have sought to sharpen the methodological tools for capturing these transfers, there has been no fundamental shift from Schmitt's paradigm. Even Peterson's 'closure' opened up the political-theological aspects of liturgy and the political action of the church itself and, by implication, of other religious organizations. The identification of the genealogical and structural dimensions of political theology, and its conceptual and institutional arms, is already present and fully elucidated by Schmitt in the early 1920s. As an analytical framework, then, very much is left, despite later developments, refinements and qualification, of the political theology as set out by Carl Schmitt one hundred years ago. While the answer to our first question is clear, the answer to the second might be much more difficult.

Politics as confession

A more difficult question concerns what is left of the critical function performed by this political theology. If the point was simply to show the 'false religiosity' of politics, then political theology would be a species of ideology critique, a means to reveal the ways in which hegemony and class or other forms of domination are maintained and legitimated. However, if the point of political theology is to call attention to the neglected or unacknowledged theology that animates politics, including that which imagines itself progressive, then in what way can it be critical? The following poses that question in relation to what might be called an instance of what we have just called institutional political theology: the re-emergence of public penitence as a form of political action.

The example concerns the emergence of public rituals to express solidarity with those fighting racism, in particular in recent 'anti-racist' politics in the United States and elsewhere. One case in point would be the ritual performed by Democratic members of Congress on 8 June 2020 on the introduction of the Justice in Policing bill soon after the police murder of George Floyd. In photographs of that event, the members of Congress are pictured kneeling on their right knees in silence with bowed heads for eight minutes and forty-six seconds in Ghanaian *kente* silk stoles. Similar ceremonies have been undertaken by professional sportspeople at the beginning of athletic contests for several years, not without political contestation, and there appears to have been an amplification of them during the protests of 2020.

One way to grasp these events is through the distinction that Michel Foucault (1993) made between two types or tendencies of confession: *exagoreusis* and *exomologesis*. For him, the dominant line is *exagoreusis*. This is the practice by which the truth of the subject is produced through its verbalization to a superior. It was first found within monastic institutions and involves an analytical and continuous verbalization of thoughts, in a relation of complete obedience to the will of the spiritual father (Foucault 1993: 215–19). It contains two elements that will come to be increasingly important in Christianity and generalized to all the faithful in the modern practice of confession: the principle of obedience and the necessity of confession to the spiritual father who listens as the image of God. For Foucault this attention to the movement of one's inner thoughts, their pure or impure origins, and the necessity of the avowal of them to a master, will become fundamental not only in the history of Christianity but in the eventual formation of the welfare state, too. This genealogy forms a part of the Foucauldian critique of modes of 'subjectification' by the human sciences, of the 'psy' disciplines and of the therapies of the welfare state. However, in keeping with the ideal he discerned in the nascent neoliberalism of France in the seventies (2008: 259–60), Foucault would imagine liberation as a maximization of self-government and minimization of domination, conceived as a fixing of identity or subjectivity. Politics, then, would be a kind of 'de-subjectification', or, as we would put it today in the language of progressive managerialism, 'transformation' of the self.

Exagoreusis is shadowed by another set of penitential or confessional practices called *exomologesis* (Foucault 2008: 213). This entails techniques of fasting and self-mortification, such as wearing a hair shirt, pouring ashes on one's head or scarring of one's body. Through such practices, the penitent dramatizes the 'willing of his own death as a sinner' and thus acts as a dramatic self-renunciation, a 'self-revelation' that 'is, at the same time, a self-destruction' (Foucault 2008: 214, 215). As Tertullian would have it, the sinner must 'publish himself' (*publicatio sui*) through rituals of humiliation to choose the path to purity (Foucault 2008: 214). For Foucault, *exomologesis* 'was the theatrical representation of the sinner as dead or as dying (2008: 214)'. The penitents in early Christian communities, as noted by Jerome, engaged in a kind of ritual renunciation of the flesh itself. They would prostrate themselves, often at the doors of churches, before the clergy and other pure persons such as widows or virgins. However, rather than a specific event, *exomologesis* is more 'a way of life acted out at all times out of an obligation to show oneself' (Foucault 2008: 214). The salient point about such rituals is that they are collective and public rather than individualized and private; that is, the penitents petition for entry into the *ekklēsia* or assembly of those who will be saved. It is a confession taken not under the priestly 'vow of silence', but under the full gaze of publicity.

What is important about these public or 'performative confessions' (Herrero 2019: 1049) is that individuals petition to become members of a community, purifying themselves of sin, so that they may take their place in a community of charismatic believers. The diversity consultant Robyn DiAngelo argues in her bestselling book *White Fragility* that white supremacy requires that white people continuously fight the evil within and join with others in such work. It is 'the lifelong work that is uniquely ours, challenging our complicity with and investment in racism' (DiAngelo 2018: 33). This message was given a particular political form during the protests of 2020, as attested by social and mass media images and videos. One video posted by a Rwandan journalist shows a group of hundreds of white people taking collective pledges.[2] They raise up their hands, or 'take a knee', reciting and together repeating affirmations that they promise to live without 'racism, anti-blackness, or violence', to 'give up' white privilege, to 'use my voice in the most uplifting way possible', 'to love my black neighbours the same as my white ones' and 'to do everything in my power to educate my communities'. While these are all laudable sentiments, their ritualization in an oath or pledge bears an uncanny resemblance to certain kinds of Christian practices of collective expiation of sin – those of *exomologesis*.

These public affirmations to conquer an inner evil are a part of the wider function of acclamations in political and religious assemblies. Acclamations are important, affect-generating, components of both formal assembly (political conventions, rallies, inauguration ceremonies) and protests. Two elementary examples from recent experience and radically different political positions would be 'Lock Her Up', the reverse acclamation directed by Trump at his opponent Hillary Clinton in 2016, and 'No Justice, No Peace', which is identified with anti-globalization activism through to the Black Lives Matter protests of 2020. There is today an easy movement of such political acclamations to the virtual assembly of social media. Since Kantorowicz (1946), as we noted, mediaeval historians have known of the relation between liturgical acclamations and political acclamations, extending into modern times. A similar movement occurs in our own example of public and performative confession when the practices of the public protest are taken up by actual religious groups. Thus, white members of a church in Houston kneel before Black devotees and ask God the Father 'for forgiveness from our black brothers and sisters for years and years of racism'.[3] The performative confessions we are witnessing add another element to acclamation. While acclamations generally effect an identification (or the opposite) with a proposition, decision or a leader, and to that extent attest to a form of truth, the performative, public confession requires a particular coming to terms with one's own inner resistances, evil, transgressions, guilt or sins, and thus a more radical entry into the community of believers. Such a practice demands the fundamental transformation of the self within rituals of the production of truth, and is thus a specific kind of what Foucault called *alèthurgie* (see Herrero, this volume).

In this respect, *exomologesis* might be regarded as a specific kind of acclamation, as Herrero suggests (2019). In his lectures of 1980, Foucault notes that for the Greeks, *omologein* means 'to say the same thing... to be in agreement, to give one's assent, to agree on something with someone' (2008: 201–2). Thus, *exomologesis* is the public manifestation of agreement, not simply the act of agreement. What is at stake is not simply a truth, but the manifestation of both the truth and the subject's adherence to the truth. As Foucault will put it in a quite striking phrase in his course summary, *exomologesis* makes 'the act of assertion an object of assertion' (2008: 322). These observations are captured perfectly in the phrase used in recent protests: 'white silence is violence'. The speaker not only acclaims his/her anti-racism but also demands that others break their silence and join the charismatic community of anti-racists. This exhortation to others can be understood as not only asserting that 'white silence is violence', but also demanding that the hearer, like the speaker, breaks that silence. Failure to do so is therefore neither a space of neutrality, a moment of consideration, an act of passive resistance, nor a sign of apathy, but is immediately an act of violence and complicity in centuries of violence and oppression.

Foucault thus understands the demand for self-transformation can be something more than a form of private confession or personal avowal as we know it. However, in his insistence of the focus on the 'subjectifying' practices of confessional expertise within the welfare state, he fails to grasp the relevance of this insight for his present. For our part, this public avowal is fast becoming the key political act of the present. It is a specific type of political acclamation/avowal in which the subject not only identifies with the leader, the policy or the ideal, but also seeks to combat his/her own shortcomings in a public confessional that will transform the self and permit entry into a political community. The members of the community cannot remain satisfied with their own transformation but must demand it of others, including casual observers and bystanders.

Institutional political theology

To return to Carl Schmitt, what we witness here is a transposition not of theological concepts but an apparent movement of institutional practices from a religious into a political domain and back again. Such a movement has been observed before in relation to acclamations and oaths, and arguably Foucault's account of modern therapeutic expertise within the welfare state can be read as a genealogy of the practice of the individualized or auricular confession, the obligatory nature of which was confirmed by the Council of Trent. Here we have presented a new theological-political case of the movement of public penitential rituals into the political domain.

If Schmitt's institutional political theology traced the relation between the Roman Church and the modern state, a complementary one might be had by understanding Max Weber's distinction between church and sect. Like the membership of the modern state, a church in Weber's view is an organization that accepts people high and low, humble and mighty, sinners and saved. But to engage in the public expiation of guilt and public pledges is to petition entry into what Weber called a 'community of personally charismatic individuals', which is what constitutes a sect rather than a church (Weber 1978: 1204–11). Because only its members are capable of salvation, the sect is 'anti-political', precludes universality and forms an 'aristocracy' comprised of the '*visible* communities of saints' (Weber 1978: 1208, 1204, original emphasis). Paradoxically, the sect has an elective affinity with liberal democracy in that it unequivocally demands freedom of conscience as the basis of all other rights and asserts the 'inalienable personal right of the governed against any power' (Weber 1978: 1208–9).

Clearly, the turn to a sect-like politics is not solely a preserve of 'progressive' politics. Some of those charged with the Capitol riot of 6 January 2021 asserted on the social media that they were 'called' to do what they did by President Trump. Similarly, the proliferation of highly sophisticated conspiracy-theory literature about Covid-19 pandemic restrictions and the emergence of movements contesting official narratives about it such as the Querdenker (the 'lateral thinkers') in Germany and the *gilets aranconi* (the 'bright orange vests') in Italy, indicate a broader confessionalization of politics. These movements contest what they see as a medical fascism exercised by a global cabal of corporations and international organizations (the WHO, the WEF, the Gates Foundation) in the name of the right of the governed to manage their own health, taking up themes of lifestyle, naturism, organic foods and farming, natural remedies, mutual aid and so forth (for instance, Mercola and Cummins 2021).

This observation of sect-like behaviour of both progressive and reactionary political movements enables us to gain a sense of the critical potential of such a political theology. It allows us to ask: what happens when politics stops taking the form of universality based on citizenship and begins to resemble the formation of communities of fully 'awakened' individuals exhorting others to undertake their own public pledges and acclamations and contest official narratives and taken-for-granted truths? Further, we can ask: what happens when progressive politics shifts its attention from the struggle against exploitation and economic inequality articulated in relation to the exercise of the political and juridical powers of the state to a struggle against our inner selves, and the enemy that is inscribed within our souls? Political theology in this sense might give 'progressive' politics a greater clarity about what it is doing and what forces it is invoking in moving towards such confessional and sect-like institutional practices and forms. It asks us to examine the costs of such a move, which forsakes the formal domain of politics with its emphasis on broad coalition building and policy detail, and the dangers of the enthusiasms such a politics unleashes. One of the clear dangers is the collapse of a common ground on which the political is played out in liberal democracy and the possibility of positions of neutrality.

The sociologist Robert Bellah (1967) drew attention to the 'civil religion in America' that was characteristic of the mid-twentieth-century manifestation of belief in the symbols and rituals of the American way of life (see Schwarzkopf, this volume). At a minimum, such a civil religion is under immense stress. The conflict over public monuments is part of this. So is the contestation between narratives of the founding moments of American history, as provoked by the *New York Times'* 1619 Project. The micropolitics of self-transformation might well have created many spaces of subjective experimentation and tolerance of difference. However, the abandonment of the struggle against exploitation and economic inequality and its replacement with penitential acts of self-assertion have reduced politics to a contest between communities of virtuosi who confront one another as mutually incompatible and incomprehensible groups of charismatic individuals. As labour unions and the welfare state have been decimated by neoliberal governing and contemporary capitalism, and even liberalism abandons the idea of a neutral state mediating between conflicting interests, the proliferation of confessional politics begins to resemble more the civil wars of Europe in the early modern period than the social politics of the twentieth century.

In 1960, Carl Schmitt appears to come to the hope that the process of de-theologization of politics would lead to a continuing commitment to a value-neutral legal order characteristic of the liberal constitutional state. In the essay, 'The Tyranny of Values' (discussed at length by Schwarzkopf, this volume), he would decry the kind of politics that proclaims the partisan and value-laden character of all aspects of life. He indicated the 'immanent aggressiveness of values', such that '[w]hoever asserts their validity must make them valid' (Schmitt 2018: 33, 31). The trajectory of Schmitt's thought led him then to not only understand the process of 'secularization' through which the modern constitutional state was formed but also to place hope in the kind of neutrality that a liberal legislative order could offer as a protection against deadly competing values. This was not merely a transposition of concepts but of an institutional transfer in which the universality of a church is replaced by the universality of citizenship within a state. Later refinement of political theology makes clear that this transference is a fragile one and that it is possible for the political and its institutional practices to regain a theological character. But Schmitt's late diagnosis appears perilously thin in the face of what an institutional political theology of forms of confession can reveal. What is at stake are immanently aggressive *values*, to be certain, but these are embedded in the permanent performance of different ways of life claiming rights of self-government and exclusive title to truth. The confessional conflict that arises today attests not merely to a difference of values as something one does or does not hold but a potentially (and sometimes actually) lethal conflict between virtuosi claiming to belong to visible communities of saints that allow no space of neutrality, and no place of silence for consideration and questioning.

Conclusion

I have argued that political theology enables us to grasp the inescapable theological and religious foundations of our political commitments and practices. It allows us to grasp, as well as the fundaments of political legitimation, order and social cohesion, the illimitable forces, enthusiasms and passions that can be conjured through such practices. It might be that a politics that seeks to fight inequality and oppression requires the tethering of such forces to foster the sense of movement and change. But it might also be that the awakening of spirits and demons call forth communities radically opposed to each other and committed to irreconcilable faiths. The choice of such a politics would need to be justified in a particular conjuncture, such as the one that characterized the Trump years, and in particular the summer of 2020. However, if politics is not to descend into the nether regions of confessional conflict and civil war, nor of the rise of a sovereign dictatorship, such an approach must only be temporary. As Weber would put it (1994: 369), the revelatory experience of radical truth, self-transformation and commitment will need to give way to the 'slow, strong drilling through hard boards', of tedious meetings, the counting of numbers, the forming of alliances and organizations and the development of policies. This is the case whether one imagines that a change will come from a reform of existing institutions or their overturning.

We have argued, then, that despite later qualifications and refinements, much of Schmitt's programme of political theology remains intact as an analytical strategy. We might now add that the intelligibility gained through such analysis will allow us to gain clarity over the potentials and limitations, as well as what is at stake, in various radical and progressive political practices and tactics. The form of study inaugurated by *Political Theology* one hundred years ago alerts us to, and cautions us about, the explosive forces they contain.

Notes

1. A corollary of Agamben's position is that political theology can do perfectly well without a notion of secularization. See the passage following this sentence: 'It is not necessary to share Schmitt's thesis on secularization in order to affirm that political problems become more intelligible and clear if they are related to theological paradigms' (Agamben 2011: 229).
2. Unfortunately, there is no information on when and where in the United States the video was recorded. It was posted on Twitter on 3 June 2020 and can be found here: twitter.com/theophilebrave/status/1268151120653844481?fbclid=IwAR1kQhK0_SYSbSaqbDhqJTBzz0vS5nj7KXIt-rgKhUrNOVC8WpOCe9fRq28
3. See '"Powerful moment": White parishioners kneel, ask for black community's forgiveness in George Floyd's hometown' (2020), *The Indian Express*, 2 June. Available online: https://indianexpress.com/article/trending/trending-globally/george-floyd-kneel-viral-video-6438938/?fbclid=IwAR01pWSgOmPCYY6EGajqBwSquiLn4UlvIvr582a9SE-YVQXoK4jJYNL2Wjg

References

Afary, J. and K. B. Anderson (2005), *Foucault and the Iranian Revolution: Gender and the Seductions of Islam*, Chicago, IL: University of Chicago Press.

Agamben, G. (2009), *The Signature of All Things: On Method*, trans. L. D'Isanto with Kevin Atell, New York: Zone Books.

Agamben, G. (2011), *The Kingdom and the Glory: For a Theological Genealogy of Economy and Government*, trans. M. Chiesa with M. Mattarini, Stanford CA: Stanford University Press.
Assmann, J. (2005), 'Political Theology: Religion as Legitimizing Fiction in Antique and Early Modern Critique', in B. Giesen and D. Šuber (eds), *Religion and Politics. Cultural Perspectives*, 193–203, London: Leiden.
Bakunin, M. (1973), *Selected Writings*, ed. A. Lehning, London: Jonathan Cape.
Bellah, R. (1967), 'Civil Religion in America', *Daedalus: Journal of the American Academy of Arts and Sciences*, 96 (1): 1–21.
Blumenberg, H. (1985), *The Legitimacy of the Modern Age*, trans. R. M. Wallace, Cambridge, MA: MIT Press.
DiAngelo, R. (2018), *White Fragility: Why It's So Hard for White People to Talk About Racism*, New York: Beacon Press.
Foucault, M. (1993), 'About the Beginning of the Hermeneutics of the Self', *Political Theory*, 21 (2): 198–227.
Foucault, M. (2008), *The Birth of Biopolitics: Lectures at the Collège de France, 1978–9*, trans. G. Burchell, Houndsmill: Palgrave Macmillan.
Heron, N. (2018), *Liturgical Power: Between Economic and Political Theology*, New York: Fordham University Press.
Herrero, M. (2015), 'On Political Theology: The Hidden Dialogue between C. Schmitt and Ernst H. Kantorowicz in *The King's Two Bodies*', *History of European Ideas*, 41 (8): 1164–77.
Herrero, M. (2019), 'Acclamations: A Theological-Political Topic in the Crossed Dialogue between Erik Peterson, Ernst H. Kantorowicz and Carl Schmitt', *History of European Ideas*, 45 (7): 1045–57.
Kantorowicz, E. (1946), *Laudes Regiae: A Study in Liturgical Acclamations and Mediaeval Ruler Worship*, Berkeley, CA: University of California Press.
Marx, K. (1975), *Early Writings*, ed. L. Colletti, Harmondsworth: Penguin.
Mauss, M. and P. Fauconnet (2005), 'Sociology', in M. Mauss (ed.), *The Nature of Sociology*, 1–30, New York: Durkheim Press/Berghahn Books.
Mercola, J. and R. Cummins (2021), *The Truth About COVID-19: Exposing the Great Reset, Lockdowns, Vaccine Passports, and the New Normal*, London: Chelsea Green Publishing.
Peterson, E. (2011), *Theological Tractates*, trans. M. J. Hollerich, Stanford, CA: Stanford University Press.
Schmitt, C. (1985), *Political Theology: Four Chapters on the Concept of Sovereignty*, trans. G. Schwab, Chicago, IL: University of Chicago Press.
Schmitt, C. (1996), *Roman Catholicism and Political Form*, trans. G. L. Ulmen, Westport, CT: Greenwood Press.
Schmitt, C. (2003), *The Nomos of the Earth in the International Law of the Jus Publicum Europæum*, trans. G. L. Ulmen, New York: Telos Press.
Schmitt, C. (2008), *Political Theology II: The Myth of the Closure of any Political Theology*, trans. M. Hoelzl and G. Ward, Cambridge: Polity Press.
Schmitt, C. (2018), *The Tyranny of Values and Other Texts*, trans. S. G. Zeitlin, Candor, NY: Telos Press.
Singh, D. (2018), *Divine Currency: The Theological Power of Money in the West*, Stanford, CA: Stanford University Press.
Sohm, R. (1958), *Outlines of Church History*, trans. M. Sinclair, Boston: Beacon Press.
Ulmen, G. L. (1996), 'Introduction', in C. Schmitt (ed.), *Roman Catholicism and Political Form*, ix–xxxvi, Westport, CT: Greenwood Press.

Weber, M. (1978), *Economy and Society: An Outline of Interpretive Sociology*, ed. G. Roth and C. Wittich, Berkeley, CA: University of California Press.

Weber, M. (1994), 'The Profession and Vocation of Politics', in P. Lassman and R. Speirs (eds), *Political Writings*, 309–69, Cambridge: Cambridge University Press.

Chapter 2

THE POPULIST PROMISE IN CARL SCHMITT'S POLITICAL THEOLOGY

Tim Christiaens

Jan-Werner Müller defines populism as 'a particular moralistic imagination of politics, a way of perceiving the political world that sets a morally pure and fully unified [. . .] people against elites who are deemed corrupt or in some other way morally inferior' (2016: 19–20). Populist movements imagine the people as an originally unified political agent with a single will unjustly distorted by official political institutions. Politicians allegedly refuse to listen to the people and, instead, do the bidding of financial elites, migrants, Muslims and/or cultural Marxists. This project is not only anti-elitist, but also anti-pluralist: divisions within the people are considered accidental distortions of what 'true, morally pure citizens' think. But can a people ever be one? Underlying the populist rhetoric of not only Donald Trump and Matteo Salvini, but also Jean-Luc Mélenchon and Nicolas Maduro, is the promise that the people are, in fact, one and possess a singular, morally impeccable will. As Hardt and Negri observe in the context of right-wing populism, 'the central point is that the unity of the people is always characteristic of the (real or imagined – sometimes primordial) past social order that the right-wing movements seek to defend against aliens, to reclaim, and to redeem' (2017: 50). Populism imagines an original unity of the people in turmoil and promises to reunify the people through political action.

This nostalgia for popular unity is nothing new. Throughout modernity, many political thinkers have wondered how to maintain popular unity in a context of increasing pluralism. In pre-modern times, the common Christian faith allowed to cultivate some form of social cohesion, but once this had dissolved, the emerging modern nation state struggled to represent 'the will of the people' as a single voice. In this chapter, I discuss Carl Schmitt's response to the problem of popular unity, a thinker close to the hearts of populists today (Abts and Rummens 2007: 405–24; Müller 2016: 19–20; Scheuerman 2019: 1170–85). According to Schmitt, a democracy can properly function only if the populace forms a 'homogenous medium' (2005: 13). 'Democracy requires, therefore, first homogeneity and second – if the need arises – elimination or eradication of heterogeneity' (Schmitt 1988: 9). If this requirement is not fulfiled, the state should purportedly even suspend the rule of law to violently enforce social homogeneity and produce what Schmitt in

Politische Theologie calls 'a normal situation' (2005: 13). I argue that this nostalgia for popular unity forms the core of Schmitt's project of political theology. The latter is not just a historical research programme, but also an existential project aimed at bridging the perceived gap between rulers and the ruled. According to Schmitt, the state must restructure itself along the lines of the Catholic Church in order to construct a harmonious body politic analogous to the Christian community's unity in the body of Christ.

I argue that Schmitt's project of revitalizing state authority by turning towards theology is misguided and that this error shows some of the dangers posed by contemporary populism. Schmitt imagines the Church solely as an institution that has held vastly different interpretations of the Bible together in a so-called '*complexio oppositorum*' (1996: 7), but he ignores the times the Church was riven by violent conflict. The history of the Catholic Church is not only a success story of vastly different people brought together in worship of God; it is also the story of fanatic zealots persecuting and killing each other in the name of God, from inquisitorial witch-hunts to millenarian revolts. Similarly, the populist promise not only entails popular unity through shared rituals and traditions, but also fosters fanatic zeal among its followers. After clarifying Schmitt's critical diagnosis of liberalism and how he imagines political theology as an existential project can reignite the political legitimacy of the state, I will turn to Jan Assmann's critique of political monotheism to lay bare the violent potential in the populist promise of popular unity.

Schmitt's anti-elitist diagnosis of liberalism

Schmitt lived through one of the most turbulent periods in Western politics when he wrote *Politische Theologie* in 1922. He had just witnessed the devastation of the First World War and Germany's unfair treatment at the Paris Peace Conference. The short-lived Weimar Republic, on the other hand, was one of the least stable regimes of twentieth-century Europe (McCormick 1997; Balakrishnan 2000; Kennedy 2004). Understandably, Schmitt lets his political thought start from the Catholic doctrine of Original Sin: humankind is to be regarded as inherently prone to evil (2007: 58). Wherever human beings meet, there is an inevitable danger of enmity and violence. Political thought should, according to Schmitt, subsequently devote its attention to institutions that restrain this potential for violence. In Schmitt's view, this means that the state ought to monopolize the decision over who the enemy is (Böckenförde 1998: 39; Esposito 2015: 4). He subscribes to a strong version of sovereignty as a last resort against social chaos: whenever the populace risks devolving into civil war, the sovereign should suspend the rule of law and intervene in order to forcefully impose stability. Instead of dissolving into a myriad of enmities, the people thereby become a political unity under the sovereign's authority.

Liberalism, however, disavows this human potential for evil and conflict, according to Schmitt (2007: 58). Instead of grounding the legal order in a sovereign institutive decision, it, first, argues on moral grounds that all political decisions must derive from pre-established, general and abstract laws (Schmitt 1988: 42). Any decision emanating from the sovereign outside the law is derided as illegitimate arbitrariness. In the framework of government by law, the foundation of legitimacy is, in other words, legality itself: a political decision is good if and only if it is the outcome of rational legal procedures. Whatever is decided through such a legal system – independently of whether it leads to silk blouses or poison gas – is thus *ipso facto* good. From an institutional perspective, liberalism grants parliament the monopoly over legislation, making it the core of the entire state apparatus. The executive is purportedly merely an institution that implements parliamentary laws. Liberalism, secondly, reduces political representation to the deputation (*Vertretung*) of social interests (Schmitt 1996: 25–6). It only sees a plurality of social groups, each defending its own interests. Politicians supposedly 'represent' the people only insofar as they 'stand in' for these constituencies. It would be impractical to gather all individual citizens together in parliament to debate legislation, so the liberal order devises rules to allow a small elite of people to represent the manifold interests of society at large. In this scenario, there is no popular unity over and above social plurality. There are only atomized voters with each her own opinions and interests. Parliament is subsequently nothing more than the aggregation of their votes articulated through the electoral system and managed by political elites.

Schmitt fears, however, that government by mere law and deputation cannot restrain the forces of the political if there is no sovereign imposing order and homogeneity on the populace (Kalyvas 2009: 142). Liberal states allegedly lack the strength to negate human sinfulness. The law risks becoming an instrument of political strife instead of its restrainer. Schmitt predicts that, in a liberal order, opposing factional interests in society will not submit to the rules of an open discussion, but will only use the representative system to fortify their own positions. Politics then becomes the mere continuation of civil war by other means. Not only does the liberal value of state neutrality allow non-liberal factions to openly defy and undermine the legal order (Schmitt 2004: 27), but the lack of state institutions that transcend oppositions in civil society also leads to the people shattering into a manifold of competing interest groups. Each group builds its own institutions and bureaucracy to occupy and use political positions of power to expand its own influence (Schmitt 2004: 13). At best, this leads to a multiparty corporatism where different constituencies govern via political compromises in an 'unending conversation' (Schmitt 1988: 36). Liberal elites presumably engage in open discussion between competing opinions where ultimately the truth prevails, but, in reality, 'modern mass democracy has made argumentative public discussion a mere formality' (Schmitt 1988: 6). The grand rhetoric of parliamentary debate constitutes a mere façade for the prosaic forms of corrupted elitist politicking.

At its worst, however, liberal power politics leads to temporary parliamentary majorities abusing their hold on the state apparatus to solidify their position and exclude rivalling groups (Schmitt 2004: 31–2). By adapting electoral regulations, parliamentary voting thresholds or voting districts, a contingent coalition of interests can perpetuate its foothold in the state apparatus. Such undertakings undercut minorities' equal chance of acquiring positions of power. Minorities could subsequently question the utility of participating in a rigged parliamentary game and turn their backs on the legal order in general. If there is no more profound sense of community or solidarity keeping the people together as a political unity, there is nothing holding minorities back from regarding the majority as an extraneous oppressor to be combated through extra-legal means. If the majority has monopolized the legal means of violence and banned the right to resistance, minorities have no other recourse than illegal means of violence. Rather than restraining the human capacity for conflict, liberalism has thus exacerbated its force setting it on a path towards civil strife (Schmitt 2004: 93).

Schmitt's political theology and the liturgical unity of the people

One can see the appeal of Schmitt's diagnosis of liberalism for populists today. He shares their anti-elitist critique of liberal bargaining democracy and defends the minorities who do not feel represented in the parliamentary system. Populist leaders likewise present 'the political establishment' as an elite of detached bureaucrats that merely seize as much benefits as possible for themselves and their direct constituents. The 'deep state', that is, the corrupted elites occupying the state apparatus, has purportedly kept the uninstitutionalized *real* will of the people out of the decision-making process (Müller 2016: 27). This constitutive betrayal allegedly grants populist movements the mandate to speak in the name of the Nixonian silent majority. Even when they lose elections, populists can refer to the uninstitutionalized populace as the sole real basis for political legitimacy.

To avert the dangers of liberalism, Schmitt advocates a strong state with an unequivocal mandate to unify the people. In *Politische Theologie*, he focuses on the extraordinary situations when the people have already broken apart and the sovereign has to intervene with brute force to re-establish public order. Almost simultaneously, however, Schmitt wrote *Römischer Katholizismus und Politische Form* to discuss how the state ought to maintain popular unity in normal times. In that text, he argues that the Church's rituals provide a symbolic basis for popular unity. Liturgies encourage Christians to imagine themselves as spiritually participating in the same mystical body of Christ. Rituals grant a certain aura to the representation of God on Earth. In Catholicism, representation *(Repräsentation)* means rendering an invisible authority from above visible in a personal and public form (McCormick 1997: 161; Kalyvas 2009: 148). According to Schmitt, the modern state must develop its own ritualistic repertoire to render 'the will of the people' visible as an embodied authority. It should imitate the Church's auratic representation of the will of God in order to increase its own political legitimacy.

According to Schmitt, 'the political power of Catholicism rests neither on economic nor military means but rather on the absolute realization of authority. [...] The Church is the concrete personal representation of a concrete personality' (Schmitt 1996: 18; McCormick 1997: 157–205; Kelly 2004: 113–34; Kalyvas 2009:

146–60; Mulieri 2018: 507–27). Rather than voicing the opinions of churchgoers from below, as in liberal deputation, the Church represents authority from above. The Church purportedly *incarnates* Christ's presence during his absence until the end of days. According to Church doctrine, Catholic priests are ordained via a lineage going all the way back to the apostles, who received their gifts (*charismata*) from God himself. This carnal link to God via apostolic succession grants priests their authority. They render visible what is structurally invisible, the loving presence of God. Clergymen – and primarily the pope at its head – are vicars of Christ: they represent God's will on Earth (Schmitt 1996: 52–3). This is not a mere act of substitution with an absent God being replaced with a present priest; thanks to apostolic succession, the clergy *embodies* God's presence (Schmitt 1996: 19). Via the mediation of the Church, believers can touch the invisible via a visible cue, a symbol, to sense their status as creatures of God. When the believers end the ceremony with the concluding word 'amen', they acclaim their shared status as creatures of God. More than thirty years later, Ernst Kantorowicz describes this popular unity in his *The King's Two Bodies* as a dialectic between the natural and mystical body of the Church (Kantorowicz 1997: 199; Kennedy 2004: 87; Esposito 2011: 68; Mulieri 2018: 521). While the consecrated host during the Eucharist constitutes the *corpus naturale* of Christ, the latter's *corpus mysticum* is the social body of believers gathered in his name. The multitude becomes a singular people under God thanks to the mediating presence of God in the flesh via the Church. The Church's representative role is a necessary and sufficient condition for the formation of the Catholic community as a political unity.

The particular advantage that Catholic representation holds over liberal deputation is its capacity to provide room for multiple different opinions simultaneously without creating internal contradictions like the liberal state does. Schmitt is astonished by the sheer diversity of Catholic creeds that submit to the same papal authority and he wishes the same cohesion for the modern state. Though Catholics come in many shapes and sizes, they all feel solidarity towards the same institution. Their common allegiance to God and his Church is presumably more important than their mutual differences. Schmitt observes that the Church has thus kept many different interpretations of Christianity together in a single institution through a so-called '*complexio oppositorum*': 'The Old and New Testament alike are scriptural canon; the Marcionite either-or is answered with an as-well-as' (1996: 7). Some would deride the Church's capacity to ally itself with multiple, opposing views as limitless opportunism, but not Schmitt. He regards it as an accomplishment in the constitution of a political unity-in-plurality (Ulmen 1996: xvii; Rasch 2019: 37). Instead of reducing representation to deputation, Catholic representation can convince very different people to submit to the same Church and a single pope.

With this presentation of the Catholic Church Schmitt seems to align himself with a distinction, developed by Ernst Troeltsch and Max Weber, between churches and sects (Weber 1985: 7–13; Troeltsch 1992: 331–43). Both German social thinkers often used this dichotomy to explain the divergence between the Catholic Church and Protestant sects. They characterized the Catholic Church as a highly institutionalized social organization that stressed the mediating role of the clergy and the sacraments between individuals and God. Individual believers were born into the Church and their salvation depended on their adherence to outward institutional expectations, only to a lesser extent on inward individual merit. Grace was administered through the Church. Modern sects, on the other hand, were voluntary associations that rejected the Catholic Church's 'objectification' of salvation in favour of salvation through practised piety and righteousness. The Christian ethic, and especially the prescriptions laid out in the Sermon on the Mount, had to permeate one's everyday conduct. One could not simply entrust one's salvation to the Church. Schmitt obviously prefers the Catholic model: by inserting the Church as mediator between believers and God, Catholicism has fostered an institution that can also mediate in conflicts between believers. It can hold vastly different interpretations of Christianity together in a *complexio oppositorum* because it holds the monopoly on the representation of God from above. Whatever these internal factions believe or do, they must keep their allegiance to the outward rituals of the Church as the sole legitimate representative of God. Because Protestant sects claim immediate connection to God, they lack this mediating force. Piety depends on individual inner devotion, not on sufficient adherence to outward rituals. Whenever a disagreement occurs, there is no hierarchical institution to overrule these opposing factions.

Schmitt wishes to confer the Catholic model unto the modern state. Representation should not concern social interests from below, but should render visible the invisible 'will of the people' *to* society (Böckenförde 1998: 49). Given that, in modern democracy, 'the people' takes the place of God at the centre of political theology, 'the people' must be represented as a sensible and personal authority in public (Schmitt 1996: 21; 2005: 49). But since the 'will of the people' is never immediately presented as such, liturgical rites and public manifestations must make it present to the populace (Balakrishnan 2000: 60). The state's main tools, according to Schmitt, are plebiscites and acclamatory practices (Agamben 2011: 171; Dean 2017b: 14; Dean 2017a: 422; Herrero 2019: 1045–57).

> A people that, as a real group gathered in a market or at another public space, acts as a collective community (like a Swiss *Landgemeinde*) is sociologically and politically beyond compare. It has a general will and expresses it differently from a people whose will is expressed as a mere addition of individually casted votes, without the public event of coming together as a group. [. . .] The real activity, capacity, and function of the people, the core of each form of popular expression, the original democratic phenomenon (*demokratisches Urphänomen*), which Rousseau as well has presented as true democracy, is the acclamation, the confirming or disconfirming cries of the gathered masses. The people acclaim a leader, the army (here identical to the people) acclaims the field marshal or *imperator*, the comrades of the people or the *Landgemeinde* acclaim a proposal. (Schmitt 1927: 33–4, my translation)

Inspired by Erik Peterson's study of acclamations in Church liturgies, Schmitt believes state liturgies requiring the physical presence and gathering of 'the people' make the latter a political and affective reality. The masses become a single political unity thanks to their common mystical body mediated by the state (Esposito 2015: 43; Vatter 2016: 251–2). As Kalyvas argues, 'the political is the realm of substantive ethical principles, of invisible and abstract values, that is, the realm of symbolization and representation in which society forges its own symbolic unity, transcending empirical divisions through some normative collective significations' (Kalyvas 2009: 149).

For Schmitt, ceremonial rituals such as presidential inaugurations, party conventions and military parades are hence not mere relics of an archaic past, but a key source of the state's political legitimacy (Dean 2017b: 111). Similarly to how the priesthood embodies the mystical presence of God, Schmitt designates political offices, especially the presidency, as visible incarnations of the general will (Kalyvas 2009: 156). A president does not merely defend the interests of his voters, but carries the will of the entire nation. Just like God's will remains a mystery if not voiced by his vicars on Earth, the will of the people remains mute if not articulated on the state level. The outcome is 'the people' as a homogenous medium, which Schmitt deems crucial for the applicability of the law (1988: 9). Normal times require that individuals regard each other as a community of friends bound by the same laws and ways of life. Political rituals represent 'the people' back at the masses like a mirror image. Formulaic phrases like 'God bless America', 'Vive la France, vive la République' or 'Deutschland über Alles' are, likewise, not mere formalities. They are signifiers that call for the people to acclaim their status as compatriots. They will shout acclamations in unison, like 'U-S-A, U-S-A, U-S-A', 'Vive le président' or 'Heil Hitler'. Such public displays of faith grant their addressees the authority to *embody* the will of the people. When the French president, for instance, ends his speech with 'Vive la France, vive la République', he invokes 'the French Republic' as a master signifier to authorize his decisions. He presumably does not act from personal motivations, but enacts the will of the people into actual policy on the people's behalf. When the French public repeat the phrase with sufficient national pride, they acclaim the president's authority to act in the name of 'the French Republic'. As Dean writes, 'rather than being merely residual symbols, these political liturgies glorify and distribute sovereignty and serve to identify ruler and the ruled' (2018: 22). Instead of voting with secret ballots – reducing public opinion to an addition of disconnected, atomized private opinion – plebiscitary democracy renders the people's consensus present in the flesh through public expressions of allegiance to the state.

> The people exist only in the sphere of publicity. The unanimous opinion of one hundred million private persons is neither the will of the people nor public opinion. The will of the people can be expressed just as well and perhaps even better through acclamation, through something taken for granted, an obvious and unchallenged presence, than through the statistical apparatus that has been constructed with such meticulousness in the last fifty years. [. . .] compared to a democracy that is direct, not only in the technical sense but also in a vital sense, parliament appears an artificial machinery, produced by liberal reasoning, while

dictatorial and Caesaristic methods not only can produce the acclamation of the people but can also be a direct expression of democratic substance and power. (Schmitt 1988: 16–17)

Schmitt prefers authoritarian democracy if that means re-grounding the legitimacy of the state on the publicity of the people (Balakrishnan 2000: 71). State liturgies symbolically confirm the political unity of rulers and the ruled as a 'people', and make it sensible in the flesh.

Fanatic zeal and politico-theological populism

The appeal of Schmitt's combination of exceptional politics and auratic representation among populist movements is understandable. Populist leaders like Donald Trump, Narendra Modi, or Matteo Salvini build their popularity on public rallies and mass acclamations (Scheuerman 2019). They need public events to convey their status as incarnations of the will of the people. Through liturgical acclamations like 'Make America great again' or '#StopTheSteal', Trump supporters *feel* their participation in a collective greater than themselves. Schmitt would have predicted, however, that regimes employing auratic practices of representation would be more stable and less prone to internal division and strife. This was clearly misguided (see Schmitt 2001; Schmitt 2012: 203–9; Bendersky 1979: 309–28; Ohanna 2019: 273–300).[1] Populist rousing tactics come at the cost of social instability and the diffusion of violence, particularly on the far-right. Pegida activists in Germany set fire to asylum centres, Italian lone wolf terrorists kill refugees and Trump's MAGA army undertakes quasi-military operations during protests and has attempted to occupy the federal parliament. Moreover, Müller points to the ironic twist that, even though populists accuse liberals of abusing political institutions to benefit their direct constituents, populists commit the same crimes even more explicitly (2016: 46). They openly redirect state resources to 'deserving, hard-working people' as opposed to parasitical elites and the undeserving poor. When their hold on state institutions reaches a critical threshold, they even redesign the state architecture to cement their hold on power, exactly what they accuse liberal majorities of doing. In Hungary, for instance, Viktor Orban's Fidesz party rewrote the constitution in 2012 to ensure that Fidesz, supposedly the only legitimate representation of the real will of the people, remains in power with limited opposition (Müller 2016: 64–6).

The core of the problem lies in Schmitt's one-sided presentation of the Catholic Church. He correctly highlights the Church's mediating role between different opposing factions; by emphasizing popular unity through symbolic rituals rather than a dogmatic creed, the Church has been able to keep its followers together in a *complexio oppositorum*. But the Church has also provided a forum for witch-trials, inquisitorial policing and the genocide of heretics. One should thus not interpret the ideal-typical distinction between churches and sects as implying that churches are entirely immune to fanatical infighting. Church history is riddled with stories of internal strife and persecution. A permanent struggle was waged over who was the better representative of God's will on Earth. This tension gave rise to the sectarian movements of, for example, Thomas Münzer and Savonarola in the Late Middle Ages, but one should not forget that Luther's Reformation also started as an internal dispute that grew into a European civil war. *Pace* Schmitt, the Church did not always manage to contain the forces of the political. The distinction between churches and sects is, in other words, more unstable than Schmitt presumes. It should not be forgotten that Troeltsch himself had already admitted that the church-type, by entrusting salvation to outward institutional devices rather than inward conversion, fosters the discontent that leads dissident voices to split off and form sects (1992: 334–6). It is in opposition to the Catholic Church's legalistic proceduralism that insurrectionary movements like Millenarianism and Protestantism emerged. At moments of crisis in Church history, when the clergy seems to give in to worldly temptation rather than successfully embodying the will of God on Earth, sects emerge to contest the Church's failed attempt at incarnation. Religious violence subsequently returns in the conflict between the Church and the sects over who can legitimately speak for God, as happened in the struggle between mediaeval heretical movements and the inquisition. Furthermore, Troeltsch nuanced the dichotomy as well by emphasizing that both emerge from the same primitive Christianity, which somewhat diminishes their stark opposition (1992: 333). As I will show with the help of contemporary German thinker Jan Assmann, both churches and sects emerge from the same monotheistic religiosity, implying that if the threat of religious fanatical violence emerges from monotheism itself, then both churches and sects are at risk of disseminating violence. Confining the issue of religious fanaticism to sects, like Schmitt attempts, is in that case no viable strategy. Although Catholic auratic representation is not usually associated with sectarian fanaticism, the two are not necessarily incompatible.

Assmann provides a helpful perspective to gauge the violent tendencies of auratic representation. According to Assmann, monotheism revolves around the following assertion:

> God is the truth, and other peoples' gods are lies. That is the theological basis of the distinction between friend and enemy. It is only on this ground and in this semantic context that the political theology of violence became truly dangerous. Carl Schmitt's political theology also stands in this revelation-theological tradition of readiness for violence. In my view, the true 'political problem' of monotheism lies here. (Assmann 2019: 240)

Assmann argues that the Abrahamic religions start from the belief in a single true God, refusing the validity of other religions. They purportedly worship the one true God, while all other gods are false idols (Assmann 2019: 239). From this moment onwards, religious community is an exclusive covenant, positing God's followers in the position of devout followers. The latter owe their entire existence to the one true God, so they must extinguish their own individual, private will to maximally internalize and enact the will of God. Any act that would contaminate the pure allegiance to God is seen as a sign of disloyalty and thus a breach of contract (Assmann 2014: 117). The faithful are indebted to God for giving them the world and their own identity. Anything not put at the service of God is an unlawful use of the Lord's gift of existence. As Sloterdijk summarizes, 'it is part and parcel of this form of personal supremacism that those who think and believe cannot be any more than mere vassals or employees of the divine sovereign – the only other option being the despicable role of infidels and disobedients' (2009: 85). Humankind bears an absolute moral responsibility to internalize and enact the will of its otherworldly Lord (Assmann 2010: 44).

A consequence of monotheism's integral devotion to a single true God is its iconoclastic tendency, ignored by Schmitt (Sloterdijk 2009: 96; Assmann 2010: 67). Schmitt emphasizes how the Catholic Church has mobilized symbols and rituals to incarnate God on Earth, but these symbols also serve another purpose. They not only endow this-worldly objects with divine qualities, but also divert the popular gaze from this world to a disembodied transcendent world beyond. From Moses' times, the aim of public rites was to focus attention away from worldly things to a God beyond this world. A suspicion thus lingered that icons would overshadow the transcendent authority they embodied. Though Catholicism has left some room for religious iconography, this suspicion has motivated Jews, Muslims and Protestants to prohibit images of God. Public liturgies in monotheism constitute collective performances of swearing allegiance to a transcendent God with whom the believers sustain an otherworldly covenant (Assmann 2010: 114). Their psychic effect is to instil a sense of gratitude and obligation to bend one's will into conformity with the will of the God beyond. Assmann draws attention to this anti-political, anti-representative tendency in liturgical praxis: the latter moves the human gaze to a duty beyond all earthly, political allegiances. There are duties far greater than those of earthly citizenship, since God's Kingdom is not of this world. This entails that God's command overrules all earthly concerns. Since God is greater than any king or emperor, his commands exceed any human commitment or ethical standard. There is nothing in this world that could limit the human servitude to God (Sloterdijk 2009: 83–4; Assmann 2010: 55). God can thus make the most outrageous demands – from killing one's own son to roaming around the desert aimlessly for forty years – with nothing to stop him. 'One must be willing to die for one's faith rather than agree to actions or beliefs known to be incompatible with true religion,' Assmann concludes (2010: 20).

This absoluteness of the covenant between God and his people makes monotheistic religions particularly prone to violence, according to Assmann and Sloterdijk (Assmann 2010: 24; Sloterdijk 2016: 46). Once allegiance is sworn to the one true God, all actions that transgress this bond are a threat to the continued existence of the community as a political unity.

> Man bears the full weight of God's address to the world, which is circumscribed in diverse models and metaphors as the loving relationship between groom and bride, as the special bond between a father and his son, a shepherd and his flock, a gardener and his vineyard, and above all – but this is no longer a metaphor

– between a ruler and his allies. Never before had man borne such a heavy responsibility towards a contractual partner. (Assmann 2010: 115)

This heavy burden fosters a hermeneutic of permanent self-suspicion in the religious community. To safeguard the covenant with God, the believers must continuously police their own thoughts and hunt down those who secretly undermine the allegiance to God. The persecution of heretics and violent purges must ensure that everyone's will aligns with the will of God at all times (Assmann 2014: 118). Whoever thus succeeds at speaking in the name of God can justify the most horrific genocides in his honour (Assmann 2010: 21). The unity-in-plurality achieved through auratic forms of representation in the Church is hence, to some extent, the product of policing the common submission to God. Biblical passages like Deuteronomy 20 confirm this policed sense of unity. They tell orthodox Jews that conquering foreign cities requires military restraint, whereas the conquest of fellow Jewish, heretical cities calls for the total annihilation of the population (Assmann 2014: 121). Orthodoxy – or what the institutional establishment labels as 'orthodoxy' – is violently policed in the name of God's absolute authority. Here the presumption that the clergy incarnates the voice of God becomes a dangerous infrastructure for religious communities: because priests embody the will of God and God's command is absolute, priests can demand horrific acts from their followers *de auctoritate Dei*. Every believer is personally bound to God and has thus a duty of integral membership (Sloterdijk 2016: 44). She must monitor herself and others to permanently obey the will of God. The Lord's sovereign command directly overrules all human laws since it is his people's duty to will what he wills.

The Catholic Church has tempered some of the iconoclastic zeal from the Old Testament. It also explicitly prohibited individual priests from independently policing orthodoxy without institutional authorization. But whenever a 'religious state of emergency' (*Ernstfall*) appears, like a natural disaster interpreted as the wrath of God, the split between friends and enemies of God reappears (Assmann 2014: 123). The monopoly on articulating the will of God has not always been stably located in the papacy. The Church's *complexio oppositorum* has regularly burst into violent conflict. From the side of the establishment, the inquisition, witch-hunts and so forth have been signs of the hermeneutic of self-suspicion policing the population; but also from below, popular revolts like the German Peasants' War (1524–5) have questioned the papacy's faithful allegiance to God. Whoever succeeds at owning the auratic representation of God on Earth has an unlimited power to declare who the enemy is and order him to be killed without committing murder. Schmitt would have accepted this power concentrated in the state, but not when popular movements or even individuals can claim the same competence. Once, however, the people are constituted through a covenant with God, the latter can, in principle, bind *everyone* to interpret and enact the will of God. The representations the Church provides in its liturgies and acclamations are, *pace* Schmitt, not meant to unify the people under the authority of the Church, but to point people's attention in unison *beyond the Church* to the transcendent God outside of this world. There is thus no guarantee that the believers do not turn on their institutions or on themselves once they believe God demands them to do so.

Assmann's critique of Schmitt's political theology is a helpful reading prism for understanding the violent tendencies of contemporary populism. For populist movements, the will of the people is not represented in electoral results, but in the plebiscitary gatherings of populist leaders. The latter are imagined as icons of the popular will. Once one accepts that there is one singular and absolute will of the people and that only the populist leaders adequately represent that will, everything becomes possible in the name of their absolute duty to the people. Once they take control over the state apparatus, populist movements are purportedly allowed to persecute by any means necessary everyone who presumably betrays the will of the people. By policing people's obedience to the populist government's command, populist movements ultimately create 'the homogenous community in whose name they had been speaking all along' (Müller 2016: 49). The incarnation of the will of the people in representatives like Trump or Salvini is not built to pacify the nation in a *complexio oppositorum*, but points the attention to an intangible, transcendent and absolute 'people' to which individuals owe their allegiance. The will of the people even transcends its populist spokespeople and makes a direct appeal to the movement's followers. Lone wolves increasingly take matters into their own hands. They target liberal elites and minorities not for the sake of Trump or Salvini themselves but in the name of the America or Italy they embody, the imaginary community that must be made whole again. Believers in the populist creed allegedly ought to devote their lives to the service of the imaginary community conveyed through populist public rallies. This duty of absolute devotion explains the extreme and violent lengths people go to in order to serve the populist cause.

Conclusion

Populist movements promise to overcome the fractured condition of modern society by demonizing supposed enemies of the people and rendering the will of the people physically present in plebiscitary events like public rallies and protests. Elections are allegedly corrupt procedures designed to distort the popular will in favour of powerful interests. By breaking these liberal institutions apart, populists promise to make the people whole again. This promise shares deep affinities with Carl Schmitt's project of political theology. He witnessed the decline of the state's democratic legitimacy in the 1920s Weimar Republic and called for a renewed alliance between the modern state and Christian theology to revitalize the authority of the state. He especially saw potential in the Catholic Church's model of representation. Instead of representing the interests and opinions from below, the Church keeps itself together by representing the mystical body of Christ from above. Representation, for the Church, is a practice of incarnating transcendent authority in the flesh and interpellating the people to commonly acclaim their submission to divine authority. According to Schmitt, the modern state should likewise use liturgical methods to render the will of the people physically tangible.

The people allegedly become a political unity by physically gathering and acclaiming their leaders as embodiments of the general will.

I have used Assmann's writings to unravel the dangers of this politico-theological project manifest in the populist promise of popular unity. In his view, auratic representation forms a political unity on the basis of an exclusive covenant with a transcendent God. Since the monotheistic believers owe their entire existence to the one true God, it is their absolute duty to reform their will to align with the will of God. The liturgies Schmitt praises for the formation of political unity thus serve to remind the believers of this duty and direct their gaze to the God beyond. There remains consequently an iconoclastic potential in the religious community. The believers cannot fully trust the Church to embody the will of God; everyone has a personal obligation to monitor himself and others for allegiance to God, leading to the permanent institution of a hermeneutic of self-suspicion with potentially violent results. Populist movements transfer the same dynamic to the political realm. The populist promise of popular unity is conveyed to plebiscitary rites that render the transcendent will of the people present in populist politicians. The people are rendered in the flesh with the populist leader as its mouthpiece. But through their acclamations, individuals are presumed to bend their will to the will of the people as expressed by the populist leader. This affective identification with 'the people' fosters an absolute duty to support the movement and protect it against its self-proclaimed enemies – whatever the costs of these actions might be. The result is a potentially violent dynamic where followers of populist movements feel obligated to commit horrendous crimes in the name of the people.

Note

1 If one considers Schmitt's own turn towards Nazism, Schmitt's misdirection has been clear from the very start. Schmitt avidly supported the Nazi regime's use of plebiscitary public gatherings and acclamations, even if they were mostly sham performances to democratically confirm what the party had already decided in advance. The end result was obviously not political stability, but a World War and one of the cruellest genocides in human history.

References

Abts, K. and S. Rummens (2007), 'Populism versus Democracy', *Political Studies*, 55 (2): 405–24.

Agamben, G. (2011), *The Kingdom and the Glory*, trans. L. Chiesa, Stanford, CA: Stanford University Press.

Assmann, J. (2010), *The Price of Monotheism*, trans. R. Savage, Stanford, CA: Stanford University Press.

Assmann, J. (2014), *From Akhenaten to Moses: Ancient Egypt and Religious Change*, Cairo: American University of Cairo Press.

Assmann, J. (2019), 'Monotheism', in S. Symons and W. Styfhals (eds), *Genealogies of the Secular: The Making of Modern German Thought*, trans. D. Steinmetz-Jenkins, 231–42. Albany, NY: SUNY Press.

Balakrishnan, G. (2000), *The Enemy: An Intellectual Portrait of Carl Schmitt*, London: Verso Books.

Bendersky, J. (1979), 'The Expendable Kronjurist: Carl Schmitt and National Socialism 1933–1936', *Journal of Contemporary History*, 14: 309–28.

Böckenförde, E. -W. (1998), 'The Concept of the Political: A Key to Understanding Carl Schmitt's Constitutional Theory', in David Dyzenhaus (ed.), *Law as Politics: Carl Schmitt's Critique of Liberalism*, 37–55, New York: Duke University Press.

Dean, M. (2017a), 'Political Acclamation, Social Media and the Public Mood', *European Journal of Social Theory*, 20 (3): 417–34.

Dean, M. (2017b), 'Three Forms of Democratic Political Acclamation', *Telos*, 179: 9–32.

Dean, M. (2018), 'What Is Economic Theology? A New Governmental-Political Paradigm', *Theory, Culture & Society*, 36 (3): 3–26.

Esposito, R. (2011), *Communitas: The Origin and Destiny of Community*, trans. T. Campbell, Stanford, CA: Stanford University Press.

Esposito, R. (2015), *Two: The Machine of Political Theology and the Place of Thought*, trans. Zakiya Hanafi, Fordham, NY: Fordham University Press.

Hardt, M., and A. Negri (2017), *Assembly*, New York: Oxford University Press.

Herrero, M. (2019), 'Acclamations: A Theological-Political Topic in the Crossed Dialogue between Erik Peterson, Ernst H. Kantorowicz and Carl Schmitt', *History of European Ideas*, 45 (7): 1045–57.

Kalyvas, A. (2009), *Democracy and the Politics of the Extraordinary*, Cambridge: Cambridge University Press.

Kantorowicz, E. (1997), *The King's Two Bodies*, Princeton, NJ: Princeton University Press.

Kelly, D. (2004), 'Carl Schmitt's Political Theory of Representation', *Journal of the History of Ideas*, 65 (1): 113–34.

Kennedy, E. (2004), *Constitutional Failure: Carl Schmitt in Weimar*, New York: Duke University Press.

McCormick, J. (1997), *Carl Schmitt's Critique of Liberalism*, Cambridge: Cambridge University Press.

Mulieri, A. (2018), 'Representation as a Political-Theological Concept: A Critique of Carl Schmitt', *Philosophy & Social Criticism*, 44 (5): 507–27.

Müller, J. -W. (2016), *What Is Populism?*, Philadelphia: University of Pennsylvania Press.

Ohanna, D. (2019), 'Carl Schmitt's Legal Fascism', *Politics, Religion & Ideology*, 20 (3): 273–300.

Rasch, W. (2019), *Carl Schmitt: State and Society*, London: Rowman & Littlefield.

Scheuerman, W. (2019), 'Donald Trump Meets Carl Schmitt', *Philosophy & Social Criticism*, 45 (9–10): 1170–85.

Schmitt, C. (1927), *Volksentscheid Und Volksbegehren: Ein Beiträg Zur Auslegung Der Weimarer Verfassung Und Zur Lehre von Der Unmittelbaren Demokratie*, Berlin: Walter de Gruyter.

Schmitt, C. (1988), *The Crisis of Parliamentary Democracy*, trans. E. Kennedy, Cambridge, MA: MIT Press.

Schmitt, C. (1996), *Roman Catholicism and Political Form*, trans. G. Ulmen, Westport: Greenwoord Press.

Schmitt, C. (2001), *State, Movement, People: The Triadic Structure of the Political Unity*, trans. S. Draghici, Corvallis: Plutarch Press.

Schmitt, C. (2004), *Legality and Legitimacy*, trans. J. Seitzer, New York: Duke University Press.
Schmitt, C. (2005), *Political Theology: Four Chapters on the Concept of Sovereignty*, trans. G. Schwab, Chicago, IL: University of Chicago Press.
Schmitt, C. (2007), *The Concept of the Political*, trans. G. Schwab, Chicago, IL: University of Chicago Press.
Schmitt, C. (2012), 'Carl Schmitt's Ultimate Emergency: The Night of the Long Knives', *The Germanic Review*, 87: 203–9.
Sloterdijk, P. (2009), *God's Zeal: The Battle of the Three Monotheisms*, trans. W. Hoban, Cambridge: Polity Press.
Sloterdijk, P. (2016), *In the Shadow of Mount Sinai*, trans. W. Hoban, Cambridge: Polity Press.
Troeltsch, E. (1992), *The Social Teaching of the Christian Churches*, 2 vols, trans. O. Wyon, Louisville, KY: Westminster/John Knox Press.
Ulmen, G. (1996), 'Introduction', in C. Schmitt (ed.), *Roman Catholicism and Political Form*, vii–xxxvi, Westport: Greenwood Press.
Vatter, M. (2016), 'The Political Theology of Carl Schmitt', in J. Meierhenrich and O. Simons (eds), *The Oxford Handbook of Carl Schmitt*, 245–68, Oxford: Oxford University Press.
Weber, M. (1985), '"Churches" and "Sects" in North America: An Ecclesiastical Socio-Political Sketch', trans. C. Loader, *Sociological Theory*, 3 (1): 7–13.

Chapter 3

POLITICAL ATHEISM

Towards a Profane Reconceptualization of the Modern State

Mikkel Flohr

The modern state remains central to contemporary politics. Rumours of its demise as a result of globalization or neoliberalism appear to have been greatly exaggerated, and responses to the global Covid-19 pandemic have amply illustrated its continued significance (Rosenberg 2005: 2–74; Barrow 2005: 123–45; Cahill 2014: 55f.; Toscano 2020: 3–23). The modern state is defined by its sovereignty. The concept of state sovereignty posits the state as a coherent subject transcending and wielding absolute power over its various institutions and the population within a given territory. However, the state only exists in and as these institutions and through the participation and obedience of the population. As such, the state cannot be said to transcend or wield absolute power over its institutions or the population in any meaningful sense (Abrams 1988: 58–89; Mitchell 1991: 77–96; Gupta 1995: 375–402; Krasner 1999). But even though the idea of the sovereign state does not correspond to the practical existence of the modern state, this idea nonetheless forms a central part of its existence, operations and reproduction. The institutions that compose the state are organized and animated precisely by the idea that they form part of and are determined by the sovereign state, as is the wider public's participation in and obedience to them. Although the modern state is not in any meaningful sense a transcendent and sovereign subject, the pervasive idea that it is, allows its various institutions to function, to some extent, *as if* they were. The idea of state sovereignty therefore cannot simply be ignored. In order to understand the modern state and its central role in modern politics, it is not enough to provide an empirical account of the state's various institutions and their operations, it is also necessary to take into account the idea that holds them together and allows them to operate within society, that is to say, the idea of the sovereign state.

My argument is that Carl Schmitt's 1922 *Political Theology: Four Chapters on the Concept of Sovereignty* provides crucial conceptual resources for such an undertaking. In this work, Schmitt argued that the idea of the sovereign state was the product of the historical secularization of the Christian notion of a transcendent and omnipotent God in early modern political thought. The notion of the state as a sovereign subject transcending and wielding absolute power over society retained the theological (transcendent) conceptual structure and legitimizing function of its precursor independently of its religious content, constituting a distinctly *political theology* that informs and organizes the ideas, organizations and practices that together constitute the modern state.

However, Schmitt remained enthralled by the idea of state sovereignty and perpetuated it as the basis of his authoritarian politics in the context of the social and political instability of the Weimar Republic. Thus, while he provided crucial insights into the theological origin and structure of the idea of state sovereignty, he remained entirely uncritical of it and failed to differentiate it from the actual (temporal) existence of the modern state in and as a part of society. It is therefore necessary to read Schmitt against Schmitt, in order to extricate his analysis of this political theology from his uncritical adherence to it. I accomplish this through the retrieval and redeployment of the origins of his concept of political theology in the inversion of Mikhail Bakunin's thought, which I leverage to reinvert Schmitt's historical and conceptual analysis of political theology as the basis of a profane reconceptualization of the modern state (see also Agamben 2009: 18).[1]

I describe this reconceptualization in terms of *political atheism*, in order to simultaneously acknowledge its roots in Schmitt's historical and conceptual analysis of political theology and my ambition of moving beyond its limitations. I take the term 'atheism' to denote the rejection of the idea of a transcendent and omnipotent God, rather than the denial of the existence of this idea and its significance to organized religion. Thus, 'political atheism' is deployed here to denote a perspective on the modern state that, on the one hand, rejects the political-theological notion of state sovereignty, but, on the other hand, remains attentive to the central importance of this idea to the practical existence and reproduction of the modern state. Political atheism is preferable to, say, political secularism, which would imply the separation of the modern state and political theology, whereas I want to insist on and critically interrogate their inherent entwinement. I outline this political atheism through a materialist critique of political theology that reinscribes Schmitt's analysis of its historical origin and conceptual structure in its social and material context and thereby makes a contribution towards the profane reconceptualization of the modern state.

My argument consists of four parts. In the first part, I excavate the relatively obscure origins of Schmitt's concept of political theology in the works of Bakunin and proceed to examine the role that they played in Schmitt's argument. In the second part, I develop an interpretation of the notion of political theology via Schmitt's 'secularization thesis', which identified the theological origin and structure of the idea of state sovereignty. In the third part, I complement my reading of Schmitt's secularization thesis with a brief historical outline of the development and content of this political theology. In the fourth and final part, I explore the conceptual connection Schmitt established between his own and Bakunin's positions, as a means of extracting Schmitt's account of political theology from his own adherence to it. I use Bakunin's materialist critique of religion as a model for formulating a materialist critique of political theology that reconsiders and reinterprets it in terms of its earthly foundation and effects and thereby provides an outline of the proposed political atheism.

The obscure origins of Schmitt's concept of political theology

Schmitt's *Political Theology* was one of the first and remains one of the most influential studies of political theology. Although Schmitt would later repeat Erik Peterson's misleading suggestion that he had 'introduced the phrase "political theology" to the literature', he appropriated the term from the nineteenth-century anarchist Mikhail Bakunin, who deployed it some five decades before Schmitt, in his 1871 'The Political Theology of Mazzini', where he criticized the influential Italian republican Giuseppe Mazzini for his celebration of state power and Christianity (Schmitt 2008; Petersen 2011: 233, n.168; Bakunin 1973a: 214–31).[2] While Schmitt does not explicitly refer to Bakunin's text in *Political Theology*, its author figures as perhaps *the* most central protagonist of this work (see Schmitt 2008: 50, 55, 64–6; Meier 2006: 79–80; Newman 2019: 21–23; Strauss 2007: 121). Moreover, his references to the text in the conclusion to the contemporary *Roman Catholicism and Political Form* show that he was familiar with it (Schmitt 1996: 36, 39; and also Ulmen 1996: xxxi, n21).[3]

Bakunin was born into the Russian nobility and studied philosophy in Germany in the early 1840s, where he fell in with the Young Hegelians, known for their radical proto-materialist critique of religion and absolutism, which Schmitt highlights in *Political Theology* as a significant part of the movement towards the 'elimination of all theistic and transcendental conceptions' (Schmitt 2008: 50–1; Giudice 1981; McLaughlin 2002; Toews 1985: 203f.; Quante 2019: 197–237; Bakunin 1973b: 37, 58).[4] At this point, Bakunin was first and foremost an adherent of revolutionary (pan-Slavic) nationalism opposed to autocratic rule and went on to become involved in a number of revolutionary movements across Europe. His participation in a failed uprising in Dresden in May 1849 led to his arrest, extradition and imprisonment in Russia. It was not until 1861 that he managed to escape and eventually return to Europe where he continued his political activism. While there are numerous indications of Bakunin's libertarian inclinations in his writings from this time, it was only after moving to Italy in 1864 that he began to formulate his characteristic and explicitly anarchist views in a series of texts that rejected the authority of both God and State (Bakunin 1971: 76f.; Pernicone 1993: 26).

Mazzini's 1871 attack on the Paris Commune and the International Workingmen's Association, which Bakunin had joined in 1868, provoked the latter to write 'The Reply of an Internationalist to Giuseppe Mazzini', which was subsequently expanded and developed into 'The Political Theology of Mazzini' (see Mazzini 2009: 153–65; Bakunin 1973a; Ravindranathan 1981: 484–93). In this polemical text, Bakunin embraced Mazzini's charges of materialism and atheism while denouncing Mazzini as 'the last high priest of an obsolescent religious, metaphysical and political idealism' (Bakunin 1973a: 214, 217). Bakunin used the term 'idealism' to denote doctrines that abstracted and elevated ideas over their social and material context as a means of legitimizing the oppression and exploitation of human beings. The central example was religion: 'divinity, once established on its heavenly throne, has become the scourge of humanity and the ally of every tyrant, charlatan, tormentor and exploiter of the popular masses' (Bakunin 1973a: 214–222; 1970: 24–8). Unfortunately, Bakunin did not develop the materialist critique of the relationship between divine and temporal authority implied here systematically in the text and the specific term 'political theology' only occurs in the title as an invective. As such, Schmitt remains the first to have systematically developed the concept of 'political theology' as part of a positive analytical (and political) project even if the term was originally appropriated from Bakunin's text (see Falk 2014: 3, n10; Augustine 1998: 237–311).[5]

But even though Bakunin did not develop a coherent concept of political theology, his materialist critique of religion and anarchist opposition to authority nonetheless played a central role in Schmitt's work. In the conclusion to *Roman Catholicism*, Schmitt identified Bakunin's attack on Mazzini as an anticipation of the Russian Revolution, the main contemporary threat to 'West European civilization'; and in a parallel set of dramatic pronouncements that conclude *Political Theology*, Schmitt reiterated Juan Donoso Cortés' apocalyptic anticipation of a 'final battle' between 'authority and anarchy', represented by the conservative, Catholic counter-revolutionaries and Bakunin 'the greatest anarchist of the nineteenth century', respectively (1996: 36, 39; 2006: 66).[6] In these passages, Bakunin figures simultaneously as the avatar of contemporary left-wing political movements challenging the authority (sovereignty) of the state and the main theoretical antagonist of Schmitt's work.

This antagonism may at first make Schmitt's appropriation and development of the term 'political theology' from this source seem rather bizarre. However, in a number of passages in *Political Theology*, Schmitt explains the common ground implicit in the direct ideological opposition between conservatives and anarchists: they both recognize God and the state as transcendent and absolute (sovereign) authorities, although they draw opposite conclusions from these insights. This enables them to appropriate analytical and theoretical insights from one another without compromising their own political position (Schmitt 2006: 55, 66; Bakunin 1973b: 38, 41–5, 48–58). Schmitt's appropriation of the term 'political theology' from Bakunin must be understood on this model, as being based on *and* in direct opposition to Bakunin (Meier 2006: 80–1; Newman 2019: 21–3, 30–3). This is, of course, not to say that Schmitt's analysis of political theology can somehow be reduced to Bakunin's text, which made no attempt at a definition of the concept. The central point is that if Schmitt's analysis of political theology was based on an inversion of Bakunin's position, it may be possible to repeat and reverse this gesture, thereby disentangling Schmitt's analysis of political theology from his normative commitment to it, as the basis of a profane critique of the idea of the sovereign state (Schmitt 2006: 66; see also Agamben 2016: 272–9).[7] But before I get ahead of myself, let me turn to explore Schmitt's analysis of political theology.

The secularization thesis

Schmitt's analysis of political theology derives from what is commonly described as the 'secularization thesis', which is elaborated at the beginning of the third chapter. Here Schmitt famously proposed:

> All significant concepts of the modern theory of the state are secularized theological concepts not only because of their historical development – in which they were transferred from theology to the theory of the state, whereby, for example, the omnipotent God became the omnipotent lawgiver – but also because of their systematic structure [. . .] only by being aware of this analogy can we appreciate the manner in which the philosophical ideas of the state developed in the last centuries. (2006: 36)

Schmitt's secularization thesis identifies two distinct but interrelated connections between theology and modern state theory: firstly, a *historical* connection consisting in the transfer and transformation of central concepts from theology into modern political thought and, secondly, a *conceptual* or *structural* connection insofar as these concepts retained the conceptual structure of their theological antecedents, that is, the reliance on a structure of transcendence. The secularization thesis thus identifies both continuity and change in the relationship between the concepts of theology and modern political theory. The historical migration of these concepts marks a change of terrain, which altered their referents and meaning, while maintaining the same systematic structure. This duality is neatly summarized in the concept of *political theology*, which simultaneously evokes the historical origins of modern 'secular' political thought in Christian theology *and* the historical movement beyond it.[8]

Here it is relevant to briefly explain my understanding of this systematic structure, which I conceive in terms of a structure of transcendence: I deliberately employ this phrase rather than just 'transcendence', to highlight the fact that this religious conception of transcendence, that was later transferred and transformed into modern political thought, was never wholly transcendent, that is, it was never entirely separate from the temporal realm it claimed to transcend, but remained connected to it and continued to intervene in and determine it (otherwise the former would be entirely inconsequential to the latter; Schmitt 2006: 36, 46–51).[9] The transcendent is transcendent only in relation to something else: the temporal realm. Crucially, the interaction of these two spheres is entirely one-directional and extends only from the transcendent to the temporal sphere. To illustrate this point, it is useful to recall Lucius Lactantius' classical etymology of the concept of religion, which he proposed derived from *religare*, meaning to bind, which he understood to refer to the fact that 'we are fastened and bound to God by this bond of piety, whence religion itself takes its name'. This bond presupposes a fundamental separation between humankind and God, the temporal and the transcendent sphere while tying the former to the latter in a hierarchical structure of transcendence (Lactantius 2008: 318). Similarly, the political-theological concept of sovereignty serves to separate the political authority of the state from its various institutions and society, while subordinating the latter to the former.

It is also important to note that the concept of secularization, which is commonly associated with the declining centrality of the church and religion in post-Reformation politics, is actually far from incompatible with such a structure of transcendence. The concept, in fact, originates in a profoundly religious context and world view. The term 'secular' comes from Latin *saeculum* meaning an age or a time period and was thus distinct from God, who was held to be eternal, existing outside of historical time. The secular, in other words, is a fundamentally theological notion that separates and subordinates that which exists within finite, created time to God. The Church was initially considered to belong to the temporal realm, even though it was primarily oriented towards the divine, but as it came to identify as the mystical body of Christ, the *corpus mysticum*, in the fourteenth century, it was reconceived as the representative of the transcendent *within* this world (Launay 2014: 932–6; Kantorowicz 1997: 194f.; Casanova 2011: 56; Lubac 2007: 13–123). The term 'secularization' [*Saecularisatio*] was first deployed in this context as a technical term in canon law, denoting a clergy-member's transfer from monastic life to live in the world among the laity. It was only after the Reformation that it came to be used to denote the acquisition of Church property by states, and it is primarily this second sense that has inspired its metaphorical deployment in the history of ideas, where it has come to denote a transition or transfer from church to state (Launay 2014: 933; Asad 2003: 192–3; Agamben 2011: 3–4). Schmitt's secularization thesis likewise denotes the transfer and transformation of theological concepts into modern political thought, but emphasizes that while this transition fundamentally altered the meaning of these concepts, they maintained a reliance on a theological structure of transcendence. As such the secularization thesis denotes neither a total break nor complete continuity between Christian theology and modern theories of the state.

The decline of the political centrality of the Church and its doctrines in the wake of the Reformation commonly associated with this notion of secularization, in other words, does not imply the decline of the political significance of theological ideas as such, but their transfer and transformation into political theology, which took over its political and legitimizing functions. Yet, Schmitt fails to consistently pursue the radical implications of his secularization thesis. Most notably, he somewhat abruptly reduces political theology to a matter of the diachronic correspondence between predominant ideas of God and the form of the state in the latter parts of the same chapter, suggesting that theistic conceptions of God corresponded to absolute monarchy and deistic conceptions of God corresponded to the modern constitutional state, which forms part of his narrative of their parallel decline (Schmitt 2006: 46–51). But this contradicts his previous argument that theological and political thought converged and developed in the form of modern political theology (rather than any resulting parallels between them). While theology and political theology can and should be distinguished – the idea of a transcendent and omnipotent God is obviously distinct from the sovereign state – the secularization thesis implies that the latter replaced the theoretical and practical legitimizing functions previously fulfilled by the former. What we might call Schmitt's 'parallelism', in other words, contradicts his secularization thesis and seems much more closely aligned with, if not directly motivated by, his normative doctrine of decisionism and will be bracketed in the following.

Schmitt's identification of the concept of sovereignty as a secularized theological concept is meant to underline its original and continued theological structure of transcendence albeit within a fundamentally different 'secularized' political discourse that profoundly changes its referent and meaning. The central point is that doctrines of political theology conceived the state as the locus of a transcendent and absolute power over society in a fundamentally theological way, independently of the Christian doctrines that gave rise to it.[10] This is the basic configuration implied by the concept of political theology here rather than any other incidental continuities with Christian theology that may have persisted alongside it (see Peterson 2011: 68–105; Blumenberg 1983: 89–101).[11]

The development of the concept of state sovereignty

Schmitt insists that the secularization thesis is the starting point of an understanding of 'the philosophical ideas of the state developed in the last centuries' and while he invokes 'all significant concepts of the modern theory of the state', his focus is the concept of sovereignty, as is evident from the subtitle of the book, 'Four Chapters on the Concept of Sovereignty', as well as its contents. At the heart of Schmitt's conception of political theology, then, is the concept of state sovereignty, whose origins and development I will now turn to examine in more detail.

The Latin term *status* and various vernacular derivatives such as *estat*, *stato* and *state* were employed in the legal and political discourse of the fourteenth century and onwards to denote a ruler's status, standing and power over their realm; over time these terms became increasingly identified with the means of maintaining this power, that is, the various institutions of government. However, they remained tied to the feudal conception of a ruler's personal dominion and did not begin to refer to an impersonal and sovereign subject transcending ruler and ruled alike until the sixteenth and seventeenth centuries (Skinner 2007: 369–79, 394–405).

The earliest identifiable precursor of the concept of sovereignty is the neologism *superanus* derived from the Latin *super* meaning over or above. Some of the earliest deployments of this concept in a political context occurred in the thirteenth century when it was used to describe the feudal authority of a ruler within a specific realm or dominion (much like the conceptual cluster preceding the state) and was commonly coupled with explicitly religious legitimations of this arrangement, for example, the doctrine of divine right (Boldt et al. 1990: 98–106; Figgis 1922: 237, 258).[12] The modern concept of state sovereignty, referring to the absolute and transcendent authority of the state itself, conceived as a sort of autonomous subject distinct from both rulers and ruled was primarily formulated in the sixteenth and seventeenth centuries by Jean Bodin, Thomas Hobbes and others (Skinner 2007: 394–5, 405). This period was marked by a series of interrelated social, political and religious conflicts that engulfed most of Europe in the wake of the Reformation and the collapse of the universal authority of the Church as well as the fragmentation of and controversy over religious doctrine, which had previously legitimized the political order. The idea of the sovereign state was formulated to fill this vacuum and provide a separate and secular source of legitimacy and stability, drawing on but fundamentally reconfiguring the idea of an omnipotent subject transcending the temporal realm and its various conflicts.

These writers drew on and developed ideas of theological origin that can be traced back to Pope Boniface VIII's 1302 identification of the Church as the 'mystical body' of Christ, a theological innovation that invested the transcendent omnipotence of God in the temporal institution of the Church headed by the pope. This move was imitated and developed in early modern legal and political thought, such as the doctrine of the king's two bodies, which reconceived the monarch as having two bodies based on the doctrine of Christ's dual nature: a natural body that was mortal and fallible and a 'mystical' body, representing the unity and power of the realm, that was considered infallible and perpetual. This redoubled the monarch's authority outside of them, where it grew increasingly independent and eventually developed into the modern concept of the state understood as an independent and sovereign subject transcending both rulers and ruled. This conception of the state as an impersonal sovereign subject drew on and replicated the structure of preceding theological doctrines but developed into a distinct and independent *political theology* (Boniface VIII 1988: 188–9; Lubac 2007: 13–123; Kantorowicz 1997: 13–23, 193–214; Hobbes 1994: 3, 109).

This political theology was constituted in and through the transfer and transformation of the theological notion of God's transcendent omnipotence into the concept of state sovereignty in early modern political thought. Sovereignty was conceptualized as the supreme power within a specific territory, transcending and determining all other social and political forces therein. In order to maintain this supremacy, it was conceived as being necessarily *indivisible*, which also meant that while it might be vested in and exercised by the monarch, it belonged solely to *the state*, conceived as the *perpetual* and *transcendent* locus of sovereignty exercise (contrary to Schmitt's insistence on the personalization of sovereignty). Sovereignty was thus conceptualized as the absolute, indivisible and perpetual power of the state, simultaneously transcending the temporal existence of the monarch, the state's various institutions and society as a whole (Bodin 1992: 1, 92; Hobbes 1994: 3, 92, 109, 135, 146; Balibar 2004: 133–54; Skinner 1978: 358; Skinner 2007: 394–539, 406).

Outline of political atheism

Schmitt argued that the significance of his secularization thesis extended beyond the identification of the theological origin and structure of the concept of state sovereignty, insisting that 'the metaphysical image that a definite epoch forges of the world has the same structure as what the world immediately understands to be appropriate as a form of its political organization' (2006: 46). Understanding this metaphysical image, that is, political theology, was also a means of grasping the political organization of this world, that is, the modern state and its existence within society.

Schmitt conceived his work as a sociology of the concept of sovereignty. He presented this sociology of concepts as a means of overcoming the contradictions of idealism and materialism, which, according to Schmitt, artificially divided the world into an ideal and a material realm and then proceeded to reduce one to the other, whereas his sociology of concepts was concerned with their correspondence (2006: 42–6).[13] But Schmitt consistently displaced the social and material sphere with its conceptualization in his descriptions, that is, 'the *conceptually represented* social structure of a certain epoch' and 'the *juristic construction* of the historical-political reality' and as such either remained caught within the realm of concepts and ideas *or* implicitly assumed that they corresponded to or otherwise structured material reality, as he appears to suggest in a number of passages, both of which return him to the realm of idealism (2006: 45–6, emphasis added). Here it is also relevant to note that Schmitt was clearly more concerned with challenging the 'radical materialist philosophy of history' than the 'similarly radical spiritualist philosophy of history', which he associated with 'the authors of the counterrevolution', who served as his historical proxies throughout the book (2006: 42). In either case, Schmitt considered the modern state only in terms of its supposed sovereignty and as such remained within and perpetuated this idealist political theology.

While Schmitt provided a convincing analysis of the historical origin and structure of the concept of state sovereignty, he did not move beyond this political theology to provide an account of its earthly foundations. However, the theoretical continuity Schmitt established between his own and Bakunin's positions provides the means of extracting his analysis of political theology from his own support for it and begin to formulate a materialist critique of it. Bakunin, of course, did not manage to formulate a critique of political theology, and his anarchism is primarily a political ideal and remains inadequate to this task (see Kelsen 1973: 61–82; Graeber 2004: 2–7).[14] However, his materialist critique of religion may serve as a model for a materialist critique of political theology and/as the basis of political atheism.

Bakunin's materialist critique of religion starts with the rejection of the structure of transcendence. From a materialist or atheist perspective, there is no transcendence and the illusion thereof must, instead, be understood as the attempt to re-signify and subordinate this world ('the temporal sphere' from a theological perspective) to the idea of a transcendent and omnipotent God and legitimize existing hierarchies. The material or temporal world is not the result of a transcendent and omnipotent God's will. Rather, this idea is itself a product of this world, the intellectual abstraction of humanity's collective power and capacities, 'everything, which seemed to constitute their power, movement, life and intelligence', invested in the abstract idea of 'spirit' or 'God' standing apart from and opposed to humanity; or as Bakunin summarizes it: 'all Gods, past and present, have owed their original existence to the fantasies of man [. . .] men, deceived by a kind of optical illusion, have only ever worshipped in their Gods their own reversed and monstrously exaggerated image' (Bakunin 1973a: 218–22).

This argument may at first appear to conform to the pattern identified and criticized by Schmitt, seemingly dividing the world into an ideal and a material sphere and reducing the former to the latter. However, Bakunin's materialism was distinctly post-Hegelian and thus presupposed the identity of subject and substance (Hegel 1977: 10; McLaughlin 2002: 156–206).[15] As such, it did not reduce the idea of God to a passive and inconsequential reflection of the social and material conditions but took seriously its significance and effects within this context. Bakunin explained that 'what we call matter or the material world by no means excludes but necessarily embraces the ideal' and proceeded to outline the historical efficacy of religious ideas in establishing and legitimizing political authority and economic exploitation throughout history: by submitting to the idea of 'God, that nothingness created out of our own power of abstraction or negation, the predominant faculty of our brain, we were abandoning society and putting all our real existence at the mercy of the prophets, tyrants and religious, political and economic exploiters of the divine idea on earth' (1973a: 219, 230; 1970: 24).

To summarize, Bakunin's materialist critique of religion consists of two interrelated arguments. Firstly, that the idea of God is an illusory projection and alienation of humanity's collective powers and capacities. Secondly, that although this idea is fundamentally illusory, it nonetheless has very real effects: it conceals these collective powers and thereby sustains political authority and economic exploitation. Based on these determinations, it is possible to anticipate two corresponding arguments of a materialist critique of political theology that together constitute an outline of political atheism: firstly, that the idea of the state transcending and determining its various institutions and society is an illusion. The state only exists in and through these institutions and, more centrally, the population's general participation in and obedience to them. As such, there is no state sovereignty nor can there ever be. The seemingly sovereign power of the state is the intellectual abstraction of the very same social forces and institutions that it purportedly transcends and determines. Secondly, while the political-theological idea of the sovereign state is fundamentally illusory, it does have very real social and material effects. It is what animates and holds together the various institutions that comprise the modern state and what motivates the population's general participation in and obedience to these institutions. The cumulative effect is what allows these institutions to continue to appear and operate as if they actually constituted a coherent transcendent and sovereign subject, thereby perpetuating themselves and/as the illusion of the sovereign state.

The hegemony of the idea of the state as a transcendent and sovereign subject is what allows its various institutions to operate as if they were part of such, which in turn perpetuates and seemingly confirms this illusion. Although the idea of the sovereign state does not reflect the actual reality of the modern state, it nonetheless informs the organization and behaviour of its various institutions and members, which produce the appearance and effect of the state as a transcendent and sovereign subject, thus giving it a strange contradictory and self-perpetuating material basis within the very same society that it seems to transcend.

Political theology both reflects and reproduces the appearance of the modern state as a transcendent and sovereign subject, in its codification of society's alienation from its own collective agency as a matter of political philosophical principle. But it is not merely a passive reflection of this social and material dynamic; this set of hegemonic ideas about the state also contributes to its perpetuation (Schmitt 1996: 17).[16] It is in this double sense, that we must reread Schmitt's claim that understanding political theology is to understand the modern state.

Political theology is central to the social and material existence and operation of the modern state and its institutions, but it is not in itself an adequate description of it, and it has therefore been necessary to complement Schmitt's account of the historical origins and conceptual structure of the notion of the sovereign state with a materialist critique of it. Bakunin's materialist critique of religion provided the conceptual model and resources necessary for such a materialist critique of political theology that, unlike Schmitt's account, can extract itself from the social and material dynamic that underpins and sustains political theology. The resulting analysis of the historical origin and conceptual structure of the idea of the modern state as a transcendent and sovereign subject, remains fundamentally indebted to Schmitt's *Political Theology*, but also moves beyond its limitations, towards a profane reconceptualization of the social and material foundations of this political theology and its practical significance to the organization and operations of the modern state in and as a part of society, which I have designated political atheism.

Political atheism provides a materialist account of political theology that reinscribes and reinterprets the idea of the sovereign state in terms of its social and material foundation and efficacy. It insists that the modern state is not and, indeed, cannot be a transcendent or sovereign subject, that it only exists in and through its various institutions and the participation of the population. However, it simultaneously highlights that the predominant idea of the modern state as a sovereign subject is what holds these institutions together and motivates the wider population's participation in and obedience to them. This allows the institutions of the modern state to operate *as if* they constituted a transcendent and sovereign subject, thereby perpetuating the political theology that underpins and sustains the modern state.

Notes

1 'Profane' comes from Latin *pro-* and *fanum* meaning in front of or otherwise outside of the temple. Here I employ the term to denote a perspective on the modern state that stands outside of political theology without denying its significance.
2 Schmitt contradicts this a little later in *Political Theology II* (2008), describing the cult of the Roman state ('*theologia politica* or *civilis*') as a relevant precedent. I would nonetheless argue that this both can and should be differentiated from the concept

of political theology pertaining to 'the modern theory of the state' that he developed almost fifty years earlier.
3   The first edition of *Political Theology* from 1922 contained a note indicating that it was written alongside an essay on 'The Political Idea of Catholicism' presumably identical to *Roman Catholicism* published the following year.
4   Bakunin (1973b) among other things contributed an article to Arnold Ruge's *Deutsche Jahrbücher für Wissenschaft und Politik* in 1842 (signed Jules Elysard).
5   Even the classical *theologia civilis* is primarily known through St. Augustine's critique of Marcus Terentius Varro (1998: 237–311).
6   Given Schmitt's fascination with Italian Fascism, it is perhaps also relevant to note that Giovanni Gentile (2002: 5–6), among others, attempted to appropriate Mazzini's legacy for this movement.
7   Note that I reject Schmitt's characterization of Bakunin as 'the theologian of the antitheological' based on the reduction of his critique of religion and state to a *decision* against them. Giorgio Agamben (2016: 272–9) has convincingly shown that Schmitt's political theology operates through inclusive exclusions that incorporate their outside and that moving beyond political theology requires a break with this structure.
8   This is not to suggest that prior Christian doctrines were not political (consider, for instance, Rom. 13:1-7; 1 Pet. 2:13-17), merely that the majority of their political functions were overtaken by discrete political doctrines after the Reformation.
9   In this regard the distinction between theistic and deistic conceptions of God that Schmitt later insists (2006) on remains irrelevant. It is seemingly mobilized to support his political commitment to personalized sovereignty vested with the power to decide on the exception (i.e. his doctrine of decisionism), which he argues is analogous to the miracle.
10 This independence, alongside the focus on the impersonal state rather than the personal power of various monarchs, separates modern political theology from preceding Christian doctrines of the divine right.
11 The secularization thesis thus understood does not imply the identity of political theology and Christianity as such nor does it pertain to modernity as a whole.
12 Hence the many contemporary references to monarchs as 'sovereigns' although sovereignty was generally considered to belong to the state and only be delegated to monarchs as representatives thereof from Jean Bodin and onwards.
13 Schmitt also uses 'correspondence' to refer to his account of diachronous parallels between conceptions of God and forms of the state in some passages, as I have already outlined (and rejected).
14 The limitations in this regard are efficiently illustrated by Hans Kelsen's 'epistemic anarchism' (1973) presented in his article 'God and the State' (a title also appropriated from Bakunin) published a few months after *Political Theology*. Here Kelsen proposed that the sovereign state was merely a hypostatized psychological representation of the unity of the legal system that should be discarded as a prerequisite of the proper scientific study of law. This approach is narrowly juristic and idealist and, as such, cannot contribute to an analysis of this idea's social and material foundation and effects. David Graeber (2004) presents a sympathetic account of the limits of anarchist theory more generally.
15 This, alongside the insistence on the collective historical agency of humanity, sets Bakunin's materialism apart from other reductive and mechanistic forms of materialism.

16   Schmitt (1996: 17) makes a related point regarding the dependence of political authority on some type of 'faith' in *Roman Catholicism*, insisting that 'no political system can survive even a generation with only naked techniques of holding power,' yet continues to neglect its material basis and efficacy.

References

Abrams, P. (1988), 'Notes on the Difficulty of Studying the State', *Journal of Historical Sociology*, 1 (1): 58–89.
Agamben, G. (2009), *What Is an Apparatus and Other Essays*, Stanford, CA: Stanford University Press.
Agamben, G. (2011), *The Kingdom and the Glory: For a Theological Genealogy of Economy and Government*, Stanford, CA: Stanford University Press.
Agamben, G. (2016), *The Use of Bodies*, Stanford, CA: Stanford University Press.
Asad, T. (2003), *Formations of the Secular: Christianity, Islam, Modernity*, Stanford, CA: Stanford University Press.
Augustine (1998), *The City of God Against the Pagans*, Cambridge: Cambridge University Press.
Bakunin, M. (1970), *God and the State*, New York: Dover.
Bakunin, M. (1971), *Bakunin on Anarchy: Selected Works by the Activist-Founder of World Anarchism*, ed. S. Dolgoff, New York: Random House.
Bakunin, M. (1973a), 'The Political Theology of Mazzini', in A. Lehning (ed.), *Mikhail Bakunin: Selected Writings*, 214–31, London: Jonathan Cape.
Bakunin, M. (1973b), 'The Reaction in Germany', in A. Lehning (ed.), *Mikhail Bakunin: Selected Writings*, 37–58, London: Jonathan Cape.
Balibar, É. (2004), *We, The People of Europe?*, Princeton, NJ: Princeton University Press.
Barrow, C. (2005), 'The Return of the State: Globalization, State Theory, and the New Imperialism', *New Political Science*, 27 (2): 123–45.
Blumenberg, H. (1983), *The Legitimacy of the Modern Age*, Cambridge, MA: MIT Press.
Bodin, J. (1992), *On Sovereignty: Four Chapters from The Six Books of the Commonwealth*, Cambridge: Cambridge University Press.
Boldt, H., W. Conze, G. Haverkate, D. Klippel and R. Koselleck (1990), 'Staat und Souveränität', in R. Koselleck, O. Brunner, W. Conze (eds), *Geschichtliche Grundbegriffe. Band 6: Historisches Lexikon Zur Politisch-Sozialen Sprache in Deutschland*, Stuttgart: Klett-Cotta.
Boniface VIII (1988), 'Unam Sanctam', in B. Tierney (ed.), *The Crisis of Church and State, 1050–1300*, 188–9, Toronto: University of Toronto Press.
Cahill, D. (2014), *The End of Laissez-Faire? On the Durability of Embedded Neoliberalism*, Cheltenham: Edward Elgar.
Casanova, J. (2011), 'The Secular, Secularizations, Secularisms', in C. Calhoun, M. Juergensmeyer and J. VanAntwerpen, *Rethinking Secularism*, 54–74, Oxford: Oxford University Press.
Falk, H. (2014), *Det Politisk-Teologiska Komplexet: Fyra Kapitel Om Carl Schmitts Sekularitet*, Gothenbury: University of Gothenburg.
Figgis, J. (1922), *The Theory of the Divine Right of Kings*, Cambridge: Cambridge University Press.
Gentile, G. (2002), *Origins and Doctrine of Fascism*, New Brunswick: Transaction Publishers.

Giudice, M. del (1981), 'The Young Bakunin and Left Hegelianism: Origins of Russian Radicalism and the Theory of Praxis', PhD diss., McGill University.
Graeber, D. (2004), *Fragments of an Anarchist Anthropology*, Chicago: Prickly Paradigm Press.
Gupta, A. (1995), 'Blurred Boundaries: The Discourse of Corruption, the Culture of Politics, and the Imagined State', *American Ethnologist*, 22 (2): 375–402.
Hegel, G. W. F. (1977), *The Phenomenology of Spirit*, Oxford: Oxford University Press.
Hobbes, T. (1994), *Leviathan: With Selected Variants from the Latin Edition of 1668*, Indianapolis: Hackett.
Kantorowicz, E. (1997), *The King's Two Bodies: A Study in Medieval Political Theology*, Princeton, NJ: Princeton University Press.
Kelsen, H. (1973), 'God and the State', in O. Weinberger (ed.), *Essays in Legal and Moral Philosophy*, 61–82, Boston: Reidel.
Krasner, S. (1999), *Sovereignty: Organized Hypocrisy*, Princeton, NJ: Princeton University Press.
Lactantius, L. (2008), *The Divine Institutes*, Washington, DC: The Catholic University of America Press.
Launay, M. de (2014), 'Secularization', in B. Cassin, E. Apter, J. Lezra, and M. Wood (eds), *Dictionary of Untranslatables*, 932–6, Princeton, NJ: Princeton University Press.
Lubac, H. de (2007), *Corpus Mysticum: The Eucharist and the Church in the Middle Ages – A Historical Survey*, Notre Dame: University of Notre Dame Press.
Mazzini, G. (2009), 'Neither Pacifism nor Terror: Considerations on the Paris Commune and the French National Assembly', in S. Recchia and N. Urbinati (eds), *A Cosmopolitanism of Nations: Giuseppe Mazzini's Writings on Democracy, Nation Building, and International Relations*, 153–66, Princeton, NJ: Princeton University Press.
McLaughlin, P. (2002), *Mikhail Bakunin: The Philosophical Basis of His Anarchism*, New York: Algora.
Meier, H. (2006), *Leo Strauss and the Theologico-Political Problem*, Cambridge: Cambridge University Press.
Mitchell, T. (1991), 'The Limits of the State: Beyond Statist Approaches and Their Critics', *American Political Science Review*, 85 (1): 77–96.
Newman, S. (2019), *Political Theology: A Critical Introduction*, Cambridge: Polity Press.
Pernicone, N. (1993), *Italian Anarchism, 1864–92*, Princeton, NJ: Princeton University Press.
Peterson, E. (2011), *Theological Tractates*, Stanford, CA: Stanford University Press.
Quante, M. (2019), 'After Hegel: The Actualization of Philosophy in Practice', in D. Moyar (ed.), *The Routledge Companion to Nineteenth Century Philosophy*, 197–237, London: Routledge.
Ravindranathan, T. R. (1981), 'The Paris Commune and the First International in Italy: Republicanism versus Socialism, 1871–2', *The International History Review*, 3 (4): 482–516.
Rosenberg, J. (2005), 'Globalization Theory: A Post Mortem', *International Politics*, 42: 2–74.
Schmitt, C. (1996), *Roman Catholicism and Political Form*, Westport, CT: Greenwood Press.
Schmitt, C. (2006), *Political Theology: Four Chapters on Sovereignty*, Chicago, IL: University of Chicago Press.
Schmitt, C. (2008), *Political Theology II: The Myth of the Closure of Any Political Theology*, Cambridge: Polity Press.

Skinner, Q. (1978), *The Foundation of Modern Political Thought. Volume Two: The Renaissance*, Cambridge: Cambridge University Press.
Skinner, Q. (2007), *Visions of Politics. Volume Two: Renaissance Virtues*, Cambridge: Cambridge University Press.
Strauss, L. (2007), 'Notes on Carl Schmitt, The Concept of the Political', in C. Schmitt, *The Concept of the Political*, 97–122. Chicago, IL: University of Chicago Press.
Toews, J. E. (1985), *Hegelianism: The Path Towards Dialectical Humanism, 1805–41*, Cambridge: Cambridge University Press.
Toscano, A. (2020), 'The State of the Pandemic', *Historical Materialism*, 28 (4): 3–23.
Ulmen, G. (1996), 'Introduction', in C. Schmitt (ed.), *Roman Catholicism and Political Form*, vii–xxxvi, Westport: Greenwood Press.

Part 2

THEOLOGY, RELIGION AND THE PUBLIC SPHERE

Chapter 4

RITUALS OF TRUTH

OATH, PUBLIC DISCUSSION, ACCLAMATION

Montserrat Herrero

Foucault adopted the term *alèthurgie,* taking the expression from the grammarian Heraclides of Pontus, as a set of verbal and non-verbal procedures conducted to discover a truth that was hidden, invisible or impossible to know (2012a: 8).[1] Moreover, *alèthurgies* are 'liturgies of truth', that is, activities that make some truth appear. Foucault points out that three kinds of liturgies were relevant for ancient societies, including oracles, oaths and testimonies. The subject of the first were gods; the subject of the second were kings; finally, the subject of testimonies were those who were neither gods nor kings (Foucault 2012a: 40). Testimonies, the simple 'yes' or 'no', is the common terrain of humans, who have been ordered by God, following Matthew's gospel, not to take oaths (Matthew 5:34–7). The difference between these three types of truth-liturgy that Foucault finds in ancient societies differ not only by the subject, as he notes, but also by their temporal valence. The rituals of truth performed by mere humans can only account for the past; but kings, who hold the stability of the political community in their hands, perform oaths to secure the future; and the gods even penetrate the future in their oracular predictions. Because of this double temporal reference, the mediaeval tradition distinguished between *juramentum assertorium* and *juramentum promissorium*.[2] Both are highly relevant to founding community: the first, where testimonies have to be given in order to establish just judgements in trials; the second, in order to bind the commitment of the will to a future and thus give stability to any kind of relationship, particularly those relating to the shaping of the political community. To such an extent are these rituals of truth relevant for the political community that usually its government requires that some acts of truth be prescribed. Foucault speaks then of 'régimes de vérité'. A truth regime involves 'what' (*ce que*) constrains the individual to a certain number of acts of truth (2012a: 91).

Taking advantage of Foucault's conceptual genius, and bearing in mind that he himself arrives at this idea in a theological-political drift, namely the analysis of Christian praxis as a device of governmentality, we have looked into Schmitt's work, searching for the rituals of truth that are present in his work as derivations of the theological-political analogy. We find at least three: oath, public discussion and acclamation, rituals of truth that in one way or another have a theological-political genealogy. The permanence of the theological-political pervades the secular institutional structure of the modern state if it wishes to prevail. The presence of 'rituals of truth' in Schmitt's constitutional theory is a mark of his move from conceptual to institutional political theology.

The Schmittian theo-political case of oaths

When affirming that all of the significant ideas in the modern state's theory are secularized theological concepts, Schmitt had the concept of sovereignty specially in mind when making the well-known analogy between miracles and the sovereign decision on the exception. However, he might easily reserve a similar centrality to the institution of the oath for exemplifying his political theology. In fact, as he wrote in several places of the *Constitutional Theory*, although the oath seems to have disappeared from public life, it will always remain a necessary institution, whatever the formula, to ensure internal disposition, so that the institutions of the modern state are not abused and their very foundations destroyed (Schmitt 2008: 69, 81, 118). It is because of their capacity to generate obligations that oaths are at the heart of the constitution of the political (Dean 2018: 67–91).

Paolo Prodi has been the first to point out the theo-political case of oaths. He describes the relevance of the oath in Western constitutional history and its decadence, echoing Schmittian political theology and applying the idea of the secularization of political concepts in modernity to the case of swearing. Certainly, he affirms, the oath is the basis of the political covenant in Western societies. It is not a formal revetment of a contract or a covenant, but a metapolitical guarantor of the political bond insofar as it implies a mutual promise between two or more persons to trust each other's word under the sight of God. The decline of the oath in our times, as a result of secularization, carries with it the crisis of the very idea of political community, asserts Prodi (1992).[3]

Certainly, in every epoch taking an oath has been considered both a civil and a religious act (Guindon 1957; Benveniste 1969; Agamben 2008).[4] The special witness evoked in oaths is precisely what guarantees truthfulness insofar as whoever commits perjury is execrated. In fact, the *execratio* that is produced by perjury and other crimes exposes the offender to divine revenge (*sacer esto*) to the extent of being precluded from human protection and being directly punished by the gods. The punishment of God who sees everything: the past, the present and even the darkest thoughts, is the guarantee of truthfulness in oaths. Benveniste, from the point of view of linguistic research, corroborates that oaths were for Indo-Europeans as much rites as juridical instruments. This dual valence was present in Ancient Greece and Rome (Benveniste 1969: 112–13, 367–75, 406–15).[5] The same could be said from the historical development of oaths in the Middle Ages and Early Modernity: oaths of coronation, oaths of alliance, vows, oaths of passage, oaths of office, oath to the succession, oath of supremacy, oath of association (see Aurell, Aurell and Herrero 2018; Condren 2006: 285).[6] In Early

Modernity also oaths were present in the generation of the Commonwealth, as we can see in the writings of Hobbes and Locke (Hobbes 1996: chapter XIV; Locke 1980: 8.121; 1968).[7] Additionally, Rousseau reserves an important role for oaths in civil religion.[8] Still in the nineteenth century we can hear Lasalle, whom Schmitt quotes in his *Constitutional Theory*, stating that 'a constitution is a pact, affirmed by oath, between king and people that establishes the fundamental principles of law-making and government in a country' (2008: 69). Adolf Reinach follows the same conviction that the law itself has the structure of a promise (1989: 147).[9]

Every legal system is based on the promise to impose a penalty on whoever commits a crime, where 'crime' still retains a moral connotation, that is, a wrong has been committed, a harm has been done. When this is lost sight of, the law is functionalized, becoming a technical means of state power devoid of the two characteristics of the oath: truthfulness and faithfulness, according to the double temporal character of oaths. Schmitt was obsessed with the exclamation, 'Be silent, theologians! *Silete theologi!* which was launched at the beginning of the modern State era by an international lawyer against theologians of both confessions' (1979: 15).[10] He describes the path of legal sciences over the last two centuries as the development of this cry (Schmitt 1990: 35–70). The substitution of divine promises, such as the respect for the given word, by the utilitarian decision of the state resulted in legal positivism: the law becomes a command of the sovereign. In the twentieth century, another step was taken, which Schmitt called the 'motorization of the law', through which the legislation process and its reform became easy and fast: the word given through the law could change in a speedy way driven by political interests of any kind. The last step emerged with liberal economism, when the law became an elastic means through which the political decisions could be formed or deformed depending on all kinds of economic interests. A moralized natural law, as well as general propositions within a theory of values, were also attempts to overcome the motorization of the law that legal positivism entails. Ultimately, the loss of theological legitimation results in the impossibility of swearing or making an oath endure, has as a consequence that the law has ceased to be a promise and has become a means to revolution (Schmitt 1978: 73–89; Herrero 2015).[11]

Certainly, after swearing an oath, our most important political commitment is making memory happen. Registering, archiving, retaining, tracing are crucial actions that make memory happen in a political community. They constitute a referential resistance to forgetfulness as much as to discursive re-appropriation. In fact, if promises have to endure over generations, they have to be in a way inscribed or scripted and accompanied by oaths or solemn declarations that imply some kind of ritual.

The theological-political derivation of Öffentlichkeit *(publicness) as a means of parliamentary governmentality*

Another ritual of truth proper to parliamentary governmental form is publicness. In particular, in the foreword to the second edition of *The Crisis of Parliamentary*

Democracy, where Schmitt defends himself against Richard Thoma's criticisms of his first edition, he makes a plea for the idea of openness of discussion for proper parliamentary government. Against the Weberian idea of the parliament as an institution for the selection of political leaders, Schmitt argues for a parliamentarism understood as a 'ritual of truth', insofar as the discussion that takes place in the parliamentary sessions makes truth appear.

Schmitt is not, therefore, as is so often interpreted, criticizing parliamentarism, but, rather, its corruption by the confusion of this kind of regime with the political form of mass democracy. Parliamentarism is, of course, the opposite of bolshevism or fascism, which are fundamentally defined by radical working-class politics, but it is also the opposite of mass democracy, which demands the homogeneity of the people and, therefore, excludes both proportional representation and open discussion of governance issues. The crisis of parliamentarism comes from its confusion with the mass democracy political form. It is the development of modern mass democracy that has made public discussion an empty formality. However, the prestige of parliamentarianism comes from the possibility of realizing political truth through open discussion, which takes on a liturgical form insofar as parliamentary sessions have their own rules that shape their own form, according to which the supposed truth is made manifest – a truth that could not be accessed in any other way. It therefore has the character of an ordeal. Where there is neither publicness nor truth, parliament transforms in a regime of secrecy, of the scoundrel: 'Parliament is in any case only "true" as long as public discussion is taken seriously and implemented,' says Schmitt (2000: 4). In fact, in a footnote Schmitt quotes the following passage of Guizot via Krabbe:

> Guizot's opinion of parliamentarism in full: 'That is in addition the character of a system that nowhere acknowledges the legitimacy of absolute power to oblige all citizens constantly and without restriction to seek truth, reason, and justice, which have to check actual power. It is this which constitutes the representative system: (1) through discussion the powers-that-be are obliged to seek truth in common; (2) through publicity the powers are brought to this search under the eyes of the citizenry; (3) through freedom of the press the citizens themselves are brought to look for truth and to tell this to the powers-that-be.' In the phrase representative system, representative refers to the representation of the (rational) people in parliament. (Schmitt 2000: 97)

This idea of the common search for truth that generates authentic representation could be seen as one of the secularized concepts of modern state theory, although Schmitt does not make this theological-political analogy explicit in an obvious way. However, if we inquire into the essay written in the same year as the *Crisis of Parliamentary Democracy*, that is, *Roman Catholicism and Political Form* (1923), we find that Schmitt clearly defends the idea of publicness as one of the most important features of an authentic political representation (Herrero 2017). The public-legal structure of the Church is an exemplar of the due publicity of the state, in the face of the whole economic fabric which moves in the sphere of privacy. Indeed, the theology of representation assumes an analogy between the juridical representation of both institutions, church and state, and in this sense is to be considered an example of political theology (Ulmen 1996: xiv). On the one hand, it shows how the Church in its task of representing Christ in history is the true heir of the Roman juridical spirit (Schmitt 1996: 18); on the other, the representative capacity of the Church is an example for political representation.

The Church represents the public scope of the faith. It is in this respect eminently public. Schmitt will rightly say that, in strict theological-political analogy a private religion will become the correlate of a corrupted parliamentarism which has lost the pathos of public discussion as the solid principle of its configuration, and dissolves itself in a trade of opinions, parties and votes and therefore, is not capable of generating the public (1996: 25–6). Years later, *Constitutional Theory* echoes the same idea:

Representation can occur only in the public sphere. There is no representation that occurs in secret and between two people, and no representation that would be a 'private matter'. In this regard, all concepts and ideas are excluded that are essentially part of the spheres of the private, of private law, and of the merely economic. (Schmitt 2008: 242)

Then, in a system of proportional representation with party lists, 'the individual party list is not there on its own account, but rather only as the means to bring about a representation of political unity that is alone essential' (Schmitt 2008: 240). In fact, in a parliamentary system this unity is made possible by public discussion. A representation that unfolds in secret, a representation that is a private affair, is a fraud. When this is the case, what goes on in the light of day is an empty formality and the really important decisions are taken with the public's back turned. Thus, parliament may be able to perform useful functions, but it is no longer the representation of the political unity of the people.

It is true that the truth made visible by the church is faith, which is dogmatically configured and requires obedience. In the parliamentary modern state, however, the truth is configured in an open discussion, which requires not obedience, but at least, says Schmitt, 'shared convictions as premises, the willingness to be persuaded, independence of party ties, freedom from selfish interests' (2000: 5). The scepticism about these attitudes makes them impossible to establish any ritual of truth. This is the crises of parliamentarianism (Vatter 2021).[12] The eclipse of faith as a common norm of coexistence gave way in non-confessional states after the privatization of religion to a parliamentary system that understood itself as a ritual of truth. It itself has been secularized with the advent of liberal ideology that dissolves any idea of privacy into an artificial struggle of interests, thus ruining the very concept of the political.

The theological-political derivation of acclamations as a means of democratic and autocratic governmentality

If in a parliamentary system the unity of the people, necessary for constructing political representation, is made possible by public discussion, in modern mass democracies the unity depends on the substantial homogeneity of the people. In this case, another ritual of truth becomes meaningful for the constitution of public representation: acclamation.

We cannot forget that for Schmitt, as he accounts in the *Crisis of Parliamentary Democracy*, Bolshevism and Fascism are, like all dictatorships, certainly anti-liberal but not necessarily anti-democratic: 'In the history of democracy there have been numerous dictatorships, caesarisms, and other more striking forms that have tried to create homogeneity and to shape the will of the people with methods uncommon in the liberal tradition of the past century' (2000: 16). Also, these kinds of regimes practise the acclamatory ritual as a central process for making truth appear.

Also, acclamations have a theological-political genealogy. In fact, Erik Peterson's *Heis Theos* (2012) disinterred the concept of acclamation in antiquity, describing it as an exclamation of an applause or triumph, of praise or reprobation proffered by a multitude.[13] He informs us that acclamations were practised during the appearance of the Caesar, as well as of every governor, at processes such as a trial or wherever a decision had to be made, or as a response to miracles. They were manifestations of a divine impulse, as well as of public opinion, in order to validate the authority of leaders, both secular and ecclesiastical (Roueché 1984: 181–99). This concern brings Peterson to research one form of acclamation in particular: that of *Heis Theos*– One God. Despite the clear monotheistic content of the Hail, Peterson insists that it was an acclamation and not a particular profession of a monotheistic faith (2012: 302). Since it was used alternatively for representing the Christian god, the Jewish god and the pagan sun god, it does not express a common monotheistic background, but, rather, shares theological-political characteristics with the emperor's cult.

Carl Schmitt transferred Peterson's thesis in *Heis Theos* to the juridical and political sphere, justifying the procedures of direct democracies, in his text from 1927, *Volksentscheid und Volksbegehren. Ein Beitrag zur Auslegung der Weimarer Verfassung und zur Lehre von der unmittelbaren Demokratie* (2014),[14] where he quotes Peterson's book, and also afterwards in *Constitutional Theory* (1928). Schmitt underlined that every political form has to include a moment of popular manifestation, but in particular, democracies and autocracies that claim for a kind of direct representation. Schmitt insisted that the natural form of the direct expression of a people's will is the assembled multitude's declaration of their consent or their disapproval (Schmitt 2008; Adam 1992: 79–83).[15] He asserted: 'Acclamation is an eternal phenomenon of the whole political community. No state without a people, no people without acclamation' (Schmitt 2014: 34).[16] Acclamation, an 'amen' of the people, is the most democratic manifestation of the will of the people to show their agreement; silence manifests their disagreement

(Schmitt 2014: 34).[17] Acclamation makes direct representation possible. Someone (the mediator, representing the people) has to be acclaimed and acclamations make of him the 'true' representation. Acclamations cannot be a continuous phenomenon, but are compatible with the juridical form. Acclamations belong to the 'extraordinary' moment of politics, using an expression coined by Kalyvas. Acclamations are an important part of exceptional moments in politics, even if they can also be performed in other circumstances. Schmitt noted: 'In times of peaceful order, these types of expression are rare and unnecessary. That no special will is perceivably expressed simply signifies the enduring consent to the existing constitution. In critical times, the no that directs itself against an existing constitution can be clear and decisive only as negation, while the positive will is not as secure' (Schmitt 2008: 132).

These acclamations are a secularized form of the ancient liturgical forms referred to by Peterson and later by Kantorowicz in *Laudes Regiae* (Herrero 2019: 1–13). This is confirmed by Schmitt when in *Politische Theologie II*, he waxed ironically about Weber's charismatic legitimacy as a Protestant derivation of ecclesiastical charisma (1970: 42).[18] In fact, Max Weber cites Rudof Sohm several times in *Economy and Society* (1978: xcvi, 216, 772, 1112).[19] In his *Kirchenrecht*, Sohm takes the step of characterizing the church as a 'charismatic organization' (Sohm 1970: 26–7), arguing that the primitive church was organized in that way without having any legal constitution ('*keine rechtliche Verfassung*'). The community character of the assembled Christians is accentuated by Sohm to the detriment of the juridical-constitutional aspect. It is, in its interpretation, the Catholic Church that deviates from that origin. Luther and Protestantism partly restored the original idea. Following this scheme Weber interprets the charismatic aspect of a domination as irrational, subjective and almost impossible to 'routinize' in any institutional aspect.

On the contrary, for Schmitt, the charismatic character of the Roman Catholic Church is due to the fact that it embodies a superior 'idea' that is expressed in a juridical form, that is, it is due to hyper-rationality. The charismatic aspect of the Church in its vision is compatible with the institutional aspect. This is one of the main differences between liturgical and political acclamations that made total identification impossible. Liturgy in the Church has 'a routine' character: circular time is implicit in the constant repetition found in the liturgical cult. It is not an extraordinary or exceptional moment of the Church. But in any case, the approval and rejection expressed by acclamations, in liturgical or secularized forms, share the very public nature of the political. Surprisingly enough, Schmitt did not make a point of political theology in relation to the case of acclamations, but – as shown – it can be seen as a corollary of his political theology of representation.

Rituals of truth in the modern state: Some conclusions

By focusing on the rituals of truth present in Schmitt's work, we have tried to show that the theological pervades the secular structure of the political community in its institutional practices. Oaths, public discussion and acclamations exemplify Schmittian political-theological cases beyond sovereignty.

All three can be seen as ritual forms of the political in which an attempt is made to unveil some kind of truth. The oath appears in the context of constitutional theory as a stabilizer of the law. Its secularization, being a merely formal secular gesture, provokes the insidiousness between legality and legitimacy that leads to a motorization of the law.

The publicity of discussion appears in the context of parliamentary government as a ritual of truth for correct political decision-making, that is, for political decision-making in which the People is represented. The theological analogue of this publicity is the representation of the church, which embodies a superior idea and personality, that of Christ. The secularization of the idea of mediation and public truth implies a transformation of representation into a trade of private interests that leads to the corruption of parliament.

The institutional ritual of truth of forms of government that claim direct representation of the people, that is, mass democracies and autocracies, such as dictatorships and caesarisms, is acclamation. Through the immediate presence of the physically assembled people, the truth of the recipient of power is made clear, who as the ruler no longer has to discuss his opinions, but to execute the trust that the people have placed in him. Acclamations were initially theological-political practices insofar as they had a double character: to affirm to the emperor that he was also a God.

Without some kind of ritual of truth, no legitimacy is constituted and the people become ungovernable. The Foucauldian conceptual tool of *alethurgy* as a ritual of truth has helped us to discover in Schmitt's work some rituals of truth that have a theological-political character. These rituals, once secularized, lose their institutional force and, as Foucault points out, give way to others that operate less at an institutional level, but more on subjectivity. In fact, Foucault also discovers another theological-political analogy when analysing the Christian rituals of truth. In fact, he refers to confession as an *alèthurgie* acting upon the subject, which allows for the constitution of a pastoral power (Foucault 2012a: 8). At the end of *Du gouvernement des vivants*, he points out the theological-political transference: the transference of an economy of salvation, a canonical system with penalties for every fault, to a juridical civil penal system (Foucault 2012a: 190). According to Foucault, the imperative 'tell me who you are', which originated in Christianity, is the fundamental imperative of Western civilization (Foucault 2012a: 143; 2012b: 201)[20], an affirmation analogical to that of Prodi, 'the oath is the basis of the political covenant in Western societies' (1992: 11). Both oath and confession are rituals of veridiction, but while in the first, God acts as an external witness, in confession his gaze looks into interiority binding truthfulness from inside.

With these questions in mind Foucault returns to Ancient Greece to analyse another form of veridiction that does not conclude in a penal system or in a kind of pastoral power: '*Parrhesia* does not produce a codified effect; it opens up an unspecified risk' (2011a: 62). Through a genealogy of the *parrhesia* – from the public orator, passing through the prince's counsellor and the minister of the modern state up to the revolutionary – Foucault tries to bring into play one of the practices of truth-telling that also implies a mode of philosophical subjectivation and veridiction, in other words, a constitution of the truthful subject. The practice called *parrhesia* is 'that attitude of the courage of the truth: having the courage to tell the truth without concealing anything and regardless of the dangers this involves' (Foucault 2011b: 339). *Parrhesia* is also an *alethurgia*, that is, a ritual of veridiction that reveals truth in the form of subjectivity, in such a way that it is interpreted as an irruption in the context in which it takes place. In this case the production of the truth about the subject does not happen in privacy as confession, but publicly, contrasting the subject's own truth with the public truth regime, which represents, in Foucault's words, 'the political dramatics of true discourse' (2011a: 69).[21] In contrast to confession and oath, in *parrhesia* the expressed truth is not regulated by a 'regime of truth'. Some similarities can be found between this second ritual of truth proper of ancient times and public discussion in parliamentary regimes. But beyond the possible similarities, Foucault's wisdom comes from considering that the rituals of truth of the new time come from devices that affect subjectivity, that is, it is the subject itself that is the site of the theological-political relation, while the rituals of truth considered by Schmitt belong to an institutional political theology.

Notes

1 He notes that until the seventeenth century the practices of astrology, divination and sorcery were normalized (Foucault 2012a: 8). Foucault quotes Jean Pierre Vernant's book, *Divination et rationalité* (1974).
2 Thomas Aquinas *Summa Theologica* II-II, Q. 89, a. 1. For a contemporary distinction between both kinds of oaths, following John Austin's theory of speech acts instead of their temporal aspect, see Condren (2006: 233–4): 'The assertory oath was in Austinian terms a constative: it attested to a state of affairs, such as one's identity in a court of law. The promissory, however, was an Austinian performative; like a wager, it was a creative act, having "constructive power". The assertory, then, could easily be synonymous with declaring and it might only require subscription to its terms. The promissory oath was more problematic and accepted as binding only on tacit conditions.'
3 Aroney, on the contrary, perceives that oaths of office and oaths of allegiance have marked the path of the authority of the modern state and continue to do so (2015). On the history of oaths, see Friesenhahn (1928). An opposed testimony can be found in Spurr, who undermines the significance of oaths and accordingly the relevance of their disappearance in political community building (2001: 37–63).
4 Benveniste has reflected on the oath in terms of the Greek and the Roman use of it from the etymological point of view (1969). Agamben has used the results of most of this historical material for a contemporary reflection, even though his archaeological studies mostly keep him in the ancient world (2008).
5 From *iurare* comes *ius iurandum*: the formula that fixes the norm. Benveniste writes: 'Le dictionnaire d'Ernout-Meillet allègue une expression *ius iurare* qui signifierait "prononcer la formule sacré qui engage", malheureusement sans donner de référence.

A notre connaissance une telle locution ne se rencontré pas. Nous n'en avons que la forme résiduelle *ius iurandum*, qui laisse subsister l'écart entre *ius* et *iuro*' (1969: 112–13). See also d'Ors (1997: §12), and Fustel De Coulanges, who points out how pronouncements on laws were ritual actions (2001).

6 Aurell, Aurell and Herrero demonstrate this assertion by means of several study cases (2018). From the Reformation, trust was severely compromised by the perceived need to impose uniformities of religious practice in the face of the feared insincerity of those forced to comply. It was the case, for example, of the Church of England with the practice of the oath of alliance in 1606.

7 It has to be simply implicit as in the case of Hobbes (1996: chapter XIV) or explicit as in the case of Locke (1980: 8.121; 1968). See also the discussion on engagement with a free state in Condren (2006: 290–313).

8 There, Rousseau praises Hobbes for daring to reunify the two 'eagle heads' in *Du contrat social* (IV, c. 8).

9 This is the thesis of Adolf Reinach, who bases the structure of law on the promise (1989: 147).

10 This foreword has not been included in the English translation.

11 In his 1978 article, Schmitt describes Hitler's rise to power as a result of a legal revolution (1978: 73–89). He argues that Hitler represents legalism's last step: legality has not only become the most important means for legitimate political power, but also a revolutionary instrument. In a modern industrial society, he adds, only legal revolutions have a chance. We know that the solution that Schmitt proposed is not simply to recover the divine or theological character of the law, but mainly a 'substantial' legal idea rooted in *nomos* instead of an 'empty' legality (Herrero 2015).

12 The theological-political derivation between faith and *Öffentlichkeit* has been well argued in chapter 5 of Vatter (2021).

13 There is not much literature on the political-theological consequences of Peterson's book except from Nichtweiss (2012: 583–642), Caronello (2002: 349–96), Hebekus (2003: 97–113) and Agamben (2011).

14 Nichtweiss points out that Erik Peterson's *Heis Theos* (1920) influenced Schmitt in what relates to the topic of acclamation (1992: 740).

15 Adam identifies three sources of inspiration for this concept in Schmitt: Roman state law, German conservatives and the role of acclamation in the church (1992: 72–83).

16 Schmitt (1927: 34): 'Truly, no State can renounce these acclamations. (...) Acclamation is an eternal phenomenon of the whole political community. No State without a people, no people without acclamation.' In the same place, he writes: 'Because the appropriate activity, capacity and function of the people, the nucleus of all popular expression, the original democratic phenomenon – what Rousseau saw as democracy in the strictest sense – is an acclamation, a cry of approval or condemnation from the assembled mass.' Because of expressions such as this one, Schmitt's work has been said to have an element of democratism. What interests the present author is not to determine if Schmitt is democratic or not, but, rather, to attempt to understand in what sense the following is true: that rigorous democracy is the same as a sovereign dictatorship. Schmitt read this thesis in Donoso Cortés's discourse on dictatorship. Recently, Andreas Kalyvas's book shed light on this question (2008).

17 Schmitt writes: '[Y]ell high and low, cry with joy or complaint, strike shields with weapons, say "Amen" to a pact of any kind or avoid this acclamation with silence' (1927: 34).

18 Schmitt writes: 'Politische Theologie ist für Peterson erledigt. Auch die große Bedeutung, die seine eigenen Forschungsergebnisse des Buches Heis Theos für Max Webers Soziologie der "charismatischen Legitimität" haben (weil die Akklamation typisch dem charismatischen Führer zuteil wird), hat ihn nicht beschäftigt. Schließlich ist sie ja nur rein Derivat säkularisierter protestantischer (von Rudolf Sohm stammender) Theologie' (1970: 42).

19 Günther Roth explains in the introduction to this English translation the Schmittian judgement, without referring to Schmitt: 'In his major work on Church Law (1892), Sohm, a devout believer and conservative columnist, had described the church not as a "legal" but a "charismatic" organization – that is, an organization established by virtue of divine inspiration, not man-made law. After using the concept of charisma in its religious connotations in the *Sociology of Religion*, Weber apparently decided that it could also denote the self-legitimation of political leadership, a usurpatory challenge from the viewpoint of patriarchal, patrimonial and bureaucratic legitimacy' (Weber 1978: xcvi). Weber himself quotes Sohm: 'The concept of "charisma" ("the gift of grace") is taken from the vocabulary of early Christianity. For the Christian hierocracy Rudolf Sohm, in his *Kirchenrecht*, was the first to clarify the substance of the concept, even though he did not use the same terminology' (1978: 216).

20 In *Mal faire, dire vrai*, Foucault writes: 'la mise en place privilégiée de l'aveu dans les pratiques pénales s'est inscrite, d'une façon générale, dans une sorte de grande juridification de la société et de la culture occidentales au Moyen-Âge, juridification qui est sensible (. . .) dans les institutions, les pratiques, les représentations propres au christianisme' (2012b: 201). See also Morris on the 'individualization' aspect of confession as one of the practices that led towards the discovery of the individual (1987: 70–5).

21 Foucault also writes: 'it is a way of telling the truth that lays one open to a risk by the very fact that one tells the truth (. . .) by binding oneself to the statement of the truth and to the act of stating the truth (. . .) in the form of a courageous act' (2011a: 66).

References

Adam, A. (1992), *Rekonstruktion des Politischen: Carl Schmitt und die Krise der Staatlichkeit, 1912–33*, Weinheim: V. C. H. Acta Humaniora.

Agamben, G. (2008), *The Sacrament of Language: An Archaeology of the Oath*, Stanford, CA: Stanford University Press.

Agamben, G. (2011), *The Kingdom and the Glory: For a Theological Genealogy of Economy and Government*, Stanford, CA: Stanford University Press.

Aroney, N. (2015), 'Faith in Public Office: The Meaning, Persistence and Importance of Oaths', in Paper in Conference Faith in Public Office. Centre for the Study of Science, Religion and Society. Emmanuel College, University of Queensland, 3 September.

Aurell, M., J. Aurell and M. Herrero (2018), *Le Sacré et la Parole. Le Serment au Moyen Age*, Paris: Classiques Garnier.

Benveniste, E. (1969), *Vocabulaire des institutions indo-européennes 2*, Paris: Les Editions de Minuit.

Caronello, G. (2002), 'La critica del monoteismo nel primo Peterson', in P. Bettiolo-Gionanni Filoramo (ed.), *Il dio mortale. Teologie politiche tra antico e contemporáneo*, 349–96, Brescia: Morcelliana.

Condren, C. (2006), *Argument and Authority in Early Modern England: The Presupposition of Oaths and Offices*, Cambridge: Cambridge University Press.

Dean, M. (2018), 'Oath and Office', *Telos*, 185: 67–91.

d'Ors, A. (1997), *Derecho privado romano*, Pamplona: Eunsa.

Foucault, M. (2011a), *The Government of Self and Others; Lectures at the College of France 1982–3*, New York: Palgrave Macmillan.

Foucault, M. (2011b), *The Courage of the Truth: The Government of Self and Others II; Lectures at the Collège de France 1983–4*, New York: Palgrave Macmillan.

Foucault, M. (2012a), *Du gouvernement des vivants*, Paris: Gallimard/Seuil.

Foucault, M. (2012b), *Mal faire, dire vrai. Fonction de l'Aveu en Justice*, Louvain: Presses Universitaires de Louvain/University of Chicago Press.

Friesenhahn, E. (1928), *Der politische Eid*, Bonn: L. Röhrscheid.

Fustel De Coulanges, N. D. (2001), *The Ancient City. A Study on the Religion, Laws, and Institutions of Greece and Rome*, Kitchener: Batoche Books.

Guindon, B. (1957), *Le serment: Son histoire, son caractère sacré*, Ottawa: Éditions de l'Université.

Hebekus, U. (2003), 'Enthusiasmus und Recht. Figurationen der Akklamation bei Ernst H. Kantorowicz, Erik Peterson und Carl Schmitt', in J. Brokoff and J. Fohrmann (eds), *Politische Theologie. Formen und Funktionen im 20. Jahrhundert*, 97–113, Paderborn: Schöningh.

Herrero, M. (2015), *The Political Discourse of Carl Schmitt: A Mystic of Order*, Lanham: Rowman & Littlefield.

Herrero, M. (2017), 'Teología política y representación en el pensamiento de Carl Schmitt', *Revista de Filosofía Aurora*, 29 (47): 377–403.

Herrero, M. (2019), 'Acclamations: A Theological-Political Topic in the Crossed Dialogue between Erik Peterson, Ernst H. Kantorowicz and Carl Schmitt', *History of European Ideas*, 45: 1–13.

Hobbes, T. (1996), *Leviathan*, Cambridge: Cambridge University Press.

Kalyvas A. (2008), *Democracy and the Politics of the Extraordinary: Max Weber, Carl Schmitt, and Hannah Arendt*, New York: Cambridge University Press.

Locke, J. (1968), *A Letter On Toleration*, Oxford: Oxford University Press.

Locke, J. (1980), *The Second Treatise of Civil Government*, Indianapolis: Hackett Publishing Company.

Morris, C. (1987), *The Discovery of the Individual 1050–1200*, Toronto: University of Toronto Press.

Nichtweiss, B. (1992), *Erik Peterson: Neue Sicht auf Leben und Werk*, Freiburg: Herder.

Nichtweiss, B. (2012), 'Nachtwort zur Entstehung und Bedeutung von Heis Theos', in E. Peterson (ed.), *Heis Theos: epigraphische, formgeschichtliche und religionsgeschichtliche Untersuchungen zur antiken Ein-Gott-Akklamation*, 583–642, Würzburg: Echter.

Peterson, E. (2012), *Heis Theos: epigraphische, formgeschichtliche und religionsgeschichtliche Untersuchungen zur antiken Ein-Gott-Akklamation*, Würzburg: Echter.

Prodi, P. (1992), *Il sacramento del potere: il giuramento político nella storia constituzionale dell' Occidente*, Bologna: Il Mulino.

Reinach, A. (1989), *Zur Phänomenologie des Rechts: Die apriorischen Grundlagen des bürgerlichen Rechts, in Sämtliche Werke. Textkritische Ausgabe in 2 Bänden*, München: Philosophia.

Roueché, C. (1984), 'Acclamations in the Later Roman Empire: New Evidence from Aphrodisias', *The Journal of Roman Studies*, 74: 181–99.

Schmitt, C. (1970), *Politische Theologie II. Legende von der Erledigung jeder Politischen Theologie*, Berlin, Duncker & Humblot.
Schmitt, C. (1978), 'The Legal World Revolution', *Telos*, 72: 73–89.
Schmitt, C. (1979), *Der Begriff des Politischen: Text von 1932 mit einem Vorwort und drei Corollarien*, Berlin: Duncker & Humblot.
Schmitt, C. (1990), 'The Plight of European Jurisprudence', *Telos*, 83: 35–70.
Schmitt, C. (1996), *Roman Catholicism and Political Form*, Westport, CT: Greenwood Press.
Schmitt, C. (2000), *The Crisis of Parliamentary Democracy*, Cambridge, MA: MIT Press.
Schmitt, C. (2008), *Constitutional Theory*, Durham, NC and London: Duke University Press.
Schmitt, C. (2014), *Volksentscheid und Volksbegehren. Ein Beitrag zur Auslegung der Weimarer Verfassung und zur Lehre von der unmittelbaren Demokratie*, Berlin and Leipzig: De Gruyter.
Sohm, R. (1970), *Kirchenrecht*, Berlin: Duncker & Humblot.
Spurr, J. (2001), 'A Profane History of Early Modern Oaths', *Transactions of the Royal Historical Society*, 11: 37–63.
Ulmen, G. (1996), 'Introduction', in C. Schmitt (ed.), *Roman Catholicism and Political Form*, vii–xxvi, Westport, CT: Greenwood Press.
Vatter, M. (2021), *Divine Democracy*, Oxford: Oxford University Press.
Vernant, J.-P. (1974), *Divination et rationalité*, Paris: Seuil.
Weber, M. (1978), *Economy and Society*, Los Angeles and Berkeley, CA: University of California Press.

Chapter 5

ATHEISM, POST-SECULARISM AND THE LEGITIMACY OF DEMOCRACY

Miguel Vatter

In the last two chapters of *Political Theology* Schmitt argues that during the nineteenth century the theory of the state began to draw all of its concepts from democratic ideas fashioned through a discourse of radical immanence which denies the existence of God. This raises the question of whether and how Schmitt believed that democracy could be legitimated at all given his previous argument, in the first two chapters, that political order requires an instance of sovereignty and that sovereignty, in turn, appeals to divine transcendence. Assuming with Schmitt that 'political theology' is a discourse of legitimacy, the question becomes: is a political theology of democracy possible? This chapter proposes the hypothesis that the contemporary turn to 'post-secularism' can be understood as a response to Schmitt's challenge by working out a political theology of democracy that is based on radical immanence and atheism.

The belief that democracy and secularism go hand in hand was consolidated during the nineteenth century. In *A Secular Age* Charles Taylor argues that modern secularism began when people were convinced to cut off their aspirations to an 'eternal' life in another world, in a Beyond, that would lend to their passage on earth a 'fullness' or absolute meaning. The project of modernity, he shows, required people to put all their energies into fulfilling the immanent goals of human flourishing, as the best way to attain a happy life (*eudaimonia*) in this world (Taylor 2007: 15–19). The discourse of post-secularism is one way in which scepticism about this promise of modernity is currently expressed at the theoretical level (Hurd 2017).[1] It sees in the late modern 'immanent framework' a potential threat to democracy and freedom, another form of the 'dialectic' of Enlightenment. Post-secularism acknowledges the political valence given to religious faith and practice in contemporary societies; it asks what happens with democracy after secularization theorems have fallen into discredit. Is some element of 'religious' transcendence necessary for contemporary democracy? How can such transcendence be conceived without thereby falling back into metaphysics or, even, legitimizing anti-democratic forms of government and their alliance with religious 'fundamentalism'? (Agar 2014).[2]

As I read him, Schmitt employs the connection between democracy and immanence as a way to question the legitimacy of democracy. For Schmitt, the legitimacy of a political and legal order relies on some appeal to transcendence. In particular, Schmitt's *Political Theology* takes aim at Hans Kelsen's defence of democracy. He considered that Kelsen's conception of 'democracy is the expression of a political relativism and a scientific orientation that are liberated from miracles and dogmas and based on human understanding and critical doubt' (Schmitt 1988: 42). As Schmitt understood it, Kelsen's attempt to employ 'methodological atheism' in order to rid both jurisprudence and state theory of its dependency on transcendence in reality only helped the cause of the 'socialist anarchism' associated with the likes of Bakunin. This development, according to Schmitt, could only be halted by providing a new and affirmative role for dictatorship within the understanding of democratic legitimacy.

My main hypothesis is that what Schmitt calls 'atheism' and 'anarchism' is better understood as the insistence and persistence of messianic discourse in the 'immanent framework' of late modernity. On this hypothesis, the claim to legitimacy of democracy would be inseparable from such a messianic discourse developed at the turn of the nineteenth century and into the twentieth century (Hägglund 2019; Caputo 2014; Bielik-Robson 2019).[3] In this article I argue that this hypothesis is perhaps best captured by Ernst Bloch's late dictum that 'only an atheist can be a good Christian; only a Christian can be a good atheist', which I shall interpret in what follows. Bloch, rather than Bakunin or Kelsen, seems to me the best exemplar of a 'socialist anarchist' during the early 1920s in Germany when Schmitt composed *Political Theology* (Rabinbach 1997). It is Bloch's 1918 *Spirit of Utopia* that brings together, perhaps for the first time in a 'systematic' way, historical materialism and messianism. While Giorgio Agamben has argued that Schmitt's *Political Theology* was an 'esoteric' polemic against Walter Benjamin's essay 'On the Critique of Violence' published in 1921, he does not consider that Benjamin's text was itself a response to Bloch's book (Agamben 2005: 53; Rosenstock 2014; 2017).[4] Perhaps more clearly and directly than Benjamin's texts, Bloch's sustained efforts to explain in what sense immanence and atheism are related to messianism offer the lineaments of a democratic political theology that contrasted Schmitt's own political theology. In what follows, I shall begin by contrasting Schmitt and Bloch in relation to the paradox of a political theology of immanence. I shall then illustrate my hypothesis by thematizing the internal relation of democracy and messianism in Habermas's and Derrida's later work.

Democracy and atheism in Schmitt's Political Theology

In the third chapter of *Political Theology* Schmitt posits that 'the metaphysical image that a definite epoch forges of the world has the same structure as what the world immediately understands to be appropriate as a form of its political organization' (1988: 46). According to this postulate, during the seventeenth and eighteenth centuries the theory of the state depended on, respectively, theist and deist theologies of transcendence. However, 'all the identities that recur in the political ideas and in the state doctrines of the nineteenth century rest on such conceptions of immanence [*Immanenzvorstellungen*]: the democratic thesis of the identity of ruler and ruled, the organic theory of the state with the identity of state and sovereignty . . . and finally Kelsen's theory of the identity of state and the legal order' (Schmitt 1988: 50). Kelsen sought to reject the juridical use of the analogy between 'God and State' in the homonymous article in 1922, the same year Schmitt's book appeared (Kelsen 1973; Vatter 2017b). Kelsen takes the devise 'God and State' from Bakunin. However, he distinguishes his position from Bakunin's anarchism by saying that his approach to jurisprudence is *methodologically* 'anarchic'; he disagrees with Bakunin's political anarchism that sees in all law simply domination. In *Political Theology* Schmitt identifies a stronger connection between Kelsen, Bakunin and Proudhon, and so between democracy, anarchism and socialism (Meier 1995; 2011; Newman 2019).[5] In the latter thinkers, Schmitt identified 'radicals who opposed all existing order' because they 'turned their ideological struggle against the belief in God as such'. Left-Hegelianism popularized the idea that 'mankind must be substituted for God . . . . This ideal of an unfolding self-conscious mankind must end in anarchic freedom' (Schmitt 1988: 51). Schmitt seems to believe that by the end of the nineteenth century democratic struggles express a deeper enmity of 'mankind' towards both God and State.

In chapter 4 of *Political Theology*, Schmitt suggests that in order to counteract this movement towards atheism and anarchism, the camp of 'catholicity' (Cardinal Newman) must adopt a theory of dictatorship, based on the 'political theology of Restoration' developed by the likes of de Maistre and Donoso Cortés. Schmitt's reasoning throughout this last chapter dedicated to counter-revolutionary political thought bears careful attention. In chapter 3, Schmitt said that the turn from transcendence to immanence in the metaphysical outlook of the nineteenth century leads to 'the formation of a new concept of legitimacy', one that is 'democratic' because based on the '*pouvoir constituant* of the people' (1988: 51; 2014: 124).[6] Yet nowhere in *Political Theology* does Schmitt expound this 'new' concept of democratic legitimacy, and so a properly 'democratic' political theology (Cristi 1997; Koekkoek 2014; Saralegui 2021).[7] Rather, by the end of chapter 3 and then in chapter 4, he leaps to a discussion of the legitimacy of dictatorship that is needed to oppose both atheism and anarchism. In later works like *Constitutional Theory*, *The Crisis of Parliamentary Democracy* and *Legality and Legitimacy*, Schmitt, indeed, strengthens the connection between democracy (the 'identity' of ruler and ruled) and 'sovereign' dictatorship (based on the representative of this identity). However, in my opinion, these works still fail to offer a political theology of immanence. Instead, they subsume democracy under the idea of dictatorship (also in the case of the Marxist-Leninist idea of a dictatorship of the proletariat), where the latter concept relies on the centrality of representation and thus of an axis of transcendence (Colón-Ríos 2020; Herrero 2015).[8]

Schmitt derives the legitimacy of dictatorship from his decisionist theory of sovereignty, which he deploys against the liberal principle of 'conversation' and Mill's principle of fallibility applied to parliamentary debate (hence Donoso Cortés's quip on liberals as being 'la clase discutidora') (Meierhenrich and Simons 2016).[9] That is why the legitimacy of dictatorship rests on the beliefs that 'every government was absolute' and that its decision was 'infallible'. Paraphrasing de Maistre, Schmitt says: 'every sovereignty acted as if it were infallible, every government was absolute – a sentence that an anarchist could pronounce verbatim, even if his intention was an entirely different one' (1988: 55). The antithesis between dictatorship and anarchism is thus reduced to the either/or between any government being good and all governments being bad (Donoso Cortés 2000: 57).[10]

Although Schmitt does not himself develop a democratic political theology, he does sketch, by way of opposition to his own beliefs, what could be taken as two principles of democratic legitimacy derived from atheism and radical immanence.

The first is related to the positive anthropology of the nineteenth century which Schmitt believes underlies anarchism. 'To the committed atheistic anarchist man is decisively good' (1988: 56). On the contrary, Donoso Cortés believes in the 'natural evil of man' and in the dogma of Original Sin (1988: 57). It is here that Schmitt cites a famous remark by Donoso Cortés drawn from his *Essays on Catholicism, Liberalism, and Socialism* (book 3, chapter 8): 'Since God has **not** said it to him: whence does he know that he is noble?'[11] [¿*De dónde sabe que es noble si Dios* **no** *se lo ha dicho*?].

It is unclear to what biblical text Donoso Cortés may be appealing. There is at least one text in the Bible (King James Version) in which God does seem to say that humanity is 'noble', namely Gen. 1:26: 'And God said, Let us make man in our image, after our likeness' and then Gen. 1:31: 'And God saw every thing that he had made, and, behold, it was very good.' In his own German translation, Schmitt substitutes Donoso Cortés's use of 'noble' for 'good': '*Woher weiß er, daß er* **gut** *ist*'. By contrast, in the Jewish tradition, since Philo Judaeus at least, 'nobility' is considered a virtue in light of the previously mentioned biblical passages (Goodenough 1969). Today, what Schmitt calls the belief in the 'goodness' of humanity should be translated in terms of the belief in human dignity as the foundation to human rights.

The second principle underlying the legitimacy of democracy is the belief in 'the natural and intrinsic [*immanenten*] truth and beauty of human life' (1988: 65). In discussing the legitimacy of nineteenth-century democracy, Schmitt had already pointed out that, unlike his own Hobbesian conception of the unity of the people, which comes from the unity of the sovereign representative, 'the unity that represents a people does not have this decisionistic character; it is an organic unity'. In chapter 4, he proceeds to project onto Bakunin and Proudhon what today we would call an 'affirmative biopolitics' (Negri 2001; Esposito 2004) that – he claims – 'paralyzes all moral and political decisions in a paradisiacal worldliness of immediate natural life and unproblematic embodiment [*in einem paradiesischen Diesseits unmittelbaren, natürlichen Lebens und problemloser 'Leib'haftigkeit*]' (Schmitt 1988: 65 – English translation modified). Here Schmitt seems to anticipate something that has become apparent in our own times, namely, that democratic legitimacy is tied up with the so-called 'politics of difference', that is, with the principle that without equal recognition of manifold forms of embodiment (marked in terms of sexual, gender, racial, ethnic differences) human beings can be neither free nor happy. For Schmitt, on the contrary, 'the core of the political idea, [is] the exacting moral decision' (1988: 65) that employs embodied difference to establish friend/enemy distinctions. This procedure is today referred to in terms of 'culture wars'. Schmitt's idea of the 'political' thus takes the form of 'a clear antithesis: (. . .) every government is necessarily absolute [versus] (. . .) [a]ll governments must be opposed for the reason that every government is a dictatorship' (1988: 66). Yet, if decisionism is legitimate for the pole defending 'catholicity' and the necessity of 'absolute' government, for Bakunin and Proudhon as exemplary of the 'socialist anarchist' no legitimate standpoint is available other than a self-contradictory one of having to decide against decisionism, and to propose a theology of the anti-theological (Schmitt 1988: 66; Stark 2013: 57).[12]

Yet, Schmitt's arguments in the third and fourth chapters of *Political Theology* do not exclude the possibility that democracy may develop its own, consistent political theology of immanence or non-dictatorial democratic legitimacy. The following interpretations of Bloch, Habermas and Derrida suggest how they attempt to develop a political theology of democracy by understanding atheism and anarchism in messianic terms. Such a political theology articulates the two principles of legitimacy of democracy criticized by Schmitt, namely, that humanity is the bearer of dignity and that embodied life is paradisaical life, in terms of two aspects of messianic discourse.

Bloch and the atheism of Christianity[13]

Bloch's late work *Atheism in Christianity* (1968) is an argument about the coincidence of atheism and messianism. The book's first exergue reads: 'only an atheist can be a good Christian; only a Christian can be a good atheist'. This text seems to speak backwards to Schmitt's opposition between atheism and Christianity, the immanence of life and the morally exacting decision between friend and enemy. Bloch's formula stands equidistant from both Schmitt and Bakunin, for both of whom atheism and Christianity are in obvious antithesis to each other. But I have also argued that this formula may stand behind Habermas's conviction that the aspiration to neutrality of the democratic state requires adopting a standpoint of 'methodological atheism' that is at the same time open to biblical normative semantic and messianic contents. Bloch argues that this paradoxical 'religious atheism' is possible because the biblical religious content that needs to be 'critically saved' turns on the doctrine of the Kingdom, and the paradoxical claim that the realization of the Kingdom (of God) is a-theistic.

The second exergue of *Atheism in Christianity* reads: 'what is decisive: to transcend without transcendence'. Again, this text can be taken to speak backwards to Schmitt: decision is not excluded, but it is featured within immanence as a paradoxical transcendence without transcendence, or the character of *not-yet* that characterizes all actuality and calls for its utopian and messianic fulfilment.[14] Also, in respect of this formula I have argued that it may influence Habermas's conviction that the context-transcending force of validity claims, without which no normative discourse is possible, does not have a transcendent origin but can be given immanently, within the lifeworld of democratic citizens. Both claims are already contained in Bloch's central politico-theological thesis that Kant's 'invisible church' should be understood as a function of the 'Utopia of (the Son of) Man' (Boer 2007; Taubes 2009; Vattimo 2002).[15]

One recalls that Schmitt thought that behind late modern atheism there was the 'Left-Hegelian' belief that 'mankind must be substituted for God . . . . This ideal of an unfolding self-conscious mankind must end in anarchic freedom' (1988: 51). Bloch takes up this conceit but argues that this replacement of God by humankind is the effective truth of Christianity. The claim that Christianity is an atheism turns on Bloch's virtuoso reading of the obscure biblical expression 'Son of Man' (Mark 8:38; Daniel 7:13). The basic idea is that Jesus Christ may not be the 'Son' of the God who is the Creator of this world, but, instead, he may be, or he may refer to, the 'Son of Man' who redeems the creation in virtue of not standing under its power.

For Bloch there are two major indications in the Old Testament that redemption may not coincide with creation, nor the redeemer with the creator. The first is found in Exodus which testifies to the fact that 'the idea of the Creator-of-the-world as well as of its Lord had to retreat continually before that of the *Spirit of the Goal* who has no fixed abode' (Bloch 1972: 94). The second is found in the Book of Job. Bloch draws attention to Job's hope for the advent of a 'redeemer' [*goel*, better translated as 'avenger'] in and through which 'in my flesh shall I see God' (Bloch 1972: 114–15). For Bloch, this 'avenger' of Job's cause against the Creator God is the messianic/promethean idea of the Son of Man as a figuration of Humanity, at once embodied and redeemed.

Bloch's highly speculative readings of the biblical text 'against its grain' retain a level of plausibility in as much as scholarly opinion is uncertain whether Jesus designates himself as Son of Man, or another person; and whether there is a connection between Jesus's use of the expression and the idea of 'son of man' found in the Book of Daniel, one of the quintessential messianic texts of the Jewish tradition. Bloch seems to think that the 'Son of Man' is related to the idea of *Adam Kadmon* (or, the 'great Man') found in the Jewish mystical tradition, and at times identified with 'humanity'. The important point is that there is a gap between the *faith* in Jesus as Son of God that is foundational for Christendom, and the *hope* through Jesus in the advent of the 'Son of Man' that leads beyond Christianity to a-theism. For Bloch, Jesus is a Kantian politico-theological actor in so far as with him, *Deus homo factus est* [God became human]. But this becoming-human of God is no longer the speculative Calvary that justifies the (Trinitarian) unity of God as Creator with God as Redeemer. The figure of the 'Son of Man', instead, separates forever the Creator God from the Redeemer, so that 'his triumphant Day at the end of days [is transformed] into the unveiling of quite a different face: the face of man' (Bloch 1972: 165). 'The words "with unveiled face" refer not only eschatologically, but also apocalyptically to our real identity as men: they un-cover what was always pointed out and reveal it as the universal Kingdom of the Son of Man . . . a figure who stands alone, without Yahweh, a-*Kyrios* and *a-theos*, at once in the true sense of *cur deus homo* [why God became man/MV]' (Bloch 1972: 170).

Bloch's virtuoso interpretation of the figure of the Son of Man culminates precisely with Kant's doctrine of the invisible church of the ethical community of republican citizens whose unity is the mystical body of this Son of Man. The idea of an 'invisible' church, as I discuss in what follows, stands opposed to the traditional doctrine of the 'visibility' of the church as the mystical body of the Son of God. For Bloch, Kant adopts 'a purely social Adam Kadmon . . . the Mystical Body and the Kingdom. Kant's mocking [of Swedenborg's mysticism/MV] was not aimed at this: *indeed, the concept of society in the form of a Great Man – of the greatest of men in the final analysis – is the mystical background of his own ethics.* Society is, for Kant, a community of intelligible worlds, of which man, because of his moral character, is a fellow-citizen. And being the ethico-religious ambience of the human race, society possesses man's intelligible form' (Bloch 1972: 157).

Earlier I drew attention to the fact that for Schmitt one of the fundamental premises of anarchism and its form of atheism is related to the principle of embodied life as the realization of paradisaical life (Agamben 2020).[16] Like Benjamin and Adorno, Bloch holds on to the biblical utopian belief in the 'resurrection' of the flesh under a Marxist formulation: the naturalization of Man and the humanization of Nature. Thus, Bloch always sought to inscribe his utopianism, or weak form of transcendence, within the radical immanence of a conception of matter. This effort finds its climax in his major work *Das Materialismusproblem, seine Geschichte und Substanz*. A small part of this work was published as a separate volume under the title *Avicenna and the Aristotelian Left* (Bloch 2019; Moir 2016).[17] Bloch's strategy turns on an appropriation of Avicenna's and Averroes's theory of the material intellect (Esposito 2015; Vatter 2017a).[18] According to his reading, mediaeval Arabic Aristotelianism contains the doctrine of 'the education of forms from a nature that is no longer passive and unqualitative, but is also almost free from the need for a transcendent Father God' (Bloch 1972: 231). I have no space in this chapter to engage the debates that arose on whether assigning 'almost freedom' to nature goes against the spirit of Marxism, and, indeed, even stand in tension with Bloch's doctrine of redemption through the 'Son of Man'. The point here is to indicate a family resemblance between Bloch's 'Left Avicennian' conception of immanent matter as vital, indeed, as creative and 'transcending' all forms, and Derrida's development of the Platonic conception of 'intelligible matter' or *khora* discussed later.

In addition, one recalls that Schmitt's sole gesture towards articulating a democratic and atheistic 'political theology' consists in his identification of Spinoza's conception of *natura naturans* with the metaphysical doublet of the idea of 'constituent power'. Bloch also identifies in this Arabic conception of formative matter a bridge to the Spinozist idea of *natura naturans* and the latter, in turn, with a conception of (eternal) 'life-force' or *conatus* in which he locates the *immanent ground of transcendence*. Bloch gives two descriptions of this 'eternal' life-force: the first is related to 'that principle within us which makes us *stand up straight*, whether this is understood in an organic or a political or a moral way' (Bloch 1972:

251). This is clearly an attempt to give a materialist and immanent foundation to the idea of human dignity (Vatter 2014; Geoghegan 1995: chapter 5, passim).[19] The second expression of this eternal life-force is 'finality' (Kant's 'highest good' of humanity) that 'comes to join morality as a second source of life-force: the finality which lay in the courage to break free from this devil's guest house, this world (. . .). Mystical sources were called on too: for example, the words of Augustine as Eckhart quotes them: "I am aware of something within me playing before my soul and illuminating it. If it could only come to fulfillment and permanence within me *it could not but be eternal life*"' (Bloch 1972: 251, emphasis mine). I emphasize here Bloch's repeated reference to a *materialistic* idea of 'eternal life' which coincides for him with the content of the messianic. This stands in deep contrast with the recent views of Martin Hägglund according to which the legitimacy of democracy depends on eliminating any faith in 'eternal life' and only valuing the survival in 'this finite life' (2019).

Habermas, Kant and the invisible church

In *Roman Catholicism and Political Form* Schmitt argues that the Catholic Church could serve as the model for the secular political form of the state due to its idea of representation: 'to represent means to make an invisible being visible and present through a publicly present one' (Schmitt 2008, 243). This idea of representation is theologically rooted in the belief that Jesus Christ is God become Man. For Schmitt, the symbolic order of modern politics still requires this function of representation, even and precisely because it assumes that the People has taken the place of God (Lefort 2006). During the German Enlightenment, spurred by Lessing, then taken up and developed by Kant and Hegel, the idea of an 'invisible church' emerged as a republican and cosmopolitical alternative to the kind of universalism previously embodied by the Christian Church as the *corpus mysticum* of Christ (Assmann 2014; Harris 1972).[20] This ideal of an 'invisible church' has now been recovered by Habermas in his interpretation of Kant as fraying the path to a post-metaphysical, political use of reason that requires a 'critical *assimilation* of religious content' (2003: 110).[21]

Kant famously argued that morality does *not* require a religious foundation of the kind offered by established religions based on divine revelation. However, he also claimed that human practical reason cannot but *hope* that human beings, in striving to fulfil their moral and legal duties, will also attain their *supernatural* happiness or blessedness *here on earth*. This is the content of what Kant calls 'philosophical faith' (Fenves 1991).[22] The 'invisible church' is a name for this messianic condition. The construct of an 'invisible church' is needed to give a *final purpose* to duty-bound action. Seen from the point of view of the individual agent, duty-bound rule-following is itself not a purposive activity because it is regulative of all teleological activity. By applying the principles of practical reason, the individual can determine whether their purposive activities ought to be pursued or not as satisfying a duty. However, when viewed from an *intersubjective perspective*, Habermas believes that it is inevitable to ask what *kind of community* is constituted if all individuals were to follow rules out of duty, and not because they are instrumental in the pursuit of certain ends they each deem to be good. What is the *final purpose* of non-purposive moral action? Kant's answer is that when all human beings are ruled solely by their duties towards the law, then God's Kingdom will be *realized on earth*. Whereas the concept of a 'Kingdom of ends' is a regulative, purely intelligible and thus unrealizable ideal for the single moral actor, God's Kingdom is a *historically effective*, sensuous ideal that is regulative for humanity as a whole (Habermas 2005: 225).

The issue is not the existence of God as such. For Kant, even if one is an atheist, as a free human being one would still have the duty to follow the moral law. The real point is that 'without purpose it is not possible to will' ['*ohne allen Zweck kann kein Wille sein*'] (Habermas 2005: 227).[23] Ultimately, for Kant and Habermas it is necessary to connect the belief in doing what is right to the belief that if people act morally, the world will become a better place. The messianic finality of rightful action is therefore an object of '*Vernunftglaube*', or philosophical faith, that being moral will do 'some good' in the overall pattern of things, that it will make a difference. The realization of God's messianic Kingdom in and through the concatenation of moral actions throughout human history takes the form of an 'invisible church' (Habermas 2005: 232).

For Habermas, the idea of an 'invisible church' refers to a people which has been formed into an 'ethical community' as a function of their belonging to a political world ruled by juridical rules under a republican constitution (Habermas 2005: 233). This 'invisible church' has as its strict correlate a constitutional republic, and therefore the 'legitimacy' of this republican and a-theist church is entirely internal to the *legality* it affords. According to Habermas, the idea of an 'invisible church' allows Kant to give up the dualism of morality and legality, the opposition between inward freedom and external coercion, that already the early Hegel would show is untenable. Habermas argues that Kant's turn to a philosophical conception of religion allowed Kant to sidestep this weakness in his moral system and to put forward an idea of 'ethical community' (*Sittlichkeit*) that corresponds to a constitutional republic, in which public happiness is achieved in and through rule-following in accordance with moral principles.

Furthermore, for Habermas the motif of the 'invisible church' in Kant's discourse is evidence of the attempt to employ the theocratic ideal of God's Kingdom on earth in order to criticize the traditional employment of the biblical image of God as Lord and Creator of the world in the establishment of the legitimacy of empire and church. Republican civil religion has always countered the political theologies employed to uphold absolute monarchies and papal sovereignty. As Bloch already showed, the emphasis on the messianic Kingdom is tendentially 'atheist' and it therefore offers another basis for a 'neutral' approach to constitutionalism (1970: 160).[24]

This messianic *and* atheistic basis for republican constitutionalism matches nicely with Habermas's two requirements for a post-secular conception of public reason. The first requirement is to maintain the 'neutrality' of the state without lending a deaf ear to religious reasons. The second requirement is to avoid construing this 'neutrality' as a function of moral and political 'relativism', that is, as a function of denying universal truth claims to all reasonable conceptions of philosophical or religious world views. For Habermas, a reference to 'absolute' truth in the realm of practical reason needs to be retained: it makes no sense, for instance, to claim that the abolition of slavery is only historically 'relative'. This is done in the Kantian strategy of translating into republican terms the ancient, biblical understanding of *messianism* as the faith in the earthly realization of God's Kingdom. In this way, Habermas suggests that a messianic faith lies at the heart of the democratic system of law. Habermas's thesis that the discourse of democratic legitimation is the result of a secularizing process of translation of religious content therefore retains not a religious as much as a *messianic* condition of possibility or underlying narrative.

Derrida and the messianicity of public reason

Derrida's most extensive discussion of the internal relation of messianism with democracy and public reason is found in his text *Faith and Knowledge*. Hägglund has interpreted this text as a declaration of 'radical atheism' underpinned by a radical denial of any trans-temporal condition, namely, of eternity and eternal life (Hägglund 2008). I read this text, on the contrary, as an attempt by Derrida to offer the metaphysical picture correlated with his conception of 'democracy to come' and based on a radical form of immanence and materialism. In other words, it is a text that can be understood as offering a basis for democratic political theology.

As is well known, in this text Derrida sets out two conceptions of faith found in the Western tradition: one related to the experience of the sacred and holy as something that is in the last instance untouched by and immune to negativity; the other related to the experience of hesitation before the otherness of the other ('la halte du scrupule (*religio*)') (Derrida 2000: 47; Derrida and Vattimo 1998).[25] Derrida's deconstruction of the first meaning of faith tied to a dialectic of immunity and auto-immunity, faith and reason, has been amply discussed in the secondary literature. However, not enough attention has been paid to the formulations Derrida employs to think about the second sense of faith as 'fidelity, the appeal to blind confidence, the testimony always beyond proof, reason, and intuition' (2000: 52).

The formula for Derrida's second approach to faith as fidelity is given as 'n + One'. 'The more than One is this n + One which introduces the order of faith or of trust in the address of the other, but also the mechanical, machine-like (. . .) division and iterability of the source' (Derrida 2000: 99).[26] I have suggested that Derrida's formula for an indeconstructible faith is actually derived from Philo's neo-Platonic interpretation of divine revelation. The 'One' ('Un') refers to the mystery of the living God which remains shrouded in its withdrawn invisibility. The '+' refers to the 'Stream' of the divine Light or Logos that issues forth from the One. And the 'n' refers to the *many* revealed or positive religions that are 'mechanically, automatically' generated as a function of the human reception or interpretation of the Stream of Light (Goodenough 1969; Vatter 2021b).[27] The effect of auto-immunity that Derrida uncovers, on this interpretation, refers to the temptation for human religion and human reason to claim that n = One, namely to claim that any one revealed religion is *the only true* religion and to adopt an alliance with human reason and technoscience to make good on this belief.

For Derrida, philosophical faith takes the form of public reason: it means being open to the incalculable effects of the formula of indeconstructible faith 'n + One', that is, to the effects of the irreligious, materialist and cosmic 'machine' that generates those conceptions of sacred, unscathed life that are called 'religions' (2000: 38).[28] Derrida's formula is Judeo-Hellenistic because it denotes a Greek, philosophical and a fortiori even 'polytheistic' approach to monotheisms as the result of what Derrida calls the 'division and iterability' (n +) 'of the source' (One). It is to be contrasted with the catholicity of faith, whose ultimate formula is Trinitarian: monotheism as polytheism, rather than the polytheism of monotheisms advocated by Derrida.

But Derrida's discussion of messianicity also addresses the demand, formulated by Bloch and Habermas, to think the possibility of a 'transcendence without transcendence' found in radical immanence and, more specifically, in materiality itself. Derrida addresses this demand by connecting messianicity to the Platonic and neo-Platonic conception of (intelligible) matter called *khora* (Falque 2014).[29] Derrida's words explicitly take up Blochian connotations:

> an invincible desire for justice is linked to this expectation [i.e., to promise] (. . .). This abstract messianicity belongs from the very beginning to the experience of faith, of believing, of a credit that is irreducible to knowledge and of a trust that 'founds' all relation to the other in testimony. *This justice (. . .) alone allows hope beyond all 'messianisms' of a universalizable culture of singularities, a culture in which the abstract possibility of the impossible translation could nevertheless be announced.* This justice inscribes itself in advance in the promise, in the act of faith or in the appeal to faith that inhabits every act of language and every address to the other. The universalizable culture of this faith (. . .) also permits a 'rational' and universal discourse on the subject of 'religion'. (Derrida 2000: 22, emphasis mine)

I think it is permissible to identify Derrida's 'universal culture of singularities' with what Bloch and Habermas call the Kingdom. Hope in the realization on earth of this Kingdom lies at the basis of what Derrida calls a '"rational" and universal discourse on the subject of "religion"' – that is, a post-Kantian aspiration – which is itself based on 'the abstract possibility of the impossible translation' of faith into reason and vice versa.

In Derrida's discussion of Platonic *khora* one can also find the Blochian motif of the 'life-force' that propels the a-theistic core of all faith. The doctrine of *khora* is an essential component of the Greek philosophical doctrine of the mystery of God as *to on*, the singular Being. For this doctrine states that the Stream of Light that comes from the hidden One makes contact with a materiality that is uncreated and entirely impassive in order for the intelligible world to be formed. This intelligible world is in turn the condition for the creation of the visible world(s) which comes about as a copy or icon or repetition of the intelligible world. In mythical parlance, the doctrine of *khora* corresponds to the cult of Demeter. The internal connection between faith and 'atheism' thus refers to the materialist, uncreated basis of messianicity.

I take it that Derrida refers to this neo-Platonic tradition – which itself underpins the metaphysics of matter of the Arabic 'Aristotelian Left' – by claiming in *Faith and Knowledge*, section 11, that the metaphor of light is internally connected to a 'public space' rooted in *khora*. In *Faith and Knowledge*, section 22, he writes: 'the chance of this desert [*khora*] in the desert [of revelation/MV] (. . .) in uprooting the tradition [of revelation/MV] that bears it, in atheologizing it, this abstraction [*khora*] without denying faith, liberates a universal rationality and the political democracy that cannot be disassociated from it.' The reference to Platonic *khora* serves Derrida – much as Bloch's motif of atheism in Christianity – to reconceive of messianic faith and the tradition of revelation in an a-theistic way in order to make possible a democratic public reason. Here Derrida's text is suggestive of the possibility that the biblical tradition(s) of divine revelation contain within them an anterior trace that is both pagan, polytheistic and philosophical, and that orients political theology in a democratic and reasonable direction.

Furthermore, Derrida's passage also contains an unconscious reference to Bloch's claim that messianic hope cannot be thought independently of the idea of *natura naturans*, of a connection between a Platonically inflected materialism and messianic hope. In Bloch the key concept was that of a 'life-force' that originates with the a-theological messianic. This idea of a deep connection between God and a form of 'eternal life' is not only mentioned but also affirmed by Derrida:

> Judaism and Islam would thus be perhaps the last two monotheisms to revolt against everything that, in the Christianizing of our world, signifies the death of God, the death in God, two non-pagan monotheisms that do not accept death anymore than multiplicity in God (. . .) by recalling at all costs that 'monotheism' signifies no less faith in the One, and in the living One, than belief in a single God [pour rappeler à tout prix que 'monothéisme' signifie autant la foi en l'Un, et en *l'Un vivant*, que la croyance en un Dieu unique]. (2000: 22, emphasis mine)

Some interpreters of Derrida's discourse on faith have placed emphasis on the supposed inescapable horizon of death and mortality that characterizes faith as sacredness and is rooted in the internal relation of living and repetition (Naas 2009: 196; Hägglund 2008). As Hägglund states in *Radical Atheism*: 'the logic of autoimmunity is radically atheist', where a-theism rejects every 'theism' linked with an idea of an immortal God, or, to put it in the language of John: to God as source of eternal life.[30] However, these readings miss the internal relation that Derrida establishes between the eternally 'living One' and his indeconstructible conception of faith as fidelity. Derrida's reference to the 'living One' casts doubt on Hägglund's connection of divine immortality with 'death'. As I understand Derrida, it is Latin Christianity and modern Enlightenment that share an auto-immunitary obsession with the attempt to 'save' life and its 'dignity' by incorporating death within God in the form of the Passion.[31] Conversely, Derrida suggests we should recover those traditions in Islam and Judaism characterized precisely by their rejection of 'death' in God. These traditions, unsurprisingly, also share a common reception of a certain Platonism, and of the mystery of Being as transmitted by Philo. They offer a vision of bare faith in the One, and the One as (eternally) living that functions as a subversive underpinning to all revealed religions of monotheism. This shared 'faith in the One' harbours the experience of a groundless bare faith as a 'bind to the other in general (. . .) as a bind between singularities prior to all social or political determination, prior to all intersubjectivity, and even prior to the opposition between the sacred (or saintly) and the profane' (Derrida 2000: 29). Platonism, Judaism and Islam multiply the faith in the One and in so doing express the generalized non-coincidence of singularity. These articulations of bare faith are indeconstructible and they harbour the experience of an openness to the other, an 'unconditional hospitality' (Derrida 2003: 204–5; Chérif 2008),[32] a community of pure singularities, that offers the ground of legitimacy for a 'democracy to come' beyond the long Western history of faith and reason.

Conclusion

In this article I assume that democracy, as a form of government, stands in need of legitimacy. I follow Schmitt's claim that discourses of legitimacy take the form of 'political theology'. Given the relation of modern democracy with a 'metaphysics' of immanence, I provide some indications as to what form a 'political theology of democracy' can take, as illustrated by the thought of Bloch, Habermas and Derrida. Their thinking suggests that the 'atheism' inherent to immanence and the 'theology' inherent to transcendence can be brought together in a democratic sense through a messianic discourse, where the messianic necessarily refers to a conception of 'eternal' life. The point of this exercise is given by the recent suspicion that the legitimacy of democracy is no longer unproblematic. This Western, modernist article of faith in democracy's legitimacy is coming under strain, partially through the so-called 'resurgence' of monotheistic religions in the public sphere, partially through the competition offered by the Chinese regime, which in many respects can be seen as offering an alternative political theology of democracy, and partially by the evidence of planetary destruction wreaked by modern civilization.

In the spirit of an open-ended concluding reflection, I believe it is also worthwhile questioning whether democracy requires legitimacy. After all, legitimacy is a requirement for rule (*archein, imperium*). But what if democracy were not, primarily, a form of rule or government, but a way of organizing living beings such that they can live under conditions of no-rule (*an-arche*)? As Derrida suggests with his idea of a democracy to-come, democracy must inherently be open to what is other, to what is most troubling to our sense of self, for better or worse.

Unlike Bakunin, I do not think that this democratic an-archy can do without law and religion. So the required an-archic conceptions of law and religion will have to be 'methodologically atheist' in ways that challenge more radically the discourse of political theology, not only, as is obvious, Schmittian political theology, but also the kind of democratic political theology I reconstruct in the case of thinkers like Habermas and even Derrida.

For the horizon within which their messianic political theology moves remains a humanist one. Bloch suggests that there is an internal connection between belief in human dignity and radical immanence, following on the Marxist dictum that human emancipation can occur only based on the emancipation of nature. However, at the end of this messianic trajectory there still stands the priority of the 'face of man'. But what if the messianic 'garden' would have another face, that of an animal, or a plant or even a rock? What changes to our conceptions of natural law and natural religion are needed in order to recognize the dignity of non-human beings?

Notes

1 This is just one possibility for how to read so-called 'postsecular' discourse, and furthermore it is limited to the Western tradition and canon. But there are other equally plausible ways to read the political motivations and stakes in the so-called 'turn to religion', such as have been advanced lately by Hurd (2017), for example.
2 For another approach to these challenges which takes Bloch as central but does not frame it within the discourse of political theology, see Agar (2014).
3 This hypothesis problematizes the claim made by Hägglund (2019) for whom any and every 'theological' content is counter-democratic, or must be radically secularized for it to be acceptable as a democratic discourse. Hägglund seems to exclude the possibility that 'atheism' is consistent with 'messianism'. However, my hypothesis is also not the same as the one of 'radical theology' based on a 'death' or 'weakness' of God (Caputo 2014). But to show this difference would exceed the limits of this chapter. For a convincing critique of the insufficiency of the latter standpoint, see Bielik-Robson (2019). I thank Montserrat Herrero and Agata Bielik-Robson for bringing up these points.
4 Agamben (2005: 53) bases his hypothesis on the claim that 'a careful examination of the footnotes and bibliographies of his [Schmitt's] writings shows that from 1915 on Schmitt was a regular reader of the journal [*Archiv für Sozialwissenschaften und Sozialpolitik*]' where Benjamin's essay appeared. Agamben fails to mention that the only citation drawn from this journal in *Political Theology* refers to an article by Kelsen of 1920. Rosenstock (2014, 2017) has recently drawn attention to Schmitt's interest in radical German Jewish political thought during these years.
5 Meier (1995, 2011) is perhaps the interpreter who most insists on the centrality of Bakunin for Schmitt's political theology. For a more recent discussion of the opposition between political theology and anarchism, see Newman (2019). See also Mikkel Flohr's chapter in the present volume.
6 In *Dictatorship* (Schmitt 2014: 124) he had already articulated the idea of a 'sovereign dictatorship' and linked it to Sieyès's *pouvoir constituant*. Awkwardly, in this early text

he also claims that this idea of constituent power derives from Spinoza's conception of *natura naturans*.

7   I subscribe to Cristi (1997) according to whom Schmitt avoided offering a political theology to go along with his interpretation of 'democratic' constituent power in *Constitutional Theory* and, instead, turned to the principle of representation which, on his reading, necessarily contains a dimension of transcendence. However, Koekkoek (2014) suggests that, at least for a brief period of time in the 1920s, Schmitt entertained the idea that Spinoza's pantheistic formula 'Deus dive Natura' could offer the basis for this immanent and democratic political theology. Saralegui, in a forthcoming book, argues that political theology is only a modern possibility, and as such there is in principle a political theology for atheism and anarchism; however, he also fails to specify where in Schmitt one would find such a discourse.

8   On Schmitt's concept of sovereign dictatorship as synonymous with constituent power, see Colón-Ríos (2020). On the role of representation in Schmitt's political theology, see Herrero (2015).

9   For these motifs in Schmitt's critique of liberalism, I refer to the essays in Meierhenrich and Simons (2016).

10 Donoso Cortés (2000: 57), in his famous speech on dictatorship, formulates the following either/or: 'One must deal with choosing between a dictatorship of insurrection and a dictatorship of Government.' Notice that Schmitt has passed from a theory of the state based on sovereignty to an account of dictatorship as a form of government.

11 The English translation of *Political Theology* unfortunately omits the negation and so makes the passage un-understandable, *sic!*

12 The relevant passage in Schmitt reads: 'Every claim of a decision must be evil for the anarchist, because the right emerges by itself if the immanence of life is not disturbed by such claims. This radical antithesis forces him [the anarchist] of course to decide against the decision; and this results in the odd paradox whereby Bakunin . . . had to become in theory the theologian of the antitheological and in practice the dictator of an antidictatorship' (1988: 66). Does Schmitt mean that Bakunin offers a political theology of democracy or is he pointing to the contradictory, thus nonsensical status of such a political theology? I opt for the latter meaning. However, Stark for example argues that 'Schmitt identified Bakunin's anarchism as an atheist political theology' (2013, 57).

13 The following sections draw from chapter 5 of my study, Vatter (2021a).

14 I do not have space here to engage the relation between Bloch's transcendence and Heideggerian ek-sistence, which could also be understood as a variant of 'transcending without transcendence'.

15 On Bloch's critique of biblical religion, see Boer (2007). On the theme of the 'invisible church' and its relation to the 'Age of Spirit' that would follow upon Christendom according to the prophecies of Joachim of Fiore, see Taubes (2009) before being taken up in a post-Heideggerian vein by Vattimo (2002).

16 For a recent articulation of the Kingdom and Paradise, see Agamben (2020) who does not, however, refer to Bloch.

17 See the 2019 English edition of Bloch, and for an interesting connection of Bloch's materialism to the 'new materialism', see Moir (2016).

18 For a discussion of this theme in contemporary Italian biopolitics, see Esposito (2015) and my discussion in Vatter (2017a).

19 I have discussed the internal relation between conatus, eternal life and *sui iuris* status (which is how I would understand Bloch's 'stand up straight') in Vatter (2014).

On Bloch's recovery of the idea of human dignity within the Marxist tradition, see Geoghegan (1995: chapter 5, passim.).
20 On the invisible church as a leitmotif of the Enlightenment, see Assmann (2014); and for the best treatment of the idea from Lessing to Hegel, see Harris (1972).
21 The interpretation of Kant I discuss here does not seem to have changed in any of its essentials in Habermas's new work, *Auch eine Geschichte der Philosophie*.
22 For a wide-ranging discussion of the motif of hope in Kant, see Fenves (1991).
23 Habermas (2005: 227) cites Kant, *On the Common Saying* A 211, note.
24 'The Kingdom [of God] remains the central religious concept (. . .). Hence the eventual transformation of the alien astral-mythical mystery, the chance to crack it into the mystery of a *citoyen* of the Kingdom and of his paradoxical relation to what has come to be. Hence, finally and above all, the greatest paradox in the religious sphere that is so rich in paradoxes: the *elimination of the deity itself* so that religious mindfulness and total hope may have a space ahead.' From *Das Prinzip Hoffnung*, 'Man's Increasing Entry into Religious Mystery', which is cited in Bloch (1970: 160).
25 The relevant passage in Derrida (2000: 47) reads: 'Let us remember the hypothesis of the two sources: on the one hand, the fiduciary-ity of confidence, trustworthiness or of trust . . . and on the other, the unscathed-ness of the unscathed (the safe and sound, the immune, the holy, the sacred, heilig).' The translation used is the one in Derrida and Vattimo (1998).
26 For two opposed possibilities of what this formulation entails, see the interpretations of Caputo and Bielik-Robson mentioned earlier.
27 For this interpretation of Philo, see Goodenough (1969). For a systematic discussion of Philo and the origins of the discourse of political theology, I refer to Vatter (2021b).
28 The relevant passage in Derrida reads: 'No to-come without some sort of messianic memory and promise, of a messianicity older than all religion (. . .). No promise (. . .) without the promise of a confirmation of the yes. This yes will have implied and will always therefore imply the trustworthiness and fidelity of a faith. No faith, therefore, nor future without everything technical, automatic, machine-like supposed by iterability' (Derrida 2000: 38).
29 On the complex background that gives rise to Derrida's use of *khora*, see Falque (2014).
30 John 5:24–27: 'Very truly I tell you, whoever hears my word and believes him who sent me has eternal life and will not be judged but has crossed over from death to life. Very truly I tell you, a time is coming and has now come when the dead will hear the voice of the Son of God and those who hear will live. For as the Father has life in himself, so he has granted the Son also to have life in himself. And he has given him authority to judge because he is the Son of Man.' As Bloch clearly perceives, the idea of 'eternal life' here is linked with the mysterious possibility of the 'Son of Man'.
31 It seems to me that Hägglund's interpretation of Hegel, as the ultimate secularization of Christianity, ultimately falls within this Trinitarian schema.
32 On these motifs, see also Derrida's discussion of 'Islam and the West' in Chérif (2008).

References

Agamben, G. (2005), *State of Exception*, Chicago, IL: University of Chicago Press.
Agamben, G. (2020), *The Kingdom and the Garden*, London and Calcutta: Seagull Books.

Agar, J. (2014), *Post-Secularism, Realism, Utopia: Transcendence and Immanence from Hegel to Bloch*, London: Routledge.
Assmann, J. (2014), *Religio Duplex: How the Enlightenment Reinvented Egyptian Religion*, Cambridge, MA: Polity Press.
Bielik-Robson, A. (2019), 'The Marrano God: Abstraction, Messianicity and Retreat in Derrida's "Faith and Knowledge"', *Religions*, 10(1), https://www.mdpi.com/387788.
Bloch, E. (1970), *Man on His Own: Essays in the Philosophy of Religion*, New York: Herder and Herder.
Bloch, E. (1972), *Atheism in Christianity*, New York: Herder and Herder.
Bloch, E. (2019), *Avicenna and the Aristotelian Left*, New York: Columbia University Press.
Boer, R. (2007), *Criticism of Heaven: Marxism and Theology*, Boston: Brill.
Caputo, J. D. (2014), 'Unprotected Religion: Radical Theology, Radical Atheism, and the Return of Anti-Religion', in E. Baring and P. E. Gordon (eds), *The Trace of God: Derrida and Religion*, New York: Fordham University Press.
Chérif, M. (2008), *Islam and the West: A Conversation with Jacques Derrida*, Chicago, IL: University of Chicago Press.
Colón-Ríos, J. (2020), *Constituent Power and the Law*, New York: Oxford University Press.
Cristi, R. (1997), 'Carl Schmitt on Sovereignty and Constituent Power', *Canadian Journal of Law and Jurisprudence*, 10 (1): 189–202.
Derrida, J. (2000), *Foi et Savoir. Les deux sources de la 'religion' aux limites de la simple raison*, Paris: Seuil.
Derrida, J. (2003), *Voyous: Deux essais sur la raison*, Paris: Galilée.
Derrida, J. and G. Vattimo (1998), *Religion*, Stanford, CA: Stanford University Press.
Donoso Cortés, J. (2000), *Selected Works of Juan Donoso Cortés*, ed. J. P. Johnson, Westport, CT: Greenwood Press.
Esposito, R. (2004), *Bios: Biopolitica e filosofia*, Turin: Einaudi.
Esposito, R. (2015), *Two: The Machine of Political Theology and the Place of Thought*, New York: Fordham University Press.
Falque, E. (2014), 'Khora ou la "Grande Bifurcation": Dialoue avec Jacques Derrida', *Archivio di Filosofia*, 82 (1/2):147–66.
Fenves, P. D. (1991), *A Peculiar Fate: Metaphysics and World-History in Kant*, Ithaca, NY: Cornell University Press.
Geoghegan, V. (1995), *Bloch*, London: Taylor & Francis.
Goodenough, E. R. (1969), *By Light, Light: The Mystic Gospel of Hellenistic Judaism*, Amsterdam: Philo Press.
Habermas, J. (2003), *The Future of Human Nature*, Cambridge: Polity Press.
Habermas, J. (2005), *Zwischen Naturalismus und Religion: Philosophische Aufsätze*, Frankfurt: Suhrkamp.
Hägglund, M. (2008), *Radical Atheism: Derrida and the Time of Life*, Stanford, CA: Stanford University Press.
Hägglund, M. (2019), *This Life: Secular Faith and Spiritual Freedom*, New York: Anchor.
Harris, H. S. (1972), *Hegel's Development: Towards the Sunlight 1770–1801*, Oxford: Oxford University Press.
Herrero, M. (2015), *The Political Discourse of Carl Schmitt: A Mystic of Order*, Lexington: Rowman & Littlefield.
Hurd, E. S. (2017), *Beyond Religious Freedom: The New Global Politics of Religion*, Princeton, NJ: Princeton University Press.
Kelsen, H. (1973), *Essays in Legal and Moral Philosophy*, Dordrecht: D. Reidel.

Koekkoek, R. (2014), 'Carl Schmitt and the Challenge of Spinoza's Pantheism Between the World Wars', *Modern Intellectual History*, 11 (2): 333–57.
Lefort, C. (2006), 'The Permanence of the Theologico-Political?', in H. de Vries (ed.), *Political Theologies: Public Religions in a Post-Secular World*, 148–87, New York: Fordham University Press.
Meier, H. (1995), *Carl Schmitt and Leo Strauss: The Hidden Dialogue*, Chicago, IL: The University of Chicago Press.
Meier, H. (2011), *The Lesson of Carl Schmitt: Four Chapters on the Distinction between Political Theology and Political Philosophy*, Chicago, IL: The University of Chicago Press.
Meierhenrich, J. and O. Simons, eds (2016), *The Oxford Handbook on Carl Schmitt*, New York: Oxford University Press.
Moir, C. (2016), 'Beyond the Turn: Ernst Bloch and the Future of Speculative Materialism', *Poetics Today*, 37 (2): 327–51.
Naas, M. (2009), 'Miracle and Machine: The Two Sources of Religion and Science in Derrida's "Faith and Knowledge"', *Research in Phenomenology*, 39: 184–203.
Negri, A. and M. Hardt (2001), *Empire*, Cambridge: Cambridge University Press.
Newman, S. (2019), *Political Theology: A Critical Introduction*, Cambridge, MA: Polity Press.
Rabinbach, A. (1997), *In the Shadow of Catastrophe: German Intellectuals Between Apocalypse and Enlightenment*, Berkeley, CA: University of California Press.
Rosenstock, B. (2014), 'Palintropos Harmonie: Jacob Taubes and Carl Schmitt "im liebenden Streit"', *New German Critique*, 41 (1): 55–92.
Rosenstock, B. (2017), *Transfinite Life: Oskar Goldberg and the Vitalist Imagination*, Bloomington, IN: Indiana University Press.
Saralegui, M. (2021), *The Politics of Time: Introduction to Carl Schmitt's Political Thought*, Santander: Cantabria University Press.
Schmitt, C. (1988), *Political Theology: Four Chapters on the Concept of Sovereignty*, Cambridge, MA: MIT Press.
Schmitt, C. (2001), *The Crisis of Parliamentary Democracy*, Cambridge: MIT Press.
Schmitt, C. (2004), *Legality and Legitimacy*, Durham, NC: Duke University Press.
Schmitt, C. (2008), *Constitutional Theory*, trans. J. Seitzer, Durham, NC: Duke University Press.
Schmitt, C. (2014). *Dictatorship: From the Origin of Modern Concept of Sovereignty to Proletarian Class Struggle*, trans. M. Hoelzl and G. Ward, London: Polity.
Stark, T. (2013), '*Complexio oppositorum*: Hugo Ball and Carl Schmitt', *October*, 146: 31–64.
Taubes, J. (2009), *Occidental Eschatology*, Stanford, CA: Stanford University Press.
Taylor, C. (2007), *A Secular Age*, Cambridge, MA: Harvard University Press.
Vatter, M. (2014), *The Republic of the Living: Biopolitics and the Critique of Civil Society*, New York: Fordham.
Vatter, M. (2017a), 'Community, Life and Subjectivity in Italian Biopolitics', in S. Prozorov and S. Rentea (eds), *The Routledge Handbook of Biopolitics*, 123–40, London and New York: Routledge.
Vatter, M. (2017b), 'The Political Theology of Carl Schmitt', in J. Meierhenrich and O. Simons, *The Oxford Handbook of Carl Schmitt*, 245–68New York: Oxford University Press.
Vatter, M. (2021a), *Divine Democracy: Political Theology After Carl Schmitt*, New York: Oxford University Press.
Vatter, M. (2021b), *Living Law: Jewish Political Theology from Hermann Cohen to Hannah Arendt*, New York: Oxford University Press.
Vattimo, G. (2002), *After Christianity*, New York: Columbia University Press.

Chapter 6

POLITICAL THEOLOGY, VALUES AND LGBTQ+ AS CIVIL RELIGION

Stefan Schwarzkopf

Schmitt and social theology

In his 1922 analysis of the concept of political theology, Schmitt surmised that all significant concepts in political-constitutional thought ('Staatslehre') are, in fact, secularized theological concepts ([1922] 2009: 43). Schmitt's famous dictum has become a widely used entry point for studies in political theology. One major consequence of this maxim is the insight that Western, secular, liberal democracies draw on a legitimizing conceptual base that they cannot construct *ex nihilo* and out of itself, so to speak. Open societies will inevitably draw on a set of concepts that carry a theological marker, a 'signature' (Dean 2013), that links these concepts back to older thought systems that are – ironically – associated with what Karl Popper called the 'enemies of open society' ([1945] 2013). In his classic 1922 work *Political Theology*, Schmitt famously used the conceptual trinity of sovereignty, decision and exception to illustrate his secularization thesis. Schmitt demonstrated how the essentially theological origins of seemingly secular and liberal political-constitutional concepts might be uncovered by paying attention to *structural analogies* between concepts from the two realms of theology and law. Famously, Schmitt described how the figure of God as almighty lawmaker morphed into the figure of the royal sovereign as lawmaker in early modern constitutional theories.

Understood as an analytic method, the search for structural analogies can be developed further, for example, with the aim to cover areas that Schmitt's original analysis left out, such as socio-economic concepts and what Drazin (2013) called 'the social life of concepts'. Over the last two decades, a new research field has emerged that exposes seemingly innocuous social and economic concepts to the same systematic analogical and genealogical analysis as proposed by Schmitt a hundred years ago with regards to political-constitutional concepts. Researchers associated with this paradigm treat Schmitt's 1922 study of the concept of sovereignty as a special case that opens the path to a wider social and economic theology. As an analytical rather than normative discipline, social and economic theology is part of a more general intellectual turn that led to theology and the social sciences problematizing each other (Boland 2019; Dean 2019; Hyman 2004;

Hynd 2016; Milbank 1990; Schwarzkopf 2020). Within the framework of social and economic theology, conceptually anchored social practices, and new movements and communities that gather around concepts, can also be exposed to a form of analysis that takes its starting point in a search for structural analogies with the theological realm. The LGBTQ+ movement and its conceptual underpinnings in liberal social philosophy is well placed to illustrate the intellectual potential of the paradigm of social and economic theology. Traditionally called 'the gay rights movement', this movement is typically understood as the poster child of a secular, open society with an entirely non- (or even anti-)theological conceptual base in ideas of individual liberty, inclusion, equality and diversity. However, if we pay closer attention to how this movement intertwines language and ritual, we uncover a very different genealogy of the LGBTQ+ agenda, one that reveals structural analogies to pre-modern Gnostic and Sabbatian sects.

Focusing on the case of the LGBTQ+ movement, this chapter will investigate the hypothesis that theological undercurrents can validate sociocultural concepts. Yet, there is more that a Schmittian reading of this movement might be able to reveal. With Schmitt, we might be able to understand how the theological valence of a set of particular sociocultural concepts might even lead to the formation of structures that resemble what Robert Bellah called a civil religion. In a short essay, originally written in 1959 and entitled *The Tyranny of Values*, Carl Schmitt warned that the proliferation of value-driven special interest groups poses a danger for a rationally organized public sphere, as such groups can morph into quasi-religious advocators of values that demand execution, inviting in turn counter-movements that insist on diametrically opposed, alternative values. In the following sections of this chapter, I will use the LGBTQ+ movement to highlight the structure – but also the limitations – of Schmitt's idea of the immanent aggression that underpins value-oriented social ideologies. The chapter thus engages with a central argument of Schmitt's 1922 book *Political Theology*, connects this argument to a relatively little-studied essay by Schmitt on the politics of values and outlines how both analyses might provide new insights into the nature of the contemporary culture wars that threaten to undermine liberal democracy.

LGBTQ+ and the spectre of civil religion

Admittedly, LGBTQ+ and theology are not obvious bedfellows. Most people would find it outright odd to analyse the gay rights movement objectively and neutrally through the prism of theological concepts. If anything, theological concepts are too often brought in position to push against the extension of common liberties to lesbian, gay, transgender and queer people. Yet, upon closer inspection, the LGBTQ+ movement might actually be understood much better when compared to a religious movement that is based on a particular theology of personhood. Seen from the perspective of the social life of theological concepts, this movement is in the process of 'upgrading' from a particularist-sectarian to an inclusive-ecclesiastical structure. In this latter form, which the global LGBTQ+ movement is taking on, this civil rights organization has the potential of becoming a public or *civil religion* of the same weight and scope that in the past was associated with the worship of nationhood and national identity.

Interpreting the LGBTQ+ movement in terms of a civil religion is rarely done, but is, in fact, a quite straightforward affair once preconceived notions and definitions of religion have been put aside. Most often, the term 'religion' is being used synonymously with 'faith' in a transcendent divine being. Consequently, since secular social movements such as LGBTQ+ do not worship a deity, they can be seen as ideological, but certainly not as religious. Following classical sociologists and anthropologists of religion such as Emile Durkheim, Rudolf Otto and Mary Douglas, we can reject this misunderstanding. Durkheim defined religion as a system of beliefs and practices *relative to sacred things* (2001). In this definition, the sacred is the origin of religion, deities, and so on – and not the other way around. As a corollary, the conceptual opposite of 'sacred' is not 'secular', but 'profane'. All groups and societies designate certain things, objects, places and people as sacred as opposed to profane, ordinary, permissible and mundane. It is around these designations of what is sacred, to be held in higher regard, to be considered as taboo and so forth, that religions emerge. Ostensibly secular social movements such as LGBTQ+ can therefore very well be organized around ideas, people, places, objects and so forth, that they regard as sacred, hence forming what sociologist Robert Bellah (1967) called a civil religion, that is, an implicit religion organized around a community's common heritage as expressed through shared beliefs, commonly observed public rituals and sacred symbols, texts, and places. Once turned back on its feet, an analysis of LGBTQ+ religiosity therefore needs to look for evidence of sacrality, not deity worship.[1]

Seen through the prism of Bellah's notion of civil religion and Durkheim's sociology of the sacred, it is not difficult to see how the LGBTQ+ movement has strategically built up a network of sacred objects, places and events. Designed to either replace or accompany older forms of Christianity, a civil religion provides followers with flags, hymns, symbols, martyrs, sacred sites and annual rituals of commemoration in order to forge the bonds that are needed to sustain the substitutes of a universal church. In the twenty-first century, and against a resurgent political particularism, movements like LGBTQ+ celebrate a secular version of the universality that formerly characterized churches. As feasts of love, colour, music, drinking, eroticism and playfulness, LGBTQ+ events such as the annual 'Pride Parades' share the enthusiastic atmosphere of religious celebrations, such as the Roman Bacchanalia, Easter parades and Carnival. There are also similarities between Pride Parades and more organized elements of religion. Many employers that sponsor the parades, for instance, encourage their employees to turn up in corporate-branded t-shirts, and participants who join the floats of non-profit organizations or who march as individuals often share similar outfits. This uniformity, but also other forms of social-symbolic interaction, helps engender a particular *spirit* among those who take part. This spirit consists of a feeling that the event celebrates something collective and transcendent, namely the universal human right to be included and feel accepted without discrimination. It is in this spirit that gifts are handed out to complete strangers: music, drinks and small tokens like flags, balloons, sweets, toys, condoms and suchlike. Crucially, these gifts are shared among the crowd to be consumed on site as a symbol of what is collectively believed in. Further, Pride Parades, like many religious rituals, celebrate martyrdom, suffering and sacrifice. Indeed, the first Pride festivals were held in commemoration of the people who had rioted on New York's Christopher Street in June 1969 and who had been violently beaten by police. Pride Parades have their own liturgy, including specific colours (the Rainbow) and appropriate music that often celebrates hedonistic themes. Other liturgical elements are the diligent preparations, the official walking route and the end point that most often consists of a central landmark, such as Copenhagen's town hall square that becomes 'Pride Square'.

Pride Parades are part of a new kind of socio-material environment for social norms and values, and they provide the scene for intensely affective, self-transcending experiences. Such experiences of collective self-transcendence are typically associated with the sacred aspects of religions. Civil religions allow groups of people an experience of rising above the mundaneness of daily life by worshipping values held in higher regard, such as shared myths and national heroes. Through its Pride Parades, the LBGTQ+ movement provides such self-transcending experiences and an affective environment that makes participants feel they stand up for something higher than themselves. These experiences then enable the performative creation of broadly integrative values and norms. In the case of LGBTQ+, these values and norms circulate around human rights and the sacredness of the person. The annual parades celebrate this sacredness and help reinforce the universal idea of love as an inalienable human right.

If the Pride Parades can be understood as the movement's sacred ritual, then the Stonewall Inn in Greenwich Village, New York, can be understood as one of the movement's most important sacred sites. The myth of Stonewall has been retold numerous times: on the night of 28 June 1969, a police raid took place, which targeted the Stonewall Inn on Christopher Street, a popular gay bar. The bar's patrons resisted, and the ensuing riots that lasted two consecutive nights helped launch the modern gay rights movement. Crucially, it is from *within* the movement itself that people have begun referring to the Stonewall Inn as a sacred site. According to LGBTQ historian Lillian Faderman, the movement had its own 'martyrs', and by that she meant the people who on 28 June stood up to police violence and started to throw bottles, rocks and coins. Tommy Lanigan-Schmidt, an eyewitness and Stonewall rioter, referred to the indignation he felt that night because the bar was considered a safe place: 'this was like sacred' (Carter 2010: 145). Celebrating the fiftieth anniversary of the riots in June 2019, National Public Radio ran a series that stated: 'The Stonewall Inn is a sacred place for many in the LGBTQ community.' Clare Hand, a self-described 'Door Dyke' in London's queer bar scene referred to 28 June as a 'sacred night'. The *New York Times* referred to the Inn on several occasions as a 'sacred place' (2015).

For a site to be considered 'sacred', it must be linked to an original extraordinary event and/or its commemoration. Such an event can come in the form of an unusual incident and an extraordinary experience, and is often either associated with or directly born out of violence. Seen from this perspective, Christian churches are considered sacred because they are sites of collective memorialization and worship of an extraordinary event connected to violence, namely the 'scapegoating' of Christ. In the case of the Stonewall Inn, its sacrality and symbolic prominence for the movement arises from the extraordinary experience of the night of 28 June 1969 as an event connected to violence – a violence that helped protect a persecuted minority from being scapegoated for larger social ills (Girard 1989). That particular night presents itself as a textbook case for Durkheim's notion of 'collective effervescence'. Numerous eyewitnesses confirmed that there seemed to be a special mood in the crowd outside the Stonewall Inn that night, an exceptional spirit bubbling up which they had not seen before during the very ordinary and frequent bar raids in Greenwich Village (Carter 2010). According to Durkheim, social communities maintain and regenerate the original feelings attached to such extraordinary moments through shared rituals, symbols and stories.

The commemoration of the original uprising in June 1969 reflects the mythical status of the Stonewall Inn as a sacred site. Local gay rights movements all over North America and Europe promoted this sacrality by naming their rallies 'Christopher Street Liberation Day' marches (CSD). These parades started in 1970 in New York, Chicago and Los Angeles, and were copied in Europe from the early 1970s onwards. The parades were designed right from the beginning as 'commemorative' marches, which feeds into the mythological and sacred nature of the site and the event. This commemorative nature allowed parade routes in Paris, Berlin and London, among other cities, to symbolically *become* Christopher Street for one day each year. The sense of having lived through an extraordinary event of liberating violence led John Paul Hudson, an activist who co-organized the first commemorative event in New York in June 1970, to experience what he described as 're-awakening' and 're-birth'. At some stage between the Stonewall riots and the organization of the first march, on 28 April 1970, Hudson said he awoke as a 'born-again radical' and moved his birthday to that day (*Today in Gay History*).

With civil religions also often come sacred texts, a fact exemplified by the rise of a 'textualist' and 'originalist' approach to the American Constitution as a sacred text of the American civil religion. In the case of the LGBTQ+ movement, the closest equivalent is the so-called 'NAMES Project AIDS Memorial Quilt', a hand-crafted and continuously growing display of the names of people who died from AIDS-related causes. In 1987, artist and gay rights activist Cleve Jones started the project of a quilt that allows individuals and communities to add new names. Today, the quilt weighs an estimated 54 tonnes. Like the travelling relic known from the Middle Ages, the quilt and parts of it can be moved from location to location. It allows people to connect to the transcendent experiences of death and suffering. The quilt becomes the site of a ritualistic litany (from Greek *litaneia* = entreaty, plea) when its public display brings in celebrities, politicians, family members and activists who publicly read out aloud the names of the people on the quilt. In the same ways as the Catholic 'Litany of the Saints' centres on singing out aloud the names of the messengers of a religious message and its martyrs, the reading out aloud of the names on the AIDS quilt uses the reiteration of the names of the dead to give death a meaning, and to create a publicly shared, collective memory in a ritualistic fashion. Since 1987, the ceremonial unfolding of the AIDS Quilt follows a particular ritual: it is put in the middle of a group of people, who before the unfolding stand in a moment of silence, and then follow a pattern of movements that slowly unfold the quilt quadrants. Some people have compared the slow and ritualistic unfolding of the quilt at public events to the military procedure that exists for folding and unfolding the American flag (Hawkins 1993). The slow pace, the careful choreography and the silence at such events make it clear that one is in the presence of a sacred object as well as a sacred text that commits to memory the victims of a virus that was too long ignored because of anti-gay prejudice.

A genealogy of anti-confessional conduct

Merely identifying the LGBTQ+ movement as a civil religion, although important and certainly contentious in its own right, would fall short of a full understanding of the revolutionary potential of this civil society movement. One issue, of course, is that the LGBTQ+ movement now rivals traditional, nationality-based civil religions. A way around this problem is that in many Western countries, Pride Parades have merged with or have been written into the mythology of older mainstream civil religions. At the Copenhagen and the London Pride Parades, one can witness a celebration of 'Danishness' and 'Britishness', with rainbow flags and Dannebrog flag and the Union Jack, respectively, flown side by side. In the United States, the Stars and Stripes has been incorporated into LGBTQ+-themed parades, the same way as contingents of gay, lesbian and transgender army and police personnel at Pride Parades now march with official emblems, uniforms and often their regimental flags.

It would be a fallacy, however, to assume that the civil-religious character of the LGBTQ+ movement was therefore unproblematic. Whether or not rainbow flags should be flown over town halls and parliament buildings during Pride Week, Obama's decision to cover the White House in rainbow colours in June 2015 and the installation of gender-neutral toilets at universities and airports suggested language changes to designate genders or non-genders (his, 'zir' and 'hir'), the introduction of gender-neutral and gay-friendly sex education as early as primary school level, the question as to whether government documents should carry binary gender-identifying 'male-female' categories or, instead, neutral non-identification boxes, the question as to whether army staff should have access to gender-affirming medical and psychological care: these and many other questions have turned into *the* most explosive issue in the ongoing culture wars in the West. The LGBTQ+ movement enters these wars as a denomination, a quasi-civil religion, which in turn gives the culture wars a denominational-religious character.

Religious ideas need social carrier groups, and German theologian Ernst Troeltsch famously differentiated between three such social structures: church, sect and mysticism (Johnson 1957). The religious idea of a 'church' is defined by the fact that its believers are born into it and that its *institutions* guarantee salvation. A 'sect' by contrast is a social structure one chooses to enter; one's membership in it needs to be reconfirmed through appropriate actions. A sect guarantees salvation not by inclusive institutions, but through exclusive rules on *behaviour and faith*. 'Mysticism', the socially most liquid of the three ideal types, is defined as the *personal internalization* of religious ideas. There are mystics, but hardly any mystic groups that would not be sects. Max Weber took up the idea of the three ideal types of the social organization of religiosity and further differentiated among different types of sects, such as those that group tightly around a charismatic personality (charismatic sects), around specific interpretations of the Bible (Protestant sects) and those that group around claims of having access to unique, 'secret' knowledge – so-called Gnostic sects.

Sects, by their very nature of being positioned against the idea of the redemptive capacity of a church as *Gnadenanstalt* (grace-giving or redemptive institution), are heretical and always take aim at what they see as accepted, ordained sociopolitical traditions and 'orders' in this world. Since sexuality as a social field is circumscribed by traditions and normative orders, sexual practices were often the target of Gnostic sects that challenged and overturned such norms. Christianity, when socially still organized as a sect, took aim at licentious Roman sexual practices as well as practices of slavery. It was socially progressive, revolutionary even, for this sect to aim for a contrasting social order based on 'family values' and a monogamous marriage shaped in the image of Adam and Eve (Brown 1988). When these values became dominant and power-infused 'church teachings', various Christian Gnostic sects began to target them because these social teachings and institutions such as the sacrament of marriage ('holy matrimony') became too closely entangled with 'the world', a fallen and evil place. Gnostic sects are characterized by their aim to develop practices that help adherents to disentangle themselves from the established ways and orders of the world. In some cases, Gnostic sects openly and very publicly defied 'normative' sexual practices in order to reject, overcome and thus disentangle themselves from the world. Paradoxically, this meant that such sects promoted the committing of sexual sins through group sex and sodomy so as to become holy.

Most prominent among such sexually libertine-Gnostic sects were the Carpocratians and the Borborites (first and second centuries AD), and later the so-called Sabbatians within Judaism (seventeenth and eighteenth centuries). The most prominent early libertine-Gnostic sect leader was Carpocrates, a Christian of whom we know only because he was the target of aggressively 'anti-heretical' writings by early Church Fathers Irenaeus and Clement of Alexandria. Carpocrates is of particular interest for us here since he provided the first theologically coherent outline of the concept of 'salvation through sin' or 'redemption through sin'. Gnostics believed in a sharp contrast between good and evil, spirit and material; they associated the former with the Christian god and the latter with a minor creator-god, a demiurge whom they identified as the god of the Old Testament. Following any form of official, institutionalized law – as the Romans and Jews did painstakingly – would have meant to tie oneself to the established order of *this* world, the world of the evil creator-god. Paradoxically, thus, Gnostics proposed that the *breaking* of these laws enabled believers to reject and overcome the world and enter a holy communion with the higher, the spiritual, god. This did not entail the breaking of laws for the sake of personal gain (theft, murder, perjury, etc.), but, rather, the targeted and systematic breaking of moral norms as a way to work on the self – namely to overcome an 'old' (earth-bound, mortal) self. For Gnostic sectarians, indulging in immoral and sinful sexual practices had therefore nothing to do with the pleasure-oriented hedonism of the pagans, but needs to be understood as an attempt to overthrow rather than accommodate the world through legal-moral and other institutional means. While the increasingly institutionalizing Christian church began to develop the confession and the public repenting of sins as a way to overcome the world, Gnostic sects developed what are, in fact, self-reflective bodily-sexual practices as a set of anti-confessional counter-conducts.

In genealogical terms, LGBTQ+ is built up *in analogy* to the Gnostic theological argument: it rejects the moralized idea of sinfulness in sexual orientation, it aims to revolutionize and overcome the restrictions of the worldly order as it is received through tradition and it promotes the idea that sexual practices can be understood as a form of reflexive work on the self. Both movements are characterized by misarchy: a profound scepticism of established power and authority (Vatter 2019). In the case of the LGBTQ+ movement, this means, for example, that the presence of uniformed police officers within Pride Parades is universally applauded because the police is often accused of targeting and criminalizing homosexuals and queers. In March 2021, the organization behind the London Pride March experienced heavy internal discussion over whether or not to allow police officers to march in uniform (Mohdin 2021). In places such as New York and Copenhagen, smaller LGBTQ organizations stage alternative marches that explicitly reject public and corporate sponsors, since these sponsors are seen as part of an overarching patriarchal, racist and capitalist power structure. Over many decades, the resistance against power began to take on the form of a confession itself. LGBTQ+ morphed from a sexual orientation into a form of identity, a particular form of subjectivity that needed to be declared and projected publicly. At the annual Pride Marches in New York and elsewhere, which began to be organized from 1970 onwards, placards appeared that called on fellow gays and lesbians to recognize their orientation as a kind of identity, and publicly declare the nature of their inner selves, their subjectivity, to others by 'uniting' and by 'coming out'.

This picture of a confessional politics is by no means homogeneous, however (Dean and Zamora 2021: 4). Parts of the LGBTQ+ movement now actually reject the ritual of 'coming out' (as homosexual, transgender, etc.) precisely because it is a form of 'confession' that only reinstitutes hetero-normative sexual customs. If there is nothing to be ashamed of, then there is nothing to 'admit' – hence why 'come out', whereto and from where? The anti-peccatory and anti-confessional elements of both Gnostics and LGBTQ+ are striking, as are the attitudes towards gender equality and even gender-irrelevance which both social movements share. Gnostics and the LGBTQ+ movement treat the body as a site of resistance against dominant discourses, and both clearly view sexuality as a power technique rather than as something 'given' and 'natural'. It is therefore most curious that Michel Foucault in his four-volume oeuvre on the *History of Sexuality*, which spans over 2000 years of history and comprises over a thousand pages, makes no mention of figures like Carpocrates and the Gnostic sects. What's more, Foucault elsewhere even positions his own stress on practices of self-transformation directly *against* the Gnostic tradition, which he identifies as purely cognitively focused on (spiritual) knowledge rather on (bodily) practices (Foucault 2005: 15–16; Carrette 2013). Foucault must have been aware of the bodily practices of the Gnostic sects, from the licentious Carpocratians and Borborites of the Antiquity, the gender-equalizing and vegetarian Cathars of the High Middle Ages, to the sex-rituals of the Jewish Sabbateans of the early modern sects that Gershom Sholem analyses in his essay *Redemption through Sin* (Sholem 1971). Perhaps he ignored all of them because they did not fit into his carefully hidden secularization thesis, which sees Greek and Stoic (pagan) practices of self-care as suppressed by a guilt-inducing, institution-oriented Christian church. The idea to develop bodily-sexual practices in order to undermine the confession as power dispositive emerged very much *within* Christian and Jewish traditions and was therefore perhaps destined to be sidelined by Foucault.

Tyranny of values

In their *misarchia* and their dislike of large-scale political and theological institutions, the Gnostic sects and the LGBTQ+ movement share what Carl Schmitt once called the 'anti-Roman affect' ([1923] 2019: 5). Schmitt's pointing out of the persistence of this affect and his methodological instrument of investigating structural analogies between theological and political concepts brings a different angle to any analysis of the rise of LGBTQ+ as movement and concept. Liberating oneself from the power dispositive of the guilt-inducing confession is, in genealogical terms, derived from a theological concept, too, namely the Gnostic concept of 'salvation through sin'. Within that concept lies the seed of the modern focus on personal values as opposed to virtues. According to Schmitt's little-known 1959 essay on *The Tyranny of Values*, modernity is characterized by a replacement of virtues by a focus on values. Whereas pre-modern political philosophy stressed the importance of virtues and virtuous behaviours for rulers and citizens, modern authors find it often difficult to make sense of virtues any longer. Thus, values come to replace them. The North-Atlantic Treaty Organization (NATO) is a case in point. Founded as a cold tool of spatial ordering around land and sea, and self-defined through its geopolitical enemy, the Soviet Union, it recreated itself as a warm 'value community' ('Wertegemeinschaft') from 1991 onwards.

The rise of value-orientation took place silently and was ironically often promoted by post-war conservatives who positioned themselves as the protectors of 'Western values', 'European values', and so forth. In late 1981, just before the invasion of the Falkland Islands by Argentina, Margaret Thatcher discussed the importance of defending 'Western values' at a meeting of the Conservative Philosophy Group. Present was a former Professor of Ancient Greek, one Enoch Powell, who disagreed with the Lady: 'Prime Minister, values exist in a transcendental realm, beyond space and time. They can neither be fought for, nor destroyed' (Schofield 2013: 346). Very few people today would align themselves with Powell's and Schmitt's scepticism. Having values – and standing up for them – is a good thing after all. Especially business schools nowadays emphasize that modern business education needs to be based on and include values such as sustainability and diversity (Duncan 2008). Valparaiso University's College of Business publishes a *Journal of Values-Based Leadership*, and the *Harvard Business Review* regularly carries articles exhorting the role of values in the shaping of future captains of industry. According to Schmitt, however, an excessive focus on values comes at the expense of the rule of law and public virtues. Values demand immediate execution and relentless implementation, something that is diametrically opposed to the spirit of disinterested interpretation and application of constitutional principles. An insistence on values led to High Court judges being labelled 'enemies of the people' by the populist newspaper, the *Daily Mail*, because their rulings did not conform to an idea of 'British values' (Breeze 2018). Says Schmitt: 'In a commonwealth whose institution provides a legislator and statute laws, it is a matter for the legislator and for the statute laws made by it to define the mediation [of values and ideas] via calculable and enforceable rules and to hinder the terror of the immediate and automatic enforcement of value' ([1959] 2011: 54).

It is almost impossible to pitch virtues against each other. It makes no sense to see the virtue of generosity somehow as the opposite of the virtue of temperance. By way of exercise, introspection and moderation, a virtuous person is supposed to find a middle ground around the virtue of bravery, without falling into the vices of cowardice ('too little') and recklessness ('too much'). In addition, a virtuous person is supposed to develop their character across a whole range of virtues, the twelve virtues in Aristotle's system and seven in Catholicism. All virtues are developmental character traits. They require constant soul-searching rather than the immediate call to arms, as in Thatcher's claim to be 'standing up for' and defending 'Western values'. A virtue acts as a guide to organize our souls, not society around us. Values, by contrast, although personally held, ultimately aim at social organization at a grand scale. They can therefore be pitted against each other, as in the case of supposedly 'Western' values of freedom and individuality against 'Eastern' values of collectivism and command-and-control. Whoever conjures up a value implicates the existence of an enemy.

For Schmitt, insisting on values means that someone or something else becomes 'valued' against, measured and devalued ([1959] 2011: 46–7). In his 1959 text, Schmitt directly pointed at the value-philosophical origins of Eugenics discourses, which after 1933 ended up with designating certain people as 'unwertes Leben' (literally: valueless life; [1959] 2011: 52). For each value that gets propounded by a sociopolitical group, another value emerges that demands equal recognition, valuation and implementation. In the United States, the insistence on freedom of choice and reproductive rights *as a value* gave birth to a 'pro-Life' movement that has now managed to send jurists who share its values to the Supreme Court. Insisting on diversity as an absolute value has fuelled the flames of the 'Identitarian' movement, which claims that if immigrants get special rights in their new home countries, such as being allowed to excuse their daughters from swimming lessons at public schools, the autochthone population deserves the same rights and protections, too. Thus emerges a spiralled logic of value against value, subgroup against sub-group: 'A multiple society, i.e., an overdeveloped pluralistic society integrating itself out of numerous heterogeneous groups, must transform the public sphere adequate to it into a training field for demonstrations in the logic of values. Group interests then present themselves as values by turning essential legal categories into significant categories of some value system adequate to them' (Schmitt [1959] 2011: 12).

Early Gnostic sects shared such a value-driven cosmology. A value-oriented person can say: my sins are, in fact, really a good thing; they are only 'sins' in the light of a corrupt order that should be overturned anyway. At the political-cultural level, this attitude underpins the LGBTQ+ movement. Various right-wing counter-movements share a similar outlook. American social conservatives, for example, invented the idea of the 'Values Voter', complete with bumper stickers ('Vote Republican – Defend American Values'; 'Proud of my Pro-Life Values'), which in turn provoke the existence of left-wing counterparts (that is, car bumper sticker with sentences such as: 'Pro-Choice, pro-LGBT, pro-Environment Feminist . . . Yes, I am a Values Voter'; 'I am proud of my San Francisco Values'). Even further to the right of the annual 'Values Voter Summits' are the supremacists and conspiracy-theorists who stormed the Washington Capitol in January 2021 because their 'values' stood above administrative processes. In the case of the QAnon movement, in particular, the analogy to the Gnostic sects is difficult to miss. For the evangelically influenced QAnoners, too, the world is split up into a sphere of God and a sphere of the Antichrist, who dominates the fallen world. This evil deity has its tentacles in all parts of public administration and top-government, but his existence is exposed by a secret insider – the messianic figure of 'Q' – who shares his secret knowledge (*gnōsis*) of the dealings of the Antichrist and his associates with those who are willing enough to see the signs and think for themselves.

It would be a grave misunderstanding to conclude that such analogizing inevitably means that LGBTQ+ and QAnon are moral equals. For a start, both movements are characterized by different visions of their own ends. In other words, their inner-worldly eschatology is not the same. For as long as worldly government exists, QAnoners will see hidden signs, clandestine groups trafficking children through seemingly innocuous pizzerias, and so forth. Theirs is a teleology without end, an infinite waiting for the messiah to reveal himself and the cabal that is *actually* ruling the world. LGBTQ+ leaders, by contrast, recognize that an inclusive society can actually be created in the here and now. Nor does the comparison of LGBTQ+ and QAnon imply that 'queers' should be criminalized again. The implications of a Schmittian reading of LGBTQ+ are very different. Such a reading would move beyond an interpretation of his *Tyranny of Values* as a mere apology for Nazi followers like himself, thus as a self-serving text of little theoretical merit in its own right (Zeitlin 2021).

Looking at the LGBTQ+ movement through the eyes of the jurist and legal scholar Schmitt, its potentially most problematic side might lie where one would least expect it, namely in its insistence on inclusion, diversity and tolerance as universal *values* rather than rights inscribed in positive law. With Schmitt, we can designate LGBTQ+ as a civil religion – but crucially, one with a sectarian-Gnostic character. Schmitt's critique of modern value-orientation allows us to see that contemporary sociopolitical struggles over LGBTQ+ as 'agenda' takes on the form of a battle between opposing sectarian denominations because they are fashioned as a war between opposing civil religions – Rainbow flag versus Confederate/MAGA flag – and as a war between values. Paying attention to the potentially perilous value-driven conflicts emerging in our societies is not to denigrate the gay rights movement. It merely highlights the challenges that are posed to a common and rationally structured public sphere when police officers begin to pin either rainbow flags on their uniforms, or alternatively the QAnon symbol, as happened in the case of Sergeant Matt Patten of the Broward County Sheriff's Office, Florida, on the occasion of a visit by Vice President Mike Pence in December 2018.

Schmitt's attention to the crucial difference between the dynamics of values and the rule of law brings elements of the LGBTQ+ movement into view that Robert Bellah might have been able to spot, but did not. Interestingly, Bellah paid almost no attention to the Gay Pride movement during his long scholarly life. Interpreting the LGBTQ+ movement as a civil religion therefore needs to move beyond Bellah's conceptualization. A civil religion need not take the social form of a church, as happened to be the case with the American civil religion of flag, constitution, pledge of allegiance and Thanksgiving. As a society, twentieth-century America fashioned its civil religion as a church because its polity was sectarian to begin with, consisting of settlers, indigenous tribes, former slaves, Eastern European Jews and culturally extremely diverse immigrant communities from Ireland, Italy, Scandinavia, Germany and Central America. Alongside the mainstream and church-like American civil religion, there emerges now a parallel civil religion in the form of LGBTQ+, which is in the process of deciding whether to remain Gnostic-sectarian or institutionalize and integrate with the church of pumpkin, Stars and Stripes. As a civil-religious sect, it would necessarily remain exclusive in character. Some parts of the LGTBQ+ movement, especially in the United States, seem to develop that way. Like the 'People's Front of Judea' in Monty Python's movie *Life of Brian*, elements of the LGBTQ+ movement are increasingly specific about who is *not* allowed to join and support them. At the New York City 'Dyke March', which is very specific about its identity as a protest march rather than a 'parade', men (gay, straight, cis, trans) are not allowed to join, but advised to stand along the route and clap if they want to show support. In 2019, some people who had joined the Dyke March in Washington, DC, with rainbow flags that featured the Star of David, were asked to leave by the organizers, since in their mind the Star symbolized an oppressive state.

Should the movement decide, by contrast, to become an all-inclusive and universal (Greek: *katholikos*) church, it would, of course, face the charge of being a conduit to corporate pink-washing, ending up with an annual Pride Parade that is an advertising show for 'Rainbow Capitalism' (Tatchell 2019). As a church-like civil religion, its value strictness would be watered down in favour of the institutionalization of grace: merely being at or sponsoring the movement's events would enable citizens and organizations to part-take in the redemptive qualities of LGBTQ+ as the new *Gnadenanstalt* (dispenser of grace) of a multicultural liberal society. The price we are all paying for LGBTQ+ *not* being a church, and for struggling against other, diametrically opposed politically religious sects, is the slow yet inescapable dissolution of a neutral public sphere into opposing value communities. Public and private sector organizations, including the judiciary and the police, have then a choice of being 'hated' by either MAGA or BLM.

Conclusion

Schmitt's analysis is not without limitations. His text is committed to a Weberian understanding of a deep gulf between instrumental rationality and value rationality. This leaves behind a touch of idealization of a rationally organized public sphere, incidentally a theme that Jürgen Habermas was working on in 1959–60, the year in which Schmitt's small text was first published. Secondly, Schmitt seems to assume that public life can more or less move ahead seamlessly by being divided into spheres where virtues get exercised and spheres where legal norms are applied. Virtues and laws can be made eternal, unchanging, reliable and predictable, thus their appeal for Schmitt. But societies change, and so do laws as well as the appeal of virtues. Crucially, it is values that drive these changes. For the rule of law to continue to be applicable and meaningful, new values need to be continuously incorporated. Very few people today would think that the discriminatory laws of the American pre-civil rights period are acceptable or 'virtuous'. It is change in values that makes us appeal to virtues and the rule of law in instances where human life is mistreated.

Despite these shortcomings, Schmitt's text is a wake-up call for those that have fallen asleep to the soothing melodies of a consensus-oriented public sphere (Smith 2021). He reminds us that whoever stresses particular values secretly aims at an enemy. Because of their pluralist and multicultural character, Western societies are now saturated with groups positioned as mutual enemies. The storming of the Capitol by armed MAGA-protesters in January 2021 confirms that we have left behind the period of the 'culture wars' of the decades between the 1960s and the 1990s, and entered into a full-blown denominational conflict akin to that of the sixteenth and seventeenth centuries. That conflict lasted a hundred years, tore apart European societies and became firmly settled only with the spatial-territorial agreements written into the Westphalian Peace Treaty of 1648. There is a possibility that the growing value-driven conflicts within European and American societies will be settled again through the mechanism of space and 'territory'. The new Westphalian Peace that is currently emerging seems to cut between urban and rural spaces, with the former increasingly in the hands of progressives and the latter in the hands of traditionalists (Rodden 2019; Wuthnow 2018). Taken to its logical and most extreme conclusion, this development might end in a kind of Belfastification of Western societies, with adherents of universal and of communal values, respectively, living in communities separated by visible and invisible peace lines.

Note

1 This section, and the following paragraphs in particular, are the preliminary outcome of a research project initiated by the author. Danish Research Council (DFF) Research Project II, Grant Number 9130-00103B: 'Beyond Pinkwash: Pride Parades and Integrative Civil Religion'. For more information, please see https://sf.cbs.dk/pride

References

Bellah, R. (1967), 'Civil Religion in America', *Dædalus: Journal of the American Academy of Arts and Sciences*, 96 (1): 1–21.

Boland, T. (2019), 'The Wholly Social or the Holy Social? Recognising Theological Tensions in Sociology', *International Journal of Philosophy and Theology*, 81 (2): 174–92.

Breeze, R. (2018), '"Enemies of the People": Populist Performances in the *Daily Mail* Reporting of the Article 50 Case', *Discourse, Context & Media*, 25 (October): 60–7.

Brown, P. (1988), *The Body and Society: Men, Women and Sexual Renunciation in Early Christianity*, New York: Columbia University Press.

Carrette, J. (2013), 'Rupture and Transformation: Foucault's Concept of Spirituality Reconsidered', *Foucault Studies*, 15: 52–71.

Carter, D. (2010), *Stonewall: The Riots that Sparked the Gay Revolution*, New York: St. Martins Griffin.

Dean, M. (2013), *The Signature of Power: Sovereignty, Governmentality and Biopolitics*, London: Sage.

Dean, M. (2019), 'What is Economic Theology? A New Governmental-Political Paradigm?', *Theory, Culture & Society*, 36 (3): 3–26.

Dean, M. and D. Zamora (2021), *The Last Man Takes LSD: Foucault and the End of the Revolution*, London: Verso.

Drazin, A. (2013), 'The Social Life of Concepts in Design Anthropology', in W. Gunn, T. Otto and R. C. Smith (eds), *Design Anthropology: Theory and Practice*, 33–50, London: Routledge.

Duncan, N. (2008), 'Developing Values in Business Education', *The European Business Review*, 20 (1): 1–6.

Durkheim, É. (2001), *The Elementary Forms of Religious Life*, trans. C. Cosman, Oxford: Oxford University Press.

Foucault, M. (2005), *The Hermeneutics of the Subject: Lectures at the College de France 1981–2*, London: Palgrave Macmillan.

Girard, R. (1989), *The Scapegoat*, Baltimore, MD: Johns Hopkins University Press.

Hawkins, P. S. (1993), 'Naming Names: The Art of Memory and the NAMES Project AIDS Quilt', *Critical Inquiry*, 19 (4): 752–79.

Hyman, G. (2004), 'The Study of Religion and the Return of Theology', *Journal of the American Academy of Religion*, 72 (1): 195–219.

Hynd, D. (2016), 'The "return of theology" to the Social and Political Sciences: A Very Brief Introduction', *Pointers: Bulletin of the Christian Research Association*, 26 (4): 14–18.

Johnson, B. (1957), 'A Critical Appraisal of the Church-Sect Typology', *American Sociological Review*, 22 (1): 88–92.

Milbank, J. (1990), *Theology and Social Theory: Beyond Secular Reason*, Oxford: Blackwell.

Mohdin, A. (2021), 'Pride in London Rejects ban on Met Police Taking Part in Parade', *The Guardian*, 5 March.

'New York City Makes Stonewall Inn a Landmark' (2015), *New York Times*, June 23.

Popper, K. ([1945] 2013), *The Open Society and its Enemies*, Princeton, NJ: Princeton University Press.

Rodden, J. A. (2019), *Why Cities Lose: The Deep Roots of the Urban–Rural Political Divide*, New York: Basic Books.

Schmitt, C. ([1922] 2009), *Politische Theologie: Vier Kapitel zur Lehre von der Souveränität*, 9th edn, Berlin: Duncker & Humblot.

Schmitt, C. ([1959] 2011), *Die Tyrannei der Werte*, 3rd edn, Berlin: Duncker & Humblot.

Schmitt, C. ([1923] 2019), *Römischer Katholizismus und Politische Form*, Stuttgart: Klett-Cotta.

Schofield, C. (2013), *Enoch Powell and the Making of Postcolonial Britain*, New York: Cambridge University Press.

Schwarzkopf, S., ed. (2020), *Routledge Handbook of Economic Theology*, London: Routledge.

Sholem, G. (1971), *The Messianic Idea in Judaism and Other Essays in Jewish Spirituality*, New York: Schocken Books.

Smith, B. (2021), 'Liberalism for Losers: Carl Schmitt's "The Tyranny of Values"', *American Affairs*, 5 (1): 222–40.

Tatchell, P. (2019), 'Pride has Sold its Soul to Rainbow-Branded Capitalism', *The Guardian*, 28 June.

Today in Gay History (2019), 'Today in Gay History: April 28, 1929'. Available online: https://www.gayinla.com/index.php/gay-los-angeles-news/archives/166-this-day-in-gay-history/11336-today-in-gay-history-april-28-1929.

Vatter, M. (2019), '"Only a God Can Resist a God": Political Theology between Polytheism and Gnosticism', *Political Theology*, 20 (6): 472–97.

Wuthnow, R. (2018), *The Left Behind: Decline and Rage in Small-Town America*, Princeton, NJ: Princeton University Press.

Zeitlin, S. G. (2021), 'Indirection and the Rhetoric of Tyranny: Carl Schmitt's *The Tyranny of Values* 1960–1967', *Modern Intellectual History*, 18 (2): 1–24.

Part 3

MODERNITY, HISTORY AND TIME

Chapter 7

CRISIS SOVEREIGNTY

POLITICAL METAPHYSICS IN CRISIS TIMES

Lotte List

Looking back not just at the last couple of decades, but also at the self-conception of those years expressed in theoretical reflection, our most recent past reads like a series of crises. Some may posit the instantaneous chock of 9/11 as the starting point of this series, others the unravelling of the global economic ecosystem during the financial crisis from 2007 onwards, but in any case, one emergency has made way for the next: economic crisis has preceded refugee crisis; refugee crisis, health crisis; and all the while, the slowly, but steadily expanding climate crisis has provided the backdrop for all the other, purportedly more acute emergencies. Unsurprisingly then, diagnosticians of the present have rallied to characterize the world of today as a time of 'universal', 'permanent' or 'chronic' crisis (Edmondson and Mladek 2017; Malm 2020; Streeck 2016; Agamben 2005: 57–9).[1] The overarching premise of these commentaries is that we have entered into a stage of capitalism where crisis is no longer a passing phenomenon disrupting the system, but itself a permanent systemic condition. The question then becomes how – and more importantly, *if* – extant political structures are able to function despite of or through this radical uncertainty.

This collective crisis consciousness is what makes Carl Schmitt acutely relevant today. While much contemporary political theory focuses on the mechanisms (or 'dispositives') of governance, that is, the system immanent management of the state apparatus, Schmitt did not believe that it was possible to understand the constitutional essence of a political system by looking at the way it functions in a state of normality. Rather, the political order reveals its true face in the moment when it encounters existential danger and the norms can no longer be trusted to uphold themselves. Schmitt's concept of sovereignty is thus a liminal concept, not just in the sense that it delimits the state, but also in the sense that it deals essentially with liminal constitutional situations. It is a concept for crisis times.

Sovereignty, I argue in the following, is inherently and reciprocally linked to crisis. Demonstration of sovereign power depends on the ability to act in crisis, and general systemic crisis necessarily raises questions of sovereignty. We have seen the signs of this relation in public debate on the power struggle between states and too-big-to-fail banks during the financial crisis, on the policy demands imposed by the 'European troika' on the Greek state in the euro crisis, on the lack of a global legislative power to counter the climate crisis and, recently, on the legitimacy of suspensions of citizens' rights in the corona crisis. When governance is business as usual, governments appear as political administrators within a neat legal framework, and sovereignty appears unproblematic and therefore invisible. However, when something happens for which the extant laws have no solution, and governments react with either passivity *or* authoritarianism, observers ask themselves under what conditions political action may legitimize itself in the future.

For example, this is the case in Wainwright and Mann's book on the ominous possibility of a new *Climate Leviathan*, which catches the problem in a simple formula: '[To] prevent tomorrow's catastrophe, to what forms of authority do we appeal today?' (2018: 134). The problem of 'so-called "governance", is really the problem of sovereignty,' they write, because climate politics is not a question of how to 'design appropriate institutions' for managing solutions to climate change, but, rather, the question of *who* will declare a climate emergency and act accordingly (Wainwright and Mann 2018: 149). Climate change represents a systemic problem, which cannot simply be handled by normal political or economic mechanisms, and it therefore forces us to reconsider the conditions of possibility of taking action. How does society respond to a problem, which is entirely new and therefore unknown in nature, a problem for which the existing legal or governmental tools are inadequate, without changing those tools? The experience of societal crisis opens up questions of authority, sovereignty and constituent power, since the crisis – such as the financial crisis or the climate crisis – apparently arises *out of* the normal functioning of political life, and the mechanisms of governance have therefore shown themselves to be an ineffective safeguard against, or even a driving force of, systemic breakdown.

In such a political conjuncture, Schmitt has become a household name. His concept of sovereignty appears to capture something in the dynamics of power at play in the crisis. It allows us to speculate about other forms of sovereignty, even as we maintain a stable definition of the concept itself. The German philosopher Joseph Vogl (2015), for instance, has argued that we can observe a 'sovereignty effect' at work in the process of the financial crisis, whereby sovereign power has been displaced and dispersed from the state to the economic sphere, specifically financial agents, as the latter have demonstrated their decisional power to impose legislature on states. The Schmittian ideal of a dictatorial or monarchic sovereign subject is thus sidelined as anachronistic, while his definition of the nature of sovereignty as the constituent power to suspend and reconstitute the law is maintained.

This chapter takes its starting point in the assumption that Schmitt's *Political Theology* is, indeed, the best source we have for thinking sovereignty in a situation of crisis. In both an analytical and a performative-political sense, Schmitt demonstrates the constitutive logic of sovereignty. However, he also inadvertently demonstrates a deeply problematic dialectics of crisis inherent to the sovereign institution. The central concept of the exception establishes not only the sovereign's decisionist omnipotence in the state of emergency, but also its essential impotence in the face of historical crisis, as I shall argue in what follows. The chapter therefore aims to gain a concept of *crisis sovereignty* by critically appropriating Schmitt's concept of sovereignty, not as an affirmative concept of state theory, but, rather, as an analytical concept of the philosophy of history of state theory. It is divided into three sections. In the first, I argue briefly that Schmitt's considerations on political theology should be read as a broader claim about the metaphysics of political thought and that his own thought should itself be viewed through this lens. In the second, I interpret the metaphysical foundation of Schmitt's concept of sovereignty as a historico-philosophical view on modernity as crisis time. And finally, in the third section, I discuss how this Schmittian notion of sovereignty has itself shaped an important concept of crisis, namely that of Reinhardt Koselleck, and through him influenced the way we think about crisis.

Political metaphysics

In order to gain a concept of crisis sovereignty through an interpretation of Schmitt's *Political Theology* it is necessary to not just reconstruct Schmitt's positive theory of sovereignty as it presents itself, but, rather, to read Schmitt against the grain as a method of going beyond his intention and appropriating the concept for ourselves. In this sense, I partake in Friedrich Balke's working hypothesis that 'the work of this "constitutional theorist" responds to a *problem*, which exceeds the horizon of the solution that he offers' (1996: 7, my translation). As Balke argues, the least fruitful way of reading Schmitt is the attempt to synthesize his various lines of argumentation into a single systematic theory, regardless of whether one relates positively to this alleged theory or posits it as a negative starting point for a critical counter-theorization. Schmitt is not a systematic thinker, although his juristic approach to the analysis of concepts may lend him the semblance of systematism. Rather, and again in line with Balke, I believe that Schmitt's attempts at a coherent theory of the state should be read as a series of experimental solutions to a problem, which he encircles while simultaneously repressing its radical challenge.

I therefore take 'political theology' to designate primarily neither a theory of the state, nor an analytical principle for a genealogy of political concepts, but, rather, as a tentative answer to an underlying problem: namely, how do political thought and political structures relate to the metaphysical preconceptions of a community? That is, I propose to read the concept of political theology more broadly as political *metaphysics*. Indeed, Schmitt himself often uses 'theology' and 'metaphysics' interchangeably (2009: 43–5).[2] One important passage in the book reads: 'The metaphysical image that a definite epoch forges of the world has the same structure as what the world immediately understands to be appropriate as a form of its political organization. The determination of such an identity is the sociology of the concept of sovereignty' (Schmitt 2009: 50–1; 2005: 46). In this sense, the political theology of Christianity is one historical example among others of such a metaphysical image, albeit the one that Schmitt is specifically interested in uncovering as the paradigm of the modern European state. It is an attempt at an answer to a broader historical question of the metaphysics of modernity, posed by Schmitt. As Schmitt himself demonstrates, however, the transcendent God of theist Christianity does not capture the modern image of the world in its entirety; rather, it struggles with the competing metaphysical principle of immanence, gaining ground from the nineteenth century onwards.

This broader approach allows us to pose the question: what then is the metaphysical assumption necessary for Schmitt's own political thought? In his polemics against legal positivism at the beginning of the first chapter of the book, Schmitt dismissingly writes: 'whether the extreme exception [Ausnahmefall] can be banished from the world is not a juridical question. Whether one has confidence and hope that it can be eliminated depends on philosophical, especially on historico-philosophical [geschichtsphilosophischen] or metaphysical, convictions' (2009: 14; 2005: 7, translation modified).[3] The intention of this passage is clearly to denounce positivists such as Hugo Krabbe and Hans Kelsen as metaphysicians who believe in what we could compare to Fukuyama's notorious 'end of history' in the sense of a finally realized human order beyond all conflict. However, it also implies that Schmitt himself operates on the basis of a metaphysical assumption: namely that the 'extreme exception' (or rather, the extreme exceptional situation) *cannot* be banished from the world. This is a metaphysical conviction in the inescapable condition of the crisis as the temporal structure of modernity.

Sovereignty and the dialectics of crisis

Of the many political concepts introduced by Schmitt, the most (in)famous and influential is arguably the concept of the *exception*. It has gained importance as a critical concept of political philosophy, not least through the works of Giorgio Agamben, notably in his *Homo Sacer* project (1995–2016), revolving around the inclusive exclusion of the outlawed homo sacer figure in Roman law and its constitutive function in the order of law. The concept of 'exception', however, is itself only a partial and limited translation of the original German *Ausnahmezustand*. In Schmitt, the *Ausnahmezustand* has (at least) two meanings and this double nature of the concept is, in fact, central if we wish to understand the dialectics of sovereignty developed in *Political Theology* (1922). This dialectics, I argue, should be understood not under the signature of the 'sovereign exception', but as *crisis sovereignty*.

The sovereign, in Schmitt's well-known definition, is he who decides on the exception, or *Ausnahmezustand*. This definition, Schmitt argues, renders the concept of the sovereign a 'liminal concept', necessarily linked to a liminal situation. The preposition 'on' (*über*) leaves open whether the sovereign decides *in* an exceptional situation or *over* the employment of exceptional means. 'It will soon become clear,' Schmitt continues, 'that the exception is to be understood to refer to a general concept in the theory of the state, and not merely to any emergency decree or state of siege' (2009: 13; 2005: 5, translation modified).[4] The concept of exception (*Ausnahmezustand*) thus refers to *both* the 'emergency decree' (*Notverordnung*) and the 'state of siege' (*Belagerungszustand*). While it is a negative qualification, demarking the exception against just 'any' case of emergency decree or state of siege, it is important to note that Schmitt anticipates two different lines of interpretation of the word 'exception': on the one hand, a legal decree issued by a state authority, and on the other, a historical situation threatening the existence of the state.

Schmitt confirms this double meaning of the concept of exception: 'It is impossible to determine with any subsumable clarity if an emergency prevails, nor can one spell out what may take place in such a case, especially when it is truly a matter of an extreme emergency *and* of how it is to be eliminated' (2009: 14; 2005: 6, emphasis added).[5] In this sense, the problem necessitating a theory of sovereignty is twofold: on the one hand, the problem of defining legally what constitutes an emergency, and on the other, the problem of choosing the means of its elimination. Neither of these problems can be solved constitutionally, Schmitt argues, since we cannot predict what the emergency will entail, and since the means to eliminate a constitutional crisis must potentially include suspending parts of the constitution itself. His solution to the problem is the decisional power of the sovereign: 'He decides whether there is an extreme emergency as well as what must be done to eliminate it. He stands outside the normally valid juridical order and, nevertheless, belongs to it' (Schmitt 2009: 14; Schmitt 2005: 7; Agamben 1998: 15).[6] These lines have been central to Agamben's critical reinterpretation of the 'logic of sovereignty', as he frames it in the first volume of *Homo Sacer* (1998: 13f.). Agamben has developed this logic as a paradoxical relation between the inside and outside of the juridical order, whereby the 'law is outside of itself' (1998: 15). At first glance, the conceptual pair of inside/outside might appear identical or at least parallel to the dual nature of the exception as both emergency situation and emergency means. Indeed, it is not, but this apparent affinity may be the reason why the inside/outside distinction has become so dominant in the reception, while the double meaning of *Ausnahmezustand* has been widely ignored (Forsthoff 1971).[7]

Schmitt himself has contributed to this line of interpretation by excluding one of the two aspects of the problem immediately after introducing it. As quoted above, Schmitt denounces the question whether it is possible to eliminate the 'extreme exception' once and for all as a matter of 'metaphysical conviction'. The question of how to exclude the exceptional situation as a historical occurrence is, he argues, a matter of historico-philosophical belief and thus outside the scope of political thought. By inference, the question of *what constitutes* an exception in the historical sense is brushed aside as speculation. The sovereign decides whether an exception exists in juridical terms, dissipating discussion as to the factual grounds for the state of exception. Yet in rejecting the question, Schmitt as mentioned inadvertently answers it, confessing his own historico-philosophical belief: that emergency situations will always and invariably arise to threaten the existence of the state. This premise, although introduced in passing, is a necessary condition for the legitimacy of the sovereign, which depends on the perceived danger of constitutional breakdown.

This analytical doctrine, then, may be applied to Schmitt's own metaphysics of modernity as crisis time. His theory of sovereignty, as we have seen, depends on the historico-philosophical assumption that the 'extreme emergency' or *Ausnahmefall* can never be completely done away with, but is, on the contrary, always present as an effective potentiality necessitating specific political structures to guard against its escalation into the chaos of absolute non-order. This is an idea of modernity as 'permanent crisis', a term that Koselleck uses to describe the Cold War global split, resulting from the revolutionary tendencies of the modern period (1973: 1). The idea, however, is as old as modernity itself. Schmitt often hails Thomas Hobbes as the father of political decisionism, citing his slogan on sovereign power, namely that '*Auctoritas non veritas facit legem*' ('Authority, not truth, makes law') (2009: 39). The authority of the sovereign is the necessary condition for law, since this cannot be based in any pre-existing ethical norm (Koselleck and Schmitt 2019: 297).[8] To Hobbes, the state of nature is not a pre-historical starting point for society, but, rather, the empty centre of the state itself (1996: 89–90).[9] It is the permanent possibility of the breakdown of the state necessitating sovereign power to uphold the social contract. Whether Hobbes was, indeed, a decisionist thinker is doubtful to say the least, but the normative vacuum of the state of nature is a basic prerequisite for the way Schmitt conceives of the constitutive function of the sovereign institution. The difference between them is that, while this function was to Hobbes quite visible in a situation of civil war and state formation, in Schmitt's present, and according to his view, it had become invisible or, we might say, repressed by a liberal desire to portray the constitutional state as a self-referential and self-reliant normative system.

While the state of nature is not any period *in* history, it is, however, a structure *of* history. It is a thesis on human nature, or 'the natural condition of mankind' (Hobbes 1996: chapter XIII), with implications for the possible courses of human history. The same is true of the state of emergency in Schmitt's work. While the power of the sovereign consists in the legal authority to declare a state of exception and employ emergency means, the basis legitimizing this authority is the historically existing state of emergency or the crisis. Without the constant possibility of constitutional or state crisis, there would be no need for a sovereign institution to keep this possibility in check. This potentiality of crisis is thus not simply extra-legal, but extra-juridical, that is, it belongs to neither the order of law nor the logical register of jurisprudence. It is external to state theory as well as to the state. This is what Schmitt means when he writes that the question belongs to the sphere of metaphysics. Although Agamben has elegantly and canonically developed 'sovereign logic' as a dialectic between the extra-legal and the intra-legal, the 'outside' locus of sovereign power to him remains an outside of the legal norm, not an outside of the sovereign logic itself (List 2020).[10] The crisis, however, is an externality in a much more concrete sense: it does not arise from within the sovereign institution, but threatens it from the outside. As an example of such an external force, one may take the Covid-19 crisis, which constituted both a shock to nation states and a legitimating basis for initiatives restricting citizens' liberties on the part of national governments (List 2020: 13).[11] The political force of the pandemic did not arise from some sovereign decision, even if it in some cases served to consolidate the perceived legitimacy of sovereign acts.

My claim, then, is that the Schmittian concept of sovereignty is dependent on a dialectics of crisis. On the one hand, sovereign power presupposes the permanent potentiality of the crisis, that is, a vision of modernity as crisis time. The institution of sovereignty entirely depends on its perceived necessity to secure the state and its order of law. As Schmitt himself admits, this necessity ultimately refers back to a metaphysical conviction. To Juan Donoso Cortés as to Hobbes, he writes, the problem at hand was the loss of the God-given monarchical mandate to rule, leaving behind a vacuum of legitimacy, which could be filled only by sovereign authority. This authority has to repeatedly re-legitimize itself by proving its capacity to overcome a pending state crisis and reinstate legal order. On the other hand, however, the crisis also poses a threat, not just to the state, but to sovereign legitimacy itself insofar as the sovereign may prove unable to act decisively in a situation of uncertainty. The institution of sovereignty is thus at one and the same time dependent upon and existentially threatened by the state crisis. It must continuously prove its necessity as well as its authoritative power by responding to crises. This dialectics with externalities, such as economic or natural forces, is lost if the concept of *Ausnahmezustand* is reduced to the formalistic conception of 'the exception'. The exception in this sense constitutes the double capacity to declare the state of exception and employ exceptionalist means, that is, the sovereign suspension of law, in order to uphold the law. Yet, this is a totalizing view of sovereign power, which ignores the fundamental insecurity so central to a thinker such as Hobbes and, implicitly, to Schmitt.

When Schmitt displaces the discussion from the dialectics of crisis to a dialectics of the sovereign exception, then, this must be seen as a performative move to strengthen the institution of sovereignty in constitutional theory. In this way, he transfers the concept from philosophy of history to the jurisprudence of state theory, excluding its metaphysical premise while underhandedly recognizing the metaphysical nature of politics. This is what the critical theorist and literary scholar Walter Benjamin recognized in his discussion of Schmitt's exceptionalist theory of sovereignty in his *Origin of the German Mourning Play* (1928). As Agamben has quite rightly noted, he subtly changes Schmitt's famous definition when he writes that the 'baroque concept [of sovereignty] emerges from a discussion of the state of emergency [*Ausnahmezustand*] and makes it the most important function of the prince to exclude it' (Benjamin 1991: 245; 2019: 49, translation modified). By switching the emphasis from the decision on the exception to the exclusion of the state of exception, Benjamin translates the discussion back into terms of history and philosophy of history. Agamben interprets this shift as the legal exclusion of the exception from the order of law, leading to a split 'between norms of law and norms of the realization of law', which to him is at the heart of the sovereign nexus itself (2005: 55–6). However, this interpretation remains caught within the jurisprudential framework of so-called sovereign logic. Instead, we should read Benjamin literally: The most important function and the raison d'être of the sovereign is to exclude the possibility of a historical actualization of the state of exception. In German baroque theatre, which is the object of Benjamin's book, this is aesthetically processed as a display of indecisiveness [*Entschlußunfähigkeit*] on the part of the prince (1991: 250). In Benjamin's view, Schmitt's sovereign is thus caught in an interplay of omnipotence and impotence, continuously forced to rely on the possibility of the very event which would threaten its existence, the state crisis.

Koselleck and the afterlife of decisionism in crisis theory

Janet Roitman, in her *Anti-Crisis*, writes with a keen eye for different levels of argumentation on the concept of crisis. She does not treat it as an epistemologically unproblematic occurrence which can be observed empirically, but, rather, as a historiographic and historico-philosophical concept that 'generates meaning in a self-referential system' (Roitman 2014: 10). Therefore, she criticizes accounts of the concept that takes its equivocal relation with an empirically extant referent in the world for granted. In a meta-theoretical reflection, she argues that 'Crisis is posited as an a priori; the grounds for knowledge of crisis are neither questioned nor made explicit. And hence contemporary narratives of crisis elude two questions: How can one *know* crisis in history? And how can one *know* crisis itself?' (Roitman 2014: 10). However, these final questions are precisely what Schmitt addressed in juridical terms and in the context of state crisis. His answer is clear, though somewhat implicit in the argumentation: Legally, we cannot know crisis in history, and we cannot know crisis itself. There is no definition available which would be able to capture the specifics of the uncertainty of crisis in advance; thus the idea of crisis transcends its reality. Therefore, the ultimate authority consists in deciding on the existence of crisis in history and on the specific conditions of crisis itself.

While Schmitt relies on a notion of crisis for his definition of sovereignty, however, he does not systematically develop it as a concept. A scholar who noticed the importance of the concept of crisis for an analysis of modernity and did extensive work on it throughout his career, was Reinhardt Koselleck. Among a group of Schmitt-inspired young researchers in the immediate after war years, Koselleck was a historian and philosopher of history and became known as an author of the discipline of conceptual history, not least with his later work on the encyclopaedia *Basic Concepts of History* (1972–97). It is well known that he was profoundly inspired by Schmitt's writings on sovereignty, and this theoretical link has only been emphasized by the 2019 publication of their letter exchange (Olsen 2011). Koselleck read several of Schmitt's early books while working on his PhD thesis (2019: 382)[12] and initiated a correspondence with their author in 1953, in the final phase of writing the thesis, which was submitted in Heidelberg in 1954. We may note that the main title of this work, *Critique and Crisis*, echoes a phrase from a 1949 essay by Schmitt on one of his heroes, the Catholic statesman Juan Donoso Cortés, which was published in book form in 1950. In this essay, in the context of a comparative analysis of the historical importance of Donoso Cortés with Bruno Bauer, Schmitt writes:

> Like no other, Bruno Bauer executed and completed the theological-philosophical critique, in its fullest sense and with all the air of destiny [*Schicksalhaftigkeit*], which was for German intellectual history of the past two centuries so intimately connected with the words *critique* and *crisis*. In Bruno Bauer, the theological and philosophical critique of reason, as well as text and Bible critique, transitioned [schlug um] into a critique of *time* [*Zeit*kritik]. But in him, as opposed to Karl Marx, it remained critical and did not evolve into a partisan annihilation of the enemy. (Schmitt 1950: 100, italics in original, my translation)

As critical concepts, the words 'critique' and 'crisis' become in Schmitt's view fateful signs for German philosophy of the eighteenth and nineteenth centuries – or, if we read the quote in a stronger sense, these words themselves contain the fate of German enlightenment. Furthermore, they are not just signatures of *intellectual* history, but also the operative elements of Bauer's '*Zeitkritik*', that is, his diagnosis of modernity. It is clear from the (quite ironical, given Schmitt's own role in the Third Reich) contrast to Marx that Schmitt shares this diagnostic, which he finds in Donoso Cortés and Bauer.

Koselleck's book likewise reads as a temporal diagnostic of modernity. The introduction opens with the claim that the 'world crisis' of the Cold War is the result of European history expanding to world history, thereby leading the world into a permanent state of crisis. The crisis, he argues, emerges from a utopian self-image on part of modern philosophy of history. The ensuing study of the concepts of critique and crisis in enlightenment thus implies a notion akin to that 'air of destiny' which Schmitt ascribed to the same period. Given the well-documented influence that Schmitt exercised on Koselleck, as well as the peculiar concurrence of the latter's book with the former's considerations on German modernity, it should thus not come as a surprise that the definition of the concept of crisis presented by Koselleck resonates with Schmitt's definition of sovereignty. In the first lines of the third chapter, Koselleck writes:

> It is in the nature of the crisis that a decision is overdue, yet remains to be made. And it is also in the nature of the crisis to leave open, *which* decision will be made. Thus the general uncertainty of a critical situation contains one certainty: that an end to the critical situation – at an indecisive time, yet decisive, under uncertain circumstances, yet certain – is imminent. (Koselleck 1973: 105; 1988: 127)

The crisis, then, in a certain sense inverts Schmitt's concept of sovereignty: Whereas the sovereign is nothing but decision, the crisis is the simultaneous necessity and lack of decision. Here, I have modified the translation to capture closer the German original; but in the MIT Press English edition of the book from 1988, the relation is obscured as the word *Entscheidung* is translated as 'solution' rather than 'decision'. A decision, however, is not the same as a solution: on the contrary, a decision is what *someone* – be it a natural or artificial person in the form of a public institution – makes in the *absence* of any reasonable solution. The certainty of which Koselleck writes is not a guarantee that the problem at the heart of the crisis will be solved, but, rather, the precarious certainty that the crisis itself opens up a power vacuum allowing for – indeed, calling for – someone to step in and reconstitute power through a sovereign decision. The fact that we do not know *who* will make *which* decision leaves this certainty existentially uncertain (*unsicher*).

In his later work on the basic concepts of history, Koselleck returns to this concept of crisis. Here, however, he argues at a different level of observation, presenting the argument as a historical reconstruction of the classic origin and modern semantic development of the word 'crisis' rather than as his *own* analytical concept. The word 'crisis', he writes in 1982, originates from the Greek κρίσις, meaning in political terms, on the one hand, separation, division or conflict, and on the other, decision (Koselleck 1982: 617). Of the two, he emphasizes the latter (Koselleck and Schmitt 2019: 164):[13] 'From this specific legal meaning, the term begins to acquire political significance. It is extended to electoral decisions, government resolutions, decisions of war and peace, death sentences and exile, the acceptance of official reports and, above all, to government decisions as such' (Koselleck 1982: 618; 2006: 359). This etymological origin of the word 'crisis' thus closely relates to Koselleck's 1954 definition of crisis as a historiographic concept – except that whereas the Greek explicitly and positively relates crisis to decision, its specific modern use renders this relation negative and problematic while simultaneously making it the image of historical time.

Although Koselleck's late work on the concept of crisis presents itself as a metatheory, the line between conceptual history and crisis theory thus blurs throughout the analysis (1989: 115).[14] Towards the end of the article, he expresses regret that contemporary media have devaluated the concept through inflation, depriving it of its original 'power to pose unavoidable, harsh and non-negotiable alternatives' (Koselleck 1982: 649; 2006: 399). In this way, he concludes his history of what the concept *was* with a judgement on what it *ought to be*. As Roitman notes, we must therefore read Koselleck's work on crisis on two levels simultaneously: as 'the orthodox historiography of the term' *and* as a historiographic theory of crisis itself which 'presupposes criteria for what counts as an event' (2014: 8). The latter aspect, I have argued, is greatly influenced by Schmitt's work and, in fact, directly relates to his concept of sovereignty. The idea of the crisis sovereign thus inverts and becomes the definitional content of the crisis concept itself.

According to Roitman, Koselleck is the 'author of perhaps the only conceptual history of crisis, which thus serves as the authoritative historiography' (2014: 7). Koselleck's importance for our conception of the history of the crisis concept cannot be stressed enough. As we have seen, however, historiography and theory of crisis are not clearly separated in Koselleck, so that what is often taken as conceptual history is mixed with elements of a specific crisis theory. Through the academic authority of Koselleck, this crisis theory has become widely cited. For instance, professor of politics and LRB pundit David Runciman, in an article on the temporality of crisis, takes his starting point in Koselleck and presupposes as a generally acceptable definition that 'A crisis may be defined as a situation characterized both by fundamental threat and fundamental choice' (2016: 4), using 'choice' interchangeably with 'decision'. Threat without the possibility of choice is not a crisis, Runciman argues, just as there can be non-critical choice where there is no threat. This broad definition of crisis does not exhaust Runciman's discussion of crisis temporality; on the contrary, his point is that it is insufficient for demarking the time of crisis. Yet, it is instructive that he considers it common sense. Koselleck's definition of the crisis as based in its relationship with decision emerges from an engagement with Schmittian decisionism. Through him, Schmitt's concept of the sovereign decision comes to influence the way crisis is conceptualized in political theories otherwise unconcerned with the latter's political theology.

Conclusion

Writing between the two world wars in a frail German republic emerging in the wake of revolution, Schmitt saw clearly the inherent and conceptually necessary link between sovereignty and crisis. This is why his *Political Theology* in 1922 has remained the most important point of reference for understanding the mechanism of sovereignty in crisis until today, and has, indeed, once more become as topical as ever. However, in a performative attempt at strengthening the theoretical base for the political institution of sovereignty, Schmitt emphasized the sovereign capacity to suspend the order of law by declaring a legal state of exception and repressed the question of dependence of this capacity on the *actual* state of exception as a historico-philosophical problem. This double nature of the exception – as the defining tool of the sovereign as well as the existential threat which it is his raison d'être to overcome – is the basis of the dialectics of crisis sovereignty. To understand what sovereignty means and how its institution is legitimized, we can therefore not limit ourselves to jurisprudence or political theory, but must recognize its roots in metaphysical beliefs pertaining to philosophy of history.

As demonstrated previously, Schmitt's decisionist theory of sovereignty had immense influence on one of the most important scholarly concepts of crisis, namely the one developed by Koselleck and institutionalized in the discipline of conceptual history. Not only was the idea of modernity as crisis time a necessary precondition for Schmitt's concept of sovereignty, but this concept in turn came to shape crisis theory until today. Of course, 'crisis' in the sense just described by no means exhausts the richness of the word. Crisis can also mean medical or personal crisis, as Koselleck has rightly argued. But in the specific sense of a systemic and societywide breakdown, this crisis concept is dependent on the notion of a centralized capacity (or incapacity) of collective decision and thus indebted to Schmitt's theory of sovereignty. As the two extremes of a tension keeping both total societal breakdown and the utopian possibility of a new social order at bay, the sovereignty-crisis nexus is at the heart of a widespread conception of modernity as crisis time. The relation between sovereignty and crisis is thus neither unilateral nor in a simple sense causal, but, rather, as core concepts of modern political thought they are dialectically interdependent.

With the dialectical concept of crisis sovereignty in hand, we can begin to understand anew the complex displays of sovereign impotence and omnipotence during times of upheaval. We cannot say that sovereigns always act resolutely and authoritatively in critical situations, nor that they always act with hesitation and reluctance. And we cannot say that crisis always engenders popular support for strong leadership, nor that it always brings forth criticism and opposition towards political leaders. What we can say, however, is that 'crisis' demands sovereign action and thus reveals the ability or lack thereof on the part of sovereigns to act, *and* that sovereignty is both dependent on crisis to legitimize its constitutional function and fundamentally threatened by that same crisis. It is important that we neither overestimate the power of draconian sovereign means to reinstitute the norm through its suspension, nor see crisis as automatically transformative of political systems. Rather, we should recognize that sovereignty *is crisis sovereignty*, and that this means that the sovereign institution is equiprimordial with its own crisis. Sovereignty only ever comes into question when it becomes problematic, and the sovereign institution is always operating in and through crisis as its locus of origin, to which it must continuously return.

Notes

1. Wolfgang Streeck (2016: 37) talks of the present phase of capitalism as an interregnum, that is, 'a time of crisis as the new normal'; and Giorgio Agamben (2005: 57–9), quoting Walter Benjamin, claims that 'the state of exception has become the rule'.
2. This identification of theology with metaphysics is especially noticeable at the beginning of chapter 3.
3. In the University of Chicago Press version, 'geschichtsphilosophisch' is translated as 'philosophical-historical', which clearly misses the point. In acknowledgement of the difficulty in translating 'geschichtsphilosophisch' into English, I follow Roitman in using the neologism 'historico-philosophical' where a rephrasing as 'philosophy of history' is not possible.
4. The English translation, contrary to the German original, qualifies the exception as a 'construct', thus formalizing what Schmitt himself does not.
5. I have modified the translation, as the English version distorts the meaning of the first sentence (changing the question of *whether* an emergency prevails to a question of the specific *details* of the emergency in question).
6. Translation modified.
7. The article on 'Ausnahmezustand' in *Historisches Wörterbuch der Philosophie*, for instance, freely oscillates between these two different meanings without noting the difference, let alone explicating it (Forsthoff 1971).

8   Schmitt would later complain that only through Heidegger's 'ceaseless word-suffocation' did his own ethics of a 'normative nothingness' become academically acceptable (Koselleck and Schmitt 2019: 297).
9   'It may peradventure be thought, there was never such a time, nor condition of war as this; and I believe it was never generally so, over all the world: but there are many places, where they live so now. [. . .] Howsoever, it may be perceived what manner of life there would be, where there were no common Power to feare; by the manner of life, which men that have formerly lived under peaceful government, use to degenerate into, in a civill Warre' (Hobbes 1996: 89–90).
10 See List (2020) for an extensive critique of Agamben's juridical formalism.
11 See List (2020) for a critique of Agamben's one-sided – and by now much criticized – take on the Covid-19 crisis in Italy.
12 On his own account, Koselleck's first encounter with Schmitt was through a number of his texts from the 1920s (Koselleck and Schmitt 2019: 382).
13 What if Koselleck had, instead, chosen to stress the former meaning? The etymology of the word 'crisis' may also be interpreted as pointing in the direction of a divide, a societal split or caesura. Then it would bring us much closer to a Marxist understanding of crisis: as the sudden manifestation of a pre-existing contradiction already inherent to capitalism in its conceived normalcy – rather than the ghostly presence-absence of (sovereign) decision. Note that what we are dealing with in Koselleck is not simply a neutral historiography of concepts, but a partisan redefinition of those same concepts. It is telling that Schmitt congratulated Koselleck on the 'non-Marxist dialectical achievement' of his thesis (Koselleck and Schmitt 2019: 164).
14 Of course, Koselleck (1989: 115) himself has reflected on the complex relationship between the observed time of the research object and the observing time of the researcher within conceptual history. The becoming conscious of the historical semantics of concepts through a reflection on their transference in history, Koselleck calls a 'methodological imperative of diachrony' to accompany all synchronic analysis. Nevertheless, when this reflection is not made explicit, as is the case in the crisis article in *Geschichtliche Grundbegriffe*, the tension between past and present disappears from the field of vision, and a slippage between historical observation of the concept of crisis and the analytical use of that same concept is made possible. When readers of the *Geschichtliche Grundbegriffe* take it as a historically authoritative source, this move is completed, and the theoretical investment in the concept is consolidated as historical 'truth'.

References

Agamben, G. (1998), *Homo Sacer: Sovereign Power and Bare Life*, trans. D. Heller-Roazen, Stanford, CA: Stanford University Press.
Agamben, G. (2005), *State of Exception*, Chicago, IL: The University of Chicago Press.
Balke, F. (1996), *Der Staat Nach Seinem Ende: Die Versuchung Carl Schmitts*, Paderborn: Wilhelm Fink Verlag.
Benjamin, W. (1991), 'Ursprung des deutschen Trauerspiels', in Rolf Tiedemann and Hermann Schweppenhäuser (eds), *Walter Benjamin, Gesammelte Schriften*, vol. I, 203–403, Suhrkamp.

Benjamin, W. (2019), *Origin of the German Trauerspiel*, trans. H. Eiland, Cambridge, MA: Harvard University Press.
Edmondson, G. and K. Mladek, eds (2017), *Sovereignty in Ruins: A Politics of Crisis*, Durham, NC: Duke University Press.
Forsthoff, E. (1971), 'Ausnahmezustand', in Joachim Ritter (ed.), *Historisches Wörterbuch der Philosophie*, 1:669–70, Schwabe Verlag. Available online: https://doi.org/10.24894/HWPh.347
Hobbes, T. (1996), *Leviathan, or The Matter, Form, & Power of a Commonwealth Ecclesiastical and Civil*, ed. R. Tuck, Cambridge: Cambridge University Press.
Koselleck, R. (1973), *Kritik und Krise: Eine Studie zur Pathogenese der bürgerlichen Welt*, Frankfurt am Main: Suhrkamp.
Koselleck, R. (1982), 'Krise', in O. Brunner, W. Conze and R. Koselleck (eds), *Geschichtliche Grundbegriffe: Historisches Lexikon zur politisch-sozialen Sprache in Deutschland*, 3:617–50, Stuttgart: Klett-Cotta.
Koselleck, R. (1988), *Critique and Crisis: Enlightenment and the Pathogenesis of Modern Society*, Cambridge, MA.: The MIT Press.
Koselleck, R. (1989), 'Begriffsgeschichte und Sozialgeschichte', in *Vergangene Zukunft: Zur Semantik geschichtlicher Zeiten*, 107–29, Frankfurt am Main: Suhrkamp.
Koselleck, R. (2006), 'Crisis', *Journal of the History of Ideas*, 67 (2): 357–401.
Koselleck, R. and C. Schmitt (2019), *Der Briefwechsel 1953–83 und weitere Materialien*, ed. J. E. Dunkhase, Frankfurt am Main: Suhrkamp.
List, L. (2020), 'Political Theology and Historical Materialism: Reading Benjamin against Agamben', *Theory, Culture & Society*, 38 (3): 117–40.
Malm, A. (2020), *Corona, Climate, Chronic Emergency: War Communism in the Twenty-First Century*, London: Verso.
Olsen, N. (2011), 'Carl Schmitt, Reinhart Koselleck and the Foundations of History and Politics', *History of European Ideas*, 37 (2): 197–208.
Roitman, J. (2014), *Anti-Crisis*, Durham, NC: Duke University Press.
Runciman, D. (2016), 'What Time Frame Makes Sense for Thinking about Crises?', in P. F. Kjaer and N. Olsen (eds), *Critical Theories of Crisis in Europe: From Weimar to the Euro*, 3–16, Lanham: Rowman & Littlefield International.
Schmitt, C. (1950), *Donoso Cortés in gesamteuropäischer Interpretation*, Cologne: Greven Verlag.
Schmitt, C. (2005), *Political Theology: Four Chapters on the Concept of Sovereignty*, trans. G. Schwab, Chicago, IL: The University of Chicago Press.
Schmitt, C. (2009), *Politische Theologie: Vier Kapitel zur Lehre von der Souveränität*, 9th edn, Berlin: Duncker & Humblot.
Streeck, W. (2016), *How Will Capitalism End? Essays on a Failing System*, London: Verso.
Vogl, J. (2015), *Der Souveränitätseffekt*, Zürich/Berlin: Diaphanes.
Wainwright, J. and G. Mann (2018), *Climate Leviathan*, London: Verso.

Chapter 8

ONE WORLD?

HISTORY AND SPACE IN SCHMITT'S POST-WAR POLITICAL THEOLOGY

Nicholas Heron

A product of the self-styled 'last knowing representative of *Ius publicum Europaeum*' (Schmitt [1950] 2018a: 60), Carl Schmitt's *Nomos of the Earth* was no mere exercise in *Ideengeschichte* in the conventional sense. Written against the backdrop of Germany's impending military defeat, Schmitt's grand historical narrative ([1950] 2003), which recounted the four hundred years of the law of nations, simultaneously sounded a lament for the demise of the state form and the Eurocentric vision of international order based on its concept. The shifting fortunes of the concept of the state nonetheless did nothing to alter Schmitt's contempt for liberalism. To be sure, the attempt of his *Political Theology* ([1922] 2005) to resuscitate the strong state from its perceived liberal torpor had failed. In more ways than one, the collapse of the German state under Nazi rule offered stark confirmation of this actuality. Yet, the detour into the arena of international law not only provided Schmitt with a forum in which to rebuild his scholarly reputation. It also enabled him to redouble his assault on liberalism from a different angle. This would now be directed against its universalist aspirations.

In the early 1950s, as he deepened engagement with the philological aspects of his topic, Schmitt added several important corollaries to the main text, which updated the historical perspective to the concerns of the present (2003: 324–55). At the same time, and in large part stimulated by these publications, he initiated a little-known correspondence with the Russian émigré philosopher Alexandre Kojève, in which the two debated the shape of the new world order following the demise of the state (Kojève and Schmitt [1998] 2001: 94–115; for commentary, see Müller 2003: 90–8). This chapter argues that the terms of this debate provide the argumentative context for the unexpected return of a political-theological register to Schmitt's writing after a hiatus of several decades, which revitalized this discourse – for and against – an increasingly globalized world. Recently, there has been a surge of interest in engaging Schmitt's political theology with questions of international order (Koskeniemmi 2004; Guilhot 2010; 2017: 69–114). Returning to the debates of the post-war period, this chapter shows how Schmitt too sought to forge this connection, even if it entailed revising the terms of his political theology to meet the demands of a post-state world. In this context, the repurposed political theology, on the one side, and the emerging discourse of globalism, on the other – which received an extreme expression in Kojève's end-of-history diagnosis – confronted one another as competing political languages.[1]

Schmitt had first become aware of Kojève's influential interpretation of Hegel in 1948 (Kojève and Schmitt 2001: 95). In Kojève himself, he found an interlocutor who was not only well informed about his recent writings, but who had already made significant use of his concept of 'the political' in an unpublished 1943 manuscript on the phenomenology of right (Kojève [1982] 2000: 134–5).[2] In many respects, he was a formidable intellectual sparring partner for Schmitt. Here was a thinker whose philosophy of right fully embraced the Schmittian definition of the political in terms of the distinction between friend and enemy, but also heralded a future reality – what he called 'the universal and homogeneous state' – when this definition would no longer apply. Not because a new definition would take its place, but because in the universal and homogeneous state there would no longer be any enemies – and hence no politics either (Kojève 2000: 137n22, 141, n. 28, 158). What Schmitt had merely intuited on the horizon – that a world without war (on the one hand) and without states (on the other) would be 'a world without the distinction of friend and enemy and hence a world without politics' ([1932] 2007: 35, 53) – was fast attaining to actuality, according to Kojève. And this was no abstract conviction to which Kojève paid simple lip service; he lived it to the utmost degree, having abandoned professional philosophy, in keeping with his infamous claim that it too was destined to disappear at the end of history (Kojève [1947] 1980: 158–9, n. 6), for a bureaucratic appointment in the post-war French government, where he was to become one of the chief architects of the European Economic Community. 'Presiding over the end of history' is how he characterized his post-war activities to the American philosopher Allan Bloom (Bloom 1990: 268).

It was the final paragraph of the first of Schmitt's corollaries, the 1953 essay 'Appropriation/Distribution/Production' ['Nehmen/Teilen/Weiden'], which set the tone for their subsequent discussion. Here, Schmitt's historical-philological analysis, which aimed at characterizing the competing political ideologies of modernity in terms of their respective sequencing of the three basic meanings of his post-war master concept, had given way to a consideration of the present problematic: that of world unity. 'Has humanity today actually "appropriated" the earth as a unity?' he asked,

> so that there is nothing more to be appropriated. Has appropriation really ceased? Is there now only division and distribution? Or does only production remain? If so, we must then ask further: Who is the great appropriator, the great divider and distributor of our planet, the manager and planner of unified world production? (Schmitt 2003: 335)

Whether the role of superintendent over a unified planet would be assumed by the legatees of the imperialist or socialist traditions remained an open question for Schmitt in 1953, even if it had been clear since the late 1930s which interpretation he favoured (2011b: 30–74). In either case, it spelled disaster. When Kojève replied that after Napoleon only production remained, Schmitt retorted with a solemn pun: a unified earth, he observed, is no longer 'grazed' (*geweidet*), but only 'eviscerated' (*ausgeweidet*) (Kojève and Schmitt 2001: 95).

For the whimsical theorist of post-history, on the other hand, it mattered little who assumed the reins. Each side, he explained to Schmitt, wanted essentially the same thing. For Kojève, both the Anglo-Saxons and the Russians were Napoleon's epigones. What Napoleon had wanted – the sublation of the state in favour of society – remained what they wanted, and had achieved, with varying degrees of success. The two world wars, accordingly, had been merely an intermezzo (Kojève and Schmitt 2001: 97). Kojève was perfectly willing to concede what Schmitt was not (even if he had been warning of this eventuality since 1922): that an alignment of 'American financiers' and 'Marxist socialists' would mean the end of politics itself (Schmitt 2005: 65). In an extraordinary confirmation of the rationale of his post-war activities, he confessed to Schmitt that after he entered the modern democratic state as a civil servant following the war, he soon became convinced that there was no longer any state left at all. The mutual 'neutralization' of the political accomplished by government, on the one hand, and parliament, on the other – two formerly political entities, he stressed – meant that the work of administration (i.e., 'grazing'), henceforth unmoored from the unpredictability of history, could proceed without interference (Kojève and Schmitt 2001: 98).

In his response, Schmitt was willing to meet his interlocutor up to a certain point. All was, indeed, finished with the state, he granted; Hobbes's 'Mortall God' was now dead. '[T]he present-day, modern administration apparatus of "provision for subsistence" ["*Daseins-Vorsorge*"],' he observed, 'is not "state" in Hegel's sense, not "government" (...) no longer capable of war or of the death penalty; and hence, also no longer historically powerful' (Kojève and Schmitt 2001: 101–2, translation modified). And yet, backpedalling from pre-war statements to the contrary, he now maintained that politics could be preserved beyond the state's obsolescence. Even in an increasingly globalized world, he now argued, meaningful enmity could still find expression. And what would ensure the perpetuation of the political 'pluriverse', and hence also the 'capacity for history', was his controversial theory of 'great spaces' (*Großräume*). 'I am of the view,' he explained to Kojève,

> that for the next stage the *magni homines* (...) will be concerned with discussion of great spaces (...) For me, 'great space' does not have the sense of a contrast to small space (...) but the sense of a contrast to world unity – which enables a plurality and therefore a meaningful enmity, and hence grounds the capacity for history [*Geschichtsfähigkeit*]; i.e. the sense of a contrast to the assumption that the cycle of time has already ended. That is what I do *not* believe. *Le cercle n'est pas encore parcouru.* Today's world dualism (of East and West, or Land and Sea) is not the final dash for unity, i.e. the end of history. Rather, it is the bottleneck through which the path to the new 'contemporary' *magni homines* leads. (Kojève and Schmitt 2001: 102, translation modified)

In Kojève and Schmitt, two distinct visions of global order confronted one another. Though united by a common frame and shared suppositions, each finally arrived at a diametrically opposed projection of the new international order that was emerging out of the collapse of modern *Staatlichkeit*. This chapter nonetheless argues that it was Kojève's end-of-history diagnosis – which for both disputants signalled the end of politics, in the sense that we have seen – that provided a new forum for Schmitt's political theology. In the eponymous book of 1922, Schmitt had been unequivocal regarding the site of his political theology: 'All significant concepts of the modern *theory of the state* are secularized theological concepts' (2005: 36, emphasis added). Three decades later, Schmitt's concession that all is over with the state would seem to imply the end for his political theology as well. But this was not the case. Coterminous with Schmitt's reinvention as an international thinker in the post-war period, is a striking re-adoption of the language of political theology in his writing. Only now, to compensate for his growing conviction that the state form is obsolete, it is displaced onto a new terrain – which, I argue, is none other than history itself. Granting the end of the state, Schmitt's political theology is now tasked with forestalling the end of history – and, together with this, the end of politics itself. In this perspective, Schmitt emerges as one of the earliest and staunchest critics of Kojève's thesis, especially in its liberal version.

In their correspondence, Kojève and Schmitt aligned in coupling what was ostensibly a temporal thesis with a distinctly spatial conceit. More visibly than in any other sphere, it was the post-war dream of world unity that presaged the end of history in their shared estimation. As early as 1939, in the very text where he introduced the *Großraum* idea into international law, Schmitt had referenced the 'dethroning of the concept of the state' (2011b: 104). The transition from a state- to a *Großraum*-based order, however, did not merely entail a shift from smaller to larger territorial units, but the development of a fundamental spatial orientation. Unlike the territorial state, which maintains its integrity relative to other states, the concrete-spatial *Großraum* idea acquires its vitality for Schmitt through opposition to a competing conception of international order: the abstract-universalistic world idea (2011a: 46–54). Thus, Schmitt distinguished two competing versions of the Monroe doctrine: the original proclamation of 1823, grounded in a principle of defence against foreign intervention, which he credited as the first instantiation of his *Großraum* idea, and Woodrow Wilson's 'imperialistic-capitalistic' reinterpretation of it, where the originally concrete-spatial meaning had been universalized and itself transformed into a pan-interventionist ideology (2011b: 83–90).

This was not to say that Schmitt's proposed application of an authentic Monroe doctrine to other parts of the globe would not entail expansion. First introduced in the immediate aftermath of Hitler's invasion of Czechoslovakia, there can be little doubt that Schmitt's conception doubtless made itself amenable to the Nazi regime's foreign policy agenda, although contemporary claims regarding the extent of Schmitt's influence were almost certainly exaggerated (Bendersky 1984: 257–9). Yet, even acknowledging the openly apologetic character of his argument, Schmitt's pluralistic *Großraum* theory articulated a major theoretical reorientation of his concept of the political that retrofitted it for a 'planetary' scale (Schmitt 2011b: 111), whose significance arguably remains undiminished today.

In his new account, spatialization and politicization went hand in hand with one another. 'Seen from the standpoint of international jurisprudence,' he wrote in 1939, 'space and political idea cannot be separated. For us, there are neither spaceless political ideas nor, conversely, idealess spaces' (2011b: 87, translation modified). Later, he added a third category to the original hendiadys. Not only space and politics, but also space and history, must remain inseparable. Viewed from this perspective, world unity assumed for Schmitt a distinctly eschatological significance: it meant nothing less than the end of the (political-historical) world.

In his reconstruction of Schmitt's preoccupation with the theme of world unity, Jean-François Kervégan has argued that one must choose between the theological Schmitt and the legal-political Schmitt (1999: 54). Yet, precisely this theme, more than any other, attests to the impossibility of keeping the two sides of this complex author apart. Restoring the theological backdrop to a set of ostensibly historiographical claims that Schmitt advanced in his struggle against world unity's philosophical-historical legitimation, this chapter argues that Schmitt's post-war historical thinking marked the resumption, albeit from an altered perspective, of his pre-war political theology. An underexplored aspect of Schmitt's enduring topicality – namely, his recalcitrance to arguments regarding the end of history – is thus revealed to have a political-theological basis.

Christian historicity

For Schmitt, the struggle against the political monism epitomized by the American Republican presidential nominee Wendell Willkie's wartime slogan 'one world' was a struggle against its philosophical-historical legitimation (Schmitt 1995: 500, 503, 601). Even as the iron curtain purported to divide the world in two, Schmitt consistently sought to emphasize the deeper unity that lay beneath a mere surface duality. No less than the communist East, so too the industrialized West, Schmitt argued in 1952, relied for its self-interpretation on an ideology of progress and human perfectibility inherited from the philosophical histories of Saint-Simon, Comte, Spencer and their popularizers. Only, now this had been intensified into what he termed a 'religion of technicity' (Schmitt 1995: 501–3). Just as the Marxist-Leninist programme projected its end point in the unity of an electrified earth, so its liberal-technocratic counterpart, Schmitt argued, figured the imminent realization of its global objective as a technical-industrial utopia – even if it acknowledged that the pace of technological progress here outstripped that of moral progress (1995: 503). It was no coincidence that Willkie's 'global' vision, formed during his 1942 world tour, had been facilitated by technical means: 'Continents and oceans are plainly only parts of a whole,' the American politician had tellingly observed, 'seen, as I have seen them, from the air' (Willkie 1943: 144; Rosenboim 2017: 74).

This new emphasis on the philosophy of history as the motor of a total process whose projected end point was the supra-political goal of world unity had been stimulated by Schmitt's engagement with Karl Löwith's now classic study *Meaning in History*. When Schmitt described the philosophy of history as a specialized concept invented by Voltaire in the eighteenth century, which had successfully outcompeted Bossuet's theology of history, it was Löwith's landmark study, which had not yet appeared in German translation, that was his tacit reference (Schmitt 1995: 505; cf. Löwith 1949: 1). In 1949, Hans Paeschke, founder and editor of the periodical *Merkur*, had commissioned Schmitt to review Löwith's book, which had been published in the United States, where Löwith – one of the most incisive critics of Schmitt's Weimar writings – had been living since 1941, following his forced emigration from Germany seven years earlier. What Schmitt produced was less a review of the work in question than a dense historiographical reflection, which staked out three possibilities for a Christian conception of history, starting from Löwith's exposé of the theological presuppositions of the modern philosophy of history (Schmitt [1950] 2009: 167–70).[3] If Löwith's 1935 critique had denounced Schmitt's decisionism as 'atheological' by turning the latter's own category of occasionalism against him (Löwith 1995: 138), Schmitt now responded by making the occasion of his Löwith review the platform for one of the most emphatically Christian statements of his entire oeuvre.[4] In so doing, he established a new programme for his political theology.

The central aim of Schmitt's review was to establish the strictly Christian provenance of what he called 'the historical' (*das Geschichtliche*). The latter, he claimed, offered an image of the world qualitatively distinct from both what preceded and what succeeded it. Löwith's study supplied the two bookends. At one end, he followed Löwith in maintaining that no form of historical thinking had been available to paganism, because it conceived the world in terms of cycles. 'The historical,' he declared, 'loses its specific meaning within the cycles of an eternal recurrence' (Schmitt 2009: 168). At the other end, he inferred from Löwith's presentation of the modern belief in progress as the secularization of an originally Jewish and Christian template, a departure from history altogether, which was fated to dissipate in the iterative structure of philosophical-historical planning (Schmitt 2009: 168). If the classical world remained in some sense 'pre-historical', the advent of the philosophy of history, by Schmitt's reckoning, augured a 'post-historical' epoch. Between the two, the properly Christian, properly historical age could be located.

It was here that Schmitt parted ways with Löwith. Löwith not only denied any direct connection between the biblical message and historical action ('the message of the New Testament,' he observed in the sole sentence Schmitt partially paraphrased in his review, 'is not an appeal to historical action but to repentance') (Löwith 1949: 196; cf. Schmitt 2009: 169). He also sought to expose the self-deception of modern historical consciousness by revealing its dependence on the provisory theology of history only subsequently articulated by Augustine and Orosius, among others. For Löwith, accordingly, it was erroneous to refer to a secular epoch of Christian history, because Christianity's consummation lay outside history altogether.[5] Hegel's philosophy of history – the most systematic expression of its kind – was thus for him as anti-Christian in its effects as it was Christian in its inspiration. Against this argument, Schmitt advanced a startling counterpoint. According to him, it was Christianity that grounded, almost in a dogmatic sense, 'the infinite uniqueness of historical reality' (Schmitt 2009: 169, translation modified). Löwith's proposition regarding the non-relationship between Christianity and history, he argued, must therefore be juxtaposed with another one, specifically formulated in order 'to keep all philosophical, ethical, or other neutralizations at bay':

> In its innermost core, Christianity is neither a morality nor a doctrine, neither a penitential sermon nor a religion in the sense of comparative religious studies, but rather a historical event of infinite, inappropriable, unoccupiable uniqueness. It is the incarnation in the Virgin Mary. (Schmitt 2009: 169–70, translation modified)

A 'Christian history' is non-sense, Löwith had concluded. 'The only, though weighty, excuse for this inconsistent compound,' he continued, '(…) is to be found in the fact that the history of the world has continued its course of sin and death in spite of the eschatological event, message, and consciousness' (Löwith 1949: 197). This 'weighty' apologia is precisely the position Schmitt defended. It enshrines his post-war historical thinking as the pendant to his pre-war political theology. Schmitt welcomed one of the central findings of Löwith's book: that the further we trace back from the modern philosophy of history to its Christian origins, the less likely we are to encounter the idea of history as an object of human planning. Not even the mechanism of divine providence was spared from this perspective (Schmitt 2009: 168; cf. Löwith 1949: 191). At the same time, he argued for the specifically Christian institution of the contingency and variety of historical reality which for Löwith was the obverse of the philosophical-historical image of history as meaningful plan. More than this, he sought to supply the incalculability of history with a transcendental basis. According to Schmitt, the 'infinite uniqueness of historical reality' has its theological paradigm in that 'historical event of infinite, inappropriable, unoccupiable uniqueness' that was the conception of the twin-natured Christ in the womb of the historical Mary. History is not meaningful for Schmitt, but its very existence is of theological significance.

This is not to say that he eschewed the eschatological perspective altogether. History remained provisional for Schmitt. But just as the first Christ-event had instituted the distinction between past and future, so only a second one would succeed in erasing it. Until then, the immanence of history must remain unattenuated. The import of the heterodox 'Marian' image of history that Schmitt received from the poet Konrad Weiß accordingly resided in its capacity to act as a 'historical counterforce against the neutralization of history'. It is Christian historicity and politicality which must be affirmed in the face of a post-historical neutralization that would see them reduced to a category of 'universal humanity', consigned to a 'museum of the past', or repurposed as an 'exchangeable costume' (a veritable storehouse of the post-historical imaginary) (Schmitt 2009: 170, translation modified).

To support this claim, Schmitt advanced his own piece of biblical evidence. The Christian tradition, he observed, has long debated the identity of the mysterious figure of the *katechon* from the Second Letter to the Thessalonians – the being or entity tasked with suppressing the appearance of the 'lawless one' and hence with deferring the end of time. In recalling this figure, which was to become a recurring trope in subsequent writings, Schmitt's concern here was to register its general significance. Far from designating a generically conservative or reactionary force, the *katechon* – which the Pauline author introduced to temper restlessness regarding Christ's promised return to an expectant messianic community – offered Schmitt a precious biblical resource in his quest to positively invest the continued course of Christian history (Schmitt 2009: 169). 'I believe in the *katechon*,' Schmitt observed in a 1947 profession of faith; 'it is the only possibility for me as a Christian to understand and find meaning in history' (2015b: 47). The meaning to which he referred was not that which rounded history's possibility off by closing the circle, but that which kept this possibility open.

Historical uniqueness

Schmitt's intellectual biographer has suggested that nowhere else across his oeuvre did the author of *Political Theology* express himself in such distinctly Christian terms (Mehring 2014: 443). Yet, the basic argument was recapitulated five years later (albeit in the absence of its theological framing) in the text where Schmitt most forcefully integrated his reflections on historiography with his postwar preoccupation with the politics of space. 'The Historical Structure of the Contemporary World-Opposition between East and West' was first published in a *Festschrift* for Ernst Jünger (Schmitt [1955] 2018b: 100–35); but it was Kojève whom Schmitt identified as the privileged addressee of this essay (Kojève and Schmitt 2001: 95–6). It is not difficult to see why. Jünger's 1953 tract *The Gordian Knot*, which frames the discussion, has only an auxiliary role to play in Schmitt's larger argument. Its mythical reflection on the relationship between East and West was soon displaced by the preferred antithesis of Schmitt's political geography: that between land and sea. Only, now the discussion of this opposition, which Schmitt had initiated more than a decade earlier (Schmitt [1942] 2015c), was given an ironic Hegelian twist.

In this essay, Schmitt too sought to fashion himself as a distinguished *lecteur* of Hegel. The sequence of the *Elements of the Philosophy of Right* where Hegel had detailed the rise of poverty in bourgeois society (§§ 243–6), he observed, was justly famous – not least because of its reception in the Marxist tradition. There Hegel had described the inner 'dialectic' of bourgeois society: its simultaneous generation of an excess of wealth, on the one hand, and an excess of poverty, on the other. As the accumulation of wealth was concentrated in the hands of fewer and fewer individuals, Hegel explained, so the mass of people descending below the expected standard of living grew larger and larger (Hegel 1991: 266–7). As an illustration of the coexistence of these twin phenomena, Hegel had offered the specific example of England. It was as an attempt to resolve its internal contradiction, Hegel argued, that this specific society had been driven out beyond itself, to establish colonies, to seek consumers (and hence the means required for its subsistence) externally, in other nations (Hegel 1991: 267–8).

It was Schmitt's contention that Hegel's formalization of bourgeois society's external development should be granted a standing equal to that accorded to the corresponding account of its internal development. 'As the earth, fixed ground and soil, is the condition of family life,' Hegel had recorded in § 247 of his treatise, 'so for industry the outward enlivening natural element is the sea.' Referencing these lines in his earlier *Nomos of the Earth*, Schmitt had characterized Hegel as the sole author to have approached the mystery of the new *nomos* that emerged at the time of the Industrial Revolution (Schmitt 2003: 49). Now he presented his own considerations on land and sea as the beginning of an attempt to unfold this mystery – and hence to bring § 247 of Hegel's *Rechtsphilosophie* to fulfilment in a manner analogous to how §§ 243–6 had been brought to fulfilment in Marxism (Schmitt 2018b: 133).

In keeping with Hegel's intuition, Schmitt located the moment of bourgeois society's global extension in the momentous decision taken by the 'island England' to abandon its prior terrestrial orientation in favour of a maritime existence. Schmitt drew a direct line between England's instigation of the Industrial Revolution, its development of unrivalled naval technology and its distinctive geographical particularity. For him, the British historian Arnold Toynbee's thesis regarding the 'almost world-wide dissemination of a technological splinter flaked off from our Western civilization since the close of the seventeenth century' should be referred to the island at large where this technological progress had originated (Toynbee 1943: 60–1; cf. Schmitt 2018b: 122–4, 128). Through its industry and technology, he argued, a European island had broken away from the European continent: it had transformed itself into a ship. But this simultaneously marked a movement outside the old state-based order. 'The island unloosed itself from the received, purely terrestrial world image and from the orders interlaced with it,' he writes,

> and from there it passed over into seeing the world consequentially from the perspective of the free sea (. . .) The island ceases to be a broken-off land and metamorphoses into a ship. The world of the free sea steps out against the stately world of the firm land as another world, with an order of life that is not stately but social (. . .) In place of the old pure terrestrial *nomos* of the earth there emerges a new *nomos*, which draws the world oceans into its order. (Schmitt 2018b: 127)

'An order of life that is not stately but social': for Schmitt, the sublation of the state in favour of society could be traced back to seventeenth-century England's heeding the call of the world's oceans opening themselves up.

In its initial phase – the age of *Ius publicum Europaeum* – the emergence of a new maritime world over against the old established a kind of equilibrium between the elements, Schmitt argued. Already in 1955, however, this was no longer the case. Now the balance, as he saw it, had tipped in favour of the sea. Much like Kojève, Schmitt did not recognize the contemporary world-dualism of East and West as a genuine opposition. Instead, he viewed it as characterized by the overwhelming predominance of one of the two sides of its prevailing antithesis over the other. But he stopped short of conceding Kojève's reproach that the categories of land and sea belonged entirely to the past (Kojève and Schmitt 2001: 99).

For Schmitt, the triumph of the smooth space of the sea over the striated space of land no more marked the advent of world unity than it did the end of human history. Instead, he spoke – for the second time – of a 'new *nomos* of the earth' (although privately he wondered whether this new *nomos* would be characterized by its absence) (2015b: 135). The old Eurocentric *nomos*, he argued, had remained in place until the time of the First World War. The circumnavigation of the earth had made it the first global order, even if balanced by the separation of the qualitatively distinct domains of land and sea. In one sense, the bipolar structure of the current world-opposition of East and West suggested the solidification of these two structuring principles into something approximating a formal opposition: what Schmitt characterized in terms of an 'antithesis of elements pure and simple' (2003: 353). After all, the East occupied a giant land mass (precisely what Mackinder had called the 'heartland'), while the West controlled the world's oceans. As always, however, Schmitt remained attentive to the deeper unity that subtended the surface duality: the shared universalism which already suggested the ascendancy of the naval perspective.

It was this recognition, Schmitt observed, that led some commentators (Kojève included) not only to see the current world-dualism as merely the prelude to a final unity, but also to suggest that this eventuality could already be discerned in the rise of a third element which would sublate the prevailing antithesis: air (Schmitt 2003: 354; cf. Kojève and Schmitt 2001: 99). Schmitt granted that this was one available interpretation. One of the two antagonists in the present global conflict would emerge victorious; the last residual form of political enmity would henceforth cease. Sole master of the world, the victor would 'appropriate the whole earth – land, sea, and air – and would divide and manage it according to his plans and ideas' (Schmitt 2003: 354). Yet, it was precisely his 'historical sense' that kept Schmitt from conceding this necessity.

Schmitt entrusted the clearest articulation of this argument to his alter ego, the historian Altmann, in the *Dialogue on New Space*, a radio-play first broadcast on the Hessischer Rundfunk in early 1955 (2015a: 51–83). According to Altmann's American interlocutor, MacFuture, the world was standing on the precipice of a new age of discovery, relative to which its sixteenth-century predecessor would pale in comparison. Today, it was the whole cosmos that was opening itself up to 'Spaceship Earth'. And, just as Columbus had set out en route to India and discovered America, so it was possible that a hitherto unknown planet was awaiting discovery in outer space, which would liberate man from Earth in the same way that the oceans had liberated him from the land (Schmitt 2015a: 76–8).[6] But such reasoning was unhistorical, Altmann cautioned. It was to provide an old answer to a new historical call. Taking up the historiographical prescription first delineated in the earlier Löwith review, he now reasserted over against MacFuture's cosmic vision the 'unrepeatable uniqueness of all great historical events' (Schmitt 2015a: 79, translation modified). Even the continuation, through repetition, of what once was historically true, he argued, soon becomes unhistorical; for, a 'historical truth is only true *once*' (Schmitt 2015a: 79; cf. 2018b: 114–15, 134).

With this last expression, Schmitt compressed his historical thinking into a memorable formula. Its impetus, however, was not merely historiographical. It was also an expression of his political theology. Modern technology had enclosed human beings on the earth, rather than opened new spaces to them beyond it, Schmitt's historian continued. The task, as he saw it, consisted in curtailing the new technology and leading it back to a concrete order. 'The human is a son of the earth,' he concluded, 'and so he shall remain as long as he remains human' (Schmitt 2015a: 81). Observing the myriad uses to which Schmitt put the figure of the *katechon* in his post-war writings, commentators have concluded that this reflected no systematic intention (Paléologue 2004: 64). In the context of his political geography, however, its function clearly coincides with that outlined in the 1950 Löwith review: to check the neutralization of history symbolized by the looming prospect of world unity. To prolong enmity beyond the liquidation of the state and thereby detain the end of history demanded a new terrestrial spatial concept. It was the pluralistic theory of *Großräume* that enabled Schmitt to imagine a 'new order of the earth' (2003: 355). In and against the first truly global age, this was his *katechon*.

Coda: From nations to empires

One world never materialized – at least, not in Schmitt's lifetime. Nonetheless, the theorist of the political continued to rally against its closure well into advanced old age (1978: 329). Of particular interest, from this perspective, was Schmitt's later use of his *Großraum* theory, which had been originally conceived as a vindication of the German *Reich* as a third way between Eastern Bolshevism and Western liberalism, to characterize the emerging political consciousness of the 'Third World'. With considerable irony, it was the global anti-colonial movements, Schmitt argued, which now worked to dissolve the prevailing dualistic-bipolar world system into a pluralistic-multipolar structure – a role he had previously envisaged for Nazi Germany (1995: 602–3).

It was no coincidence, however, that when the Berlin Wall was finally toppled, in 1989, four years after Schmitt's death, Kojève's end-of-history idea would experience a significant renewal, which transformed it into a global *cause célèbre*. With liberal democracy, Francis Fukuyama famously argued, the long evolution of political forms had arrived at the terminus of its historical development. While it may not yet cover the entire globe, its basic principles, he contended, could not be substantially improved upon (Fukuyama 1989). Issuing from a deputy director of the US State Department's policy planning staff, this was precisely what Schmitt had most feared. Almost simultaneously with the worldwide diffusion of Kojève's idea, a previously unpublished memorandum to Charles de Gaulle, dated 27 August 1945, was unearthed, which advanced a proposal for a distinctive application of Schmitt's *Großraum* concept. The memorandum came from a highly unexpected source: Kojève himself (Kojève 2004; Auffret 1990: 282–9). In it, Kojève employed a host of Schmittian terms and concepts, which suggested a close reading of Schmitt's 1939 '*Großraum* Order' essay in particular.[7]

Kojève's starting point was what he called 'the political unreality of Nations'. In different ways, he argued, both bourgeois liberalism and international socialism had consigned the essentially political entity – the nation state – to the past (Kojève 2004: 7). This much was consistent with his later correspondence with Schmitt. But both had nonetheless failed to recognize, he surprisingly added, that there was an intermediate political reality between the superseded nation and depoliticized humanity. 'Before being embodied in Humanity, the Hegelian *Weltgeist*, which has abandoned the Nations, inhabits Empires,' Kojève declared (2004: 8). The 'national' period of history was certainly over, but this was not yet the end of history as such.

This had been precisely Schmitt's position in 1939. '[T]he task of German international jurisprudence,' he wrote, 'is to find, between a merely conservative maintenance of the previous interstate way of thinking and a non-stately, non-national overreach into a universalistic global law as carried out by Western democracies, the concept of a concrete *Großraum* order which escapes both' (1995: 305). What would provide the means of this escape was the juridical concept of a German *Reich*, which would radiate its 'political idea' into the *Großraum* with respect to which it was the leading or bearing power (Schmitt 2011b: 101). Utilizing Schmitt's very language, Kojève now advocated the same for France (2004: 11–15). But also, against Germany.[8] It was in order to curtail Germany's eventual domination of Europe that, a matter of months after the capitulation of the Nazi regime, Kojève prophetically advised France to move to establish a 'Latin Empire' with its affiliated nations, Italy and Spain, while itself assuming the role of leading power. What would form the basis of this affiliation, he argued, was not only the kinship between its languages and the shared mentality among its peoples, but also – and above all – the Catholic Church (Kojève 2004: 15–17). Inadvertently reviving an antique tradition, Kojève identified his *katechon* with the Church.

Notes

1 Schmitt's critique of liberal universalism has been mobilized in the context of the anti-globalization movement, yet without its political-theological basis being recognized. See Mouffe (2005).
2 Kojève largely facilitated the reception of Schmitt in France. See Geroulanos (2011).
3 Paeschke judged Schmitt's review insufficiently focused on Löwith's book and it was published in the journal of his former student Serge Maiwald.

4 Schmitt acknowledged the acuteness of Löwith's critique via a pun entered in the margins of his personal copy: 'Gut gebrüllt, Löwith!' [Well Roared, Löwith!]. See Mehring (2014: 618, n. 93.)
5 As Hans Blumenberg has observed ([1976] 1985: 27–8), Löwith had his own motivation for pursuing this reading: the vindication of the ancient cosmology he had championed in an earlier work on Nietzsche. See Löwith [1935] (1997).
6 A decade prior to its popularization in the United States, Schmitt utilized the figure of 'Spaceship Earth' in a pejorative sense. See Schmitt (2015a: 79; 2018b: 134).
7 The connection to Schmitt has been previously noted by Müller (2003: 263) and Hooker (2009: 152, n. 86), but not yet substantiated by analysis.
8 This explains why Kojève never mentioned this document in his correspondence with Schmitt. On the memorandum's anti-Germanness, see Lepenies (2016: 15–32).

References

Auffret, D. (1990), *Alexandre Kojève: La philosophie, l'État, la fin de l'Histoire*, Paris: Grasset.
Bendersky, J. W. (1984), *Carl Schmitt: Theorist for the Reich*, Princeton, NJ: Princeton University Press.
Bloom, A. (1990), 'Alexandre Kojève', in *Giants and Dwarfs: Essays 1960–90*, 268–74, New York: Simon & Schuster.
Blumenberg, H. (1985), *The Legitimacy of the Modern Age*, trans. Robert M. Wallace, Cambridge, MA: MIT Press.
Fukuyama, F. (1989), 'The End of History?', *The National Interest*, 16: 3–18.
Geroulanos, S. (2011), 'Heterogeneities, Slave-Princes, and Marshall Plans: Schmitt's Reception in Hegel's France', *Modern Intellectual History*, 8 (3): 531–60.
Guilhot, N. (2010), 'American Katechon: When Political Theology Became International Relations', *Constellations*, 17 (2): 229–53.
Guilhot, N. (2017), *After the Enlightenment: Political Realism and International Relations in the Mid-Twentieth Century*, Cambridge: Cambridge University Press.
Hegel, G. W. F. (1991), *Elements of the Philosophy of Right*, trans. H. B. Nisbet, Cambridge: Cambridge University Press.
Hooker, W. (2009), *Carl Schmitt's International Thought*, Cambridge: Cambridge University Press.
Kervégan, J. -F. (1999), 'Carl Schmitt and "World Unity"', trans. D. Hahn, in C. Mouffe (ed.), *The Challenge of Carl Schmitt*, 55–75, London: Verso.
Kojève, A. (1980), *Introduction to the Reading of Hegel*, ed. A. Bloom, trans. J. H. Nichols, Jr, Ithaca: Cornell University Press.
Kojève, A. (2000), *Outline of a Phenomenology of Right*, trans. B. -P. Frost and R. Howse, Lanham: Rowman and Littlefield.
Kojève, A. (2004), 'Outline of a Doctrine of French Policy', trans. E. de Vries, *Policy Review*, 126: 3–40.
Kojève, A. and C. Schmitt (2001), 'Correspondence', trans. E. de Vries, *Interpretation*, 29 (1): 94–115. Originally published as 'Der Briefwechsel Kojève-Schmitt', in P. Tommisen (ed.), *Schmittiana*, vol. 6: 100–24, Berlin: Duncker & Humblot, 1998.
Koskeniemmi, M. (2004), 'International Law as Political Theology: How to Read *Nomos der Erde*?', *Constellations* 11 (4): 492–511.

Lepenies, W. (2016), *Die Macht am Mittelmeer: Französische Träume von einem anderen Europa*, Munich: Carl Hanser.
Löwith, K. (1949), *Meaning in History*, Chicago, IL: University of Chicago Press.
Löwith, K. (1995), 'The Occasional Decisionism of Carl Schmitt', trans. G. Steiner, in R. Wolin (ed.), *Martin Heidegger and European Nihilism*, 137–69, New York: Columbia University Press.
Löwith, K. (1997), *Nietzsche's Philosophy of the Eternal Recurrence of the Same*, trans. J. H. Lomax, Berkeley, CA: University of California Press.
Mehring, R. (2014), *Carl Schmitt: A Biography*, trans. D. Steuer, Cambridge: Polity.
Mouffe, C. (2005), 'Schmitt's Vision of a Multipolar World Order', *South Atlantic Quarterly*, 104 (2): 245–51.
Müller, J. -W. (2003), *A Dangerous Mind: Carl Schmitt in Post-War European Thought*, New Haven, CT: Yale University Press.
Paléologue, T. (2004), *Sous l'œil du Grand Inquisiteur: Carl Schmitt et l'héritage de la théologie politique*, Paris: Cerf.
Rosenboim, O. (2017), *The Emergence of Globalism*, Princeton, NJ: Princeton University Press.
Schmitt, C. (1978), 'Die legale Weltrevolution', *Der Staat*, 17 (3): 321–39.
Schmitt, C. (1995), *Staat, Großraum, Nomos: Arbeiten aus den Jahren 1916–69*, ed. G. Maschke, Berlin: Duncker & Humblot.
Schmitt, C. (2003), *The Nomos of the Earth in the International Law of the Jus Publicum Europaeum*, trans. G. L. Ulmem, Candor: Telos Press.
Schmitt, C. (2005), *Political Theology*, trans. G. Schwab, Chicago, IL: University of Chicago Press.
Schmitt, C. (2007), *The Concept of the Political*, trans. G. Schwab, Chicago, IL: University of Chicago Press.
Schmitt, C. (2009), 'Three Possibilities for a Christian Conception of History', trans. M. Wenning, *Telos*, 147: 167–70. Originally published as 'Drei Stufen historischer Sinngebung', *Universitas*, 5 (1950): 927–30.
Schmitt, C. (2011a), 'Großraum versus Universalism', trans. M. Hannah, in S. Legg (ed.), *Spatiality, Sovereignty and Carl Schmitt*, 46–54, London: Routledge.
Schmitt, C. (2011b), *Writings on War*, ed. and trans. T. Nunan, Cambridge: Polity Press.
Schmitt, C. (2015a), *Dialogues on Power and Space*, ed. A. Kalyvas and F. Finchelstein, trans. S. G. Zeitlin, Cambridge: Polity Press.
Schmitt, C. (2015b), *Glossarium: Aufzeichnungen aus den Jahren 1947 bis 1958*, ed. G. Giesler and M. Tielke, Berlin: Duncker & Humblot.
Schmitt, C. (2015c), *Land and Sea: A World-Historical Meditation*, trans. S. G. Zeitlin, Candor: Telos Press.
Schmitt, C. (2018a), *Ex captivitate salus*, ed. A. Kalyvas and F. Finchelstein, trans. M. Hannah, Cambridge: Polity Press.
Schmitt, C. (2018b), 'The Historical Structure of the Contemporary World-Opposition Between East and West', trans. S. G. Zeitlin, in *The Tyranny of Values and Other Texts*, 100–35, Candor: Telos. Originally published as 'Die geschichtliche Struktur des heutigen Welt-Gegensatzes von Ost und West', in A. Mohler (ed.), *Freundschaftliche Begegnungen: Festschrift für Ernst Jünger zum 60. Geburtstag*, 135–67, Frankfurt: Vittorio Klostermann, 1955.
Toynbee, A. (1943), *The World and the West*, Oxford: Oxford University Press.
Willkie, W. L. (1943), *One World*, London: Cassell.

Chapter 9

EXPLOSIVE PUBLICS IN THE INTERZONES OF POLITICAL THEOLOGY AND POLITICAL MYTHOLOGY

Christiane Mossin

The 1899 poem 'Antigonish' by William Hughes Mearns recounts a meeting on a staircase with a mystical man who 'wasn't there', yet whom the narrator nevertheless wishes away.[1] While the author remains little known, the poem has become a classic of popular culture. The enduring popularity of the poem may indicate a collective sense of a peculiar 'present absence' pervading modern social experience. Indeed, the poem can be read as capturing one of the most important insights springing from Schmitt's political theology: Modern, secularized Europe is not free of religion; religious conceptual structures survive in secular clothing in legal, political and social principles of order. From this perspective, the 'man who wasn't there' could be grasped as the transcendent source of divinity which has been lost as an unquestionable foundation of social-political order, but still inhabits the secularized world as a peculiar absent force. Present as absence.[2]

This chapter is devoted to the task of developing conceptually two different responses to the loss of an indubitable transcendent foundation of social-political life: political theology and political mythology. Mearns' poem would be apposite to both: both responses are haunted by the 'present absence' of a transcendent foundation. But they divert from each other in their ways of dealing with the loss. Political theology seeks a path of compensation, political mythology a path of rebellion.

The chapter's conceptualization of political theology builds on Schmittian definitions and historical-philosophical constructions. I shall argue that Schmitt's political theology is profoundly inscribed within a particular understanding of European modernity. The conceptualization of political mythology, however, emerges as the result of a journey undertaken by myself. This journey takes its crucial starting point in certain enigmatic remarks concerning a fundamental 'myth' of European modernity – given by Schmitt in his Hamlet-essay from 1956 (1999). Arguably, these remarks do not in themselves establish a basis for a 'political mythology' in the sense of an alternative to 'political theology'. They concern, merely, the problematic foundations of political theology. But a small opening towards other terrains may be found in connections established between 'play' and 'myth'. According to my reading, Schmitt opens the door for a possible conceptualization of a 'playing society', yet closes it immediately again.

In this idea of a 'playing society' I discern an alternative response to the modern loss of transcendent foundations. I call this response 'political mythology'. Essentially, this response foregrounds 'playing the loss', rather than compensating for it through the establishment of secular principles of social-political order. I develop the characteristics of a possible 'political mythology' on the basis of Walter Benjamin's analyses of 'allegorical existence' and Lacan's interpretation of the element of 'knowledge' in Shakespeare's *Hamlet*.

But what would be the point, today, of developing a 'political mythology' in contrast to 'political theology'?

The power and unpredictability of collective dynamics – transgressing controllability by established elites – have emerged as core factors of social-political development. Erratic voting behaviour and social movements capable of turning the tables beyond previous imagination have given rise to admiration as well as perplexity and outright fear. The internet constitutes, especially, an incontrollable, gigantic factory of parallel worlds, plots, dreams and battle-forms. From the perspective of political theology, collective power relies on unifying ideas, functioning as unquestioned, ultimate principles of (self)justification. Such ideas may foster identity-formations and (temporary) stability within political groups, but also external demonizations. Arguably, such unifying ideas – echoing the present absence of a divine foundation – may be detected within explosive social groups and movements of today. But to the extent we are confronted not only with opposed groups dedicated to identifiable beliefs and goals but also with sheer fragmentation and sporadic discursive developments, political theology falls short. It is my hope that the conceptualization of 'political mythology' developed in this chapter may offer an analytical prism by which the mechanisms of such orderless collective meaning-creation come into sight.

The chapter is composed of three parts: An interpretation of Schmitt's 'political theology'; a reading of Schmitt's Hamlet-essay offering partly a meta-reflection on the problematic foundations of modern political theology, partly an opening towards the idea of 'a playing society'; and a conceptual development of 'political mythology' building on Benjamin's concept of 'allegory' and Lacan's understanding of 'knowledge' in Hamlet.

The dangers of immanent gods: Political theology and European modernity

Schmitt develops his understanding of 'political theology' within the context of a particular historical-philosophical analysis of the logics of European modernity. His basic narrative – arguably upheld throughout his entire oeuvre, gradually developed and sophisticated – can be summarized as follows.

The religious wars of the sixteenth–seventeenth centuries left the European political order in ruins. The Catholic Church had for centuries functioned as an overall metaphysical and institutional framework of order – while allowing for legal-political pluralism in accordance with the customs of feudalism. The devastating religious wars could, however, not be settled on the basis of this framework. The modern state emerged as it provided a new foundation for a settlement of the conflict: It neutralized the fiery religious spirit by separating political power from the church. Moreover, it sought – and gradually succeeded in realizing – an end to legal-political pluralism while introducing the principle of sovereignty as a core constitutional principle (Schmitt 1950b: 62–71; 1997: 27–8, 90–1, 111–43; 1995a: 71–2, 113; also Bodin 1986).[3]

Schmitt assumes that humans, fundamentally, cannot realize themselves politically without metaphysics (1988e: 163; 1996b: 79, n. 1). In place of the religious principles of the Catholic order emerged conceptual structures of political legitimation referred to by Schmitt as 'immanent gods'. Initially, the monarch incorporated the idea of a divine principle of government on earth. Schmitt identifies, moreover, the immanent god of the Enlightenment era to be 'Human reason', the immanent god of the conservative counter-revolutionary forces of the nineteenth century to be 'Tradition', and that of the democratic age to be 'The people'. The state itself figured throughout European modernity as a 'human god', as captured by Hobbes' symbol 'Leviathan'. Such immanent gods do not amount to entirely new inventions, but carry the structural logics of inherited religious concepts. Accordingly, they may be seen as attempts to mirror the idea of a distant transcendent order on secular grounds (1996a: 43–4, 51–4, 59–68; 1950b: 72–3; 1995a: 50–60; 1995b: 139–47; 1963a: 68–9; 1963b: 80–5, 88–90; 1925: 23, 86–95; 1988d: 130, 135, 142; 1921: 116–29, 139–46; 1961: 30–41; 1988a: 21–5).

Schmitt indicates that the logic of secularization implies a movement towards ever more immanent gods. Ultimately, the human being would figure as a god to itself. He finds this to be a tendency in Russian anarchism, but also in liberalist wars carried out in the name of 'humanity' (Schmitt 1963a: 69–78; 1988c). Whether or not this historical development towards ever more immanent gods should be seen as due to inescapable logics, remains ambiguous. Crucial is, in any case, the significance Schmitt ascribes to the first step of secularization. The first step constitutes a point of no return. Once the first god has emerged in the historical terrain, transiency and eternity have entered into an entirely new, and unstable, alliance. Dubitability has become an inescapable feature of any 'god'. Even if continuously repressed, the ultimately unfounded nature of political authority has come to the forefront. Metaphysical signification operates now in the enormous shadowlands of human freedom and desire conditioned by the absent presence of a transcendent god – while paying the price of ontological vertigo.[4]

Importantly, the fact that indubitability has been lost means not that the secular gods are worshipped less intensely – as long as they last. Paradoxically, the most 'human' gods give rise to the greatest fanaticism, as Schmitt sees it. When humans begin to judge other humans on the basis of a particular standard of 'humanity', in contrast to 'inhumanity', the utmost degree of arrogance, exclusion and blind enmity has been reached. Humility and self-critique crumble, he finds, once the possibility of human gods have entered the horizons of metaphysical imagination (Schmitt 1963a: 37, 54–6, 69–78; 1963b: 94; 1950a: 110–12; 1979: 36–40). It would not be difficult to find twentieth-century examples of fanatically worshipped self-acclaimed 'human gods' (such as Hitler) and brutally excluding notions of 'humanity' (such as racial theory). As is well known, with a few exceptions (1973b; 1973a: 430–51), Schmitt avoids Nazism as a subject of critical analysis – and directs his critique against anarchism and liberalist humanism. Nazism, fascism or Stalinism would, however, constitute exceedingly strong manifestations of the dangers of human gods.

In other words, the result of the first step of 'neutralization' was not a taming of human conflictuality. Schmitt's pessimist anthropology (1963a: 36–7, 59–67, 76–7) underpins political theology no less than 'the political'. More precisely, the assumed conflictuous human nature in combination with the assumed human need for metaphysical legitimation constitutes the driving forces of political theology. This means political theology may concern unitarian principles of order, but likewise passionate polarization. In the latter instance, different groups would oppose one another, each advocating its own 'god'.

The counter-concepts of Schmitt's political theology would, I suggest, be the same as the counter-concepts of 'the political': 'entertainment' and 'play'. A 'playing society' would be an aestheticizing, entertainment-seeking society without 'seriousness'. Such a society would see the collapse of the 'political' (the intensity of friend–enemy distinctions; Schmitt 1963a: 26–40) as well as the 'political-theological' (the search for metaphysical principles as justification for conflict and lines of demarcation). Occasionally, Schmitt indicates that such a playing society might potentially materialize in the future – while leaving no doubt it would constitute a scenario of horror from his perspective. Should it happen, though, it would not mean the end of 'the political' altogether; brutal decisions concerning social order would still be taken. But it would mean the widespread negligence thereof, an escapism denying conflict and enmity. And it would mean that whatever order had been established, it would be accepted without any need for legitimation principles. The strive towards the metaphysical which characterize humans would be undermined (Schmitt 1963a: 54–8; 1999: 39–42, 71, n. 17; 1979: 11–14, 19–25, 30–1, 36–40; 1994: 26–9).

Generally, however – and most explicitly in his late work *Politische Theologie II* (1996b)[5] – Schmitt denies the possibility of a future disappearance of political theology. Conflictuality and uproar belong to the destiny of humans – and so does the establishment of 'gods' by which the parties of a conflict find meaning and self-justification. From this perspective, 'play' would not ultimately be able to threaten political theology, only constitute its dangerous counterforce.

Importantly, a complementary understanding of political theology can be detected within Schmitt's works: a general understanding he claims to be relevant in relation to numerous historical phenomena. This understanding – developed in detail in *Politische Theologie II*, but implicitly present in earlier works as well – points to the existence of various instances of human history in which politics and theology appear as 'a common bi-polar phenomenon'. By this he means to refer to phenomena in which neither politics, nor theology, is derived from the other, but is structurally bound to the other while manifesting an overall conception of the historical era in question (Schmitt 1996a: 43–4, 50–1; 1963a: 64; 1988d: 135; 1996b: 41, 57). What is important about this general understanding is that it opens up the field for all sorts of phenomena. That is, political theology need not concern the modern state, its principle of sovereignty or immanent gods; it need not even concern Christianity or monotheism. Various collective formations, be it formal organizations or loosely connected movements, today or in the past, become possible objects of political-theological analysis.

It is, however, crucial to notice what still delimits the range of political theology – even when the general understanding is taken into account. Allow me to summarize the foundations of Schmitt's 'political theology' as follows:

1. Political theology implies the existence of *overall, integrative* – rather than piecemeal, broken or disconnected – metaphysical conceptions.
2. Political theology relates to unitary rule, unfolded by comprehensive political regimes, or to polarized political groups confronting each other. The idea of human conflictuality underpins political theology, but in the sense of *groups* opposing each other. Political theology builds on *social polarization*, not social fragmentation.
3. Political theology opposes 'play', defined as 'lack of seriousness'.
4. Immanent gods – which constitute specific political-theological phenomena, relating to European modernity – are manifestations of mirroring exercises, attempts to translate a lost transcendent foundation into secular concepts.

The conception of political mythology I shall develop in what follows will depart from political theology in terms of all these four characteristics.

Reflecting or moving beyond political theology?
A reading of Schmitt's Hamlet-essay

Schmitt's 1956 essay entitled *Hamlet or Hecuba* is in many ways remarkable (Rust and Lupton 2009; Pan 2009; Frank 2010: 70–93).[6] It centres not on a sovereign hero, but on a prince incapable of deciding, acting and speaking the truth. According to Schmitt's analysis of the play, these incapabilities of Hamlet should not be grasped as symptoms of psychological weakness, but as expressions of inescapable historical structures. The historical structures Schmitt has in mind are not those referred to within the narrative itself (conditions of monarchy in late sixteenth-century Denmark). Rather, his point is that crucial historical conditions concerning English monarchy at the time of the inception and first performance of the play (around the year 1600) *broke into* the play while determining core features of its plot-structure. According to Schmitt, it was not just Hamlet, but England itself that was trapped in a situation in which truth-telling, along with sovereign decision-making and action, had become impossible.

Problematizations of sovereignty can be found in other Schmitt writings (1921: 22–3, 32; 1996a: 55, 69–70; 1994; 1997: 32–3, 45). Yet, the essay constitutes a profound deconstruction of the ideals of sovereignty often advocated by Schmitt in his pre-war writings – and for which he is famous. Most unique about the essay is, however, that it introduces the concept of 'myth' (rather than 'political theology') and indicates a peculiar connection between 'myth' and 'play'. Hereby, a new field, potentially different from political theology, is indicated – even if it remains undeveloped.

Trapped sovereignty: Connections between plot-structure and historical situation

In order to pursue the implications of Schmitt's myth–play-conceptualizations, a brief reconstruction of his analysis of the plot-structure of Hamlet – and how it relates to the impotence of sovereignty in England around the year 1600 – shall be necessary. Schmitt identifies two crucial features of ambiguity incorporated in the plot-structure of *Hamlet*. Firstly, the guilt or innocence of Hamlet's mother, Queen Gertrude, is kept ambiguous throughout the play. Secondly, the revenge-figure of the play, Hamlet, materializes as a hesitating revenger.

As for the first ambiguity, concerning the mother's possible complicity in the murder of Hamlet's father, Schmitt brings attention to another mother, outside the play, subjected to a similar suspicion. Mary Stuart's second husband, Lord Darnley, was murdered in 1567 when the couple's son, James, was only eight months old. Subsequently, the suspicion fell on Mary Stuart and her new husband, the Earl of Bothwell, whom she had married just three months after the murder.

Around the year 1600, Queen Elizabeth I was lying on her deathbed. James was King of Scotland (as James VI) and one of the candidates to succeed Elizabeth I. Schmitt argues that in this situation, the possible complicity of Mary Stuart in her husband's death constituted a 'real taboo' for those favouring James as a successor to Elizabeth I (as did Shakespeare's group). The mother's guilt could delegitimize him. On the other hand, everybody at the time knew about the suspicions. A straight denial would have been difficult to believe. Silence – an ambiguous silence full of indications and half-spoken accusations – constituted the only possible path. According to Schmitt, this ambiguous manner of dealing with the suspicions against Mary Stuart 'broke into' the play *Hamlet* and came to determine one of its most significant structural features (1999: 13–21).

As for the second ambiguity of the plot-structure, the withheld revenge, Schmitt identifies an even more significant political conflict as a historical sounding board for narrative complexities: the Protestantism–Catholicism division tearing Europe apart in the early modern period. Schmitt finds this conflict embodied in the personal fate of James as well: his mother was Catholic; his father allied with Protestant rebels; and his reign over Scotland marked by violent religious tensions and personal insecurity. Intellectually, he leaned towards Protestant conceptions, yet struggled in the inherited complex terrains of scholastic speculation and new Lutheran vocabulary.

As for the English situation, no one knew how the coming ruler would settle – or not – the religious conflict. These were years of paralysis. No significant decision could be taken, no real actions embarked on. According to Schmitt, this hesitance of the time also broke into the play and characterized its most profound plot feature: that of postponement of decision and action (1999: 22–32). Schmitt's *Hamlet*-analysis implies, in other words, that historical situations exist in which certain forms of collective knowledge *must* remain withheld and tabooed, and profound political decisions *cannot* be taken – not due to the weaknesses of particular potentates (be that Elizabeth I or her councillors, or royal relatives aspiring to inherit the throne), but due to historical conditions. The mere *possibility* of sovereign intervention seems to be ruled out in advance.

I shall argue that in order for Schmitt's position to be meaningful, a more careful interpretation of the historical conditions is required. Naturally, attempts at breaking the taboo and intervening sovereignly in the interregnum period *could* have occurred. But the legitimacy of the monarchy would hereby have been threatened. As for the religious conflict, it could not be settled on the basis of the existing order – so runs Schmitt's general narrative. A new constitutional framework, based on (relative) religious neutralization would prove necessary – a framework only in the process of being established, around the year 1600.

In short, the particular historical conditions mentioned by Schmitt only become conceivable as inescapable conditions of paralysed speech and action if we grasp them beyond their immediate reference. They concern more than the prolonged dying of Elizabeth I. They concern the institution of the monarchy as such, its chances of legitimate survival in the face of the religious wars, tearing apart the established European order.

Myth, tragedy, play and collective knowledge: Enigmas and openings

Schmitt's analysis of the connections between plot-structure and historical conditions lays the ground for what subsequently emerges as his main purpose: to liberate the concept 'tragedy' from any dependence on aesthetic contemplation and ground it in historical reality. His argument – involving striking conceptualizations of 'play' and 'myth' – can be reconstructed as follows.

The source of tragedy is always historical reality. Only because *Hamlet* derives its core from historical reality is the play capable of moving its audience tragically (Schmitt 1999: 46–7, 54). In this connection, Schmitt establishes a contrary relationship between 'play' and 'tragedy'. Generally, 'play' – or aesthetic manifestation – is characterized by a lack of seriousness and reality and serves to diminish 'tragedy' (1999: 39–42, 47).

Contrastingly, Schmitt situates 'myth' on the side of historical reality. 'Myths' correspond to living, collective knowledge – grounded in real tragedy. As such, myths function as mediators of tragedy. In antiquity, myths were already present as parts of collective reality – ready for playwrights to use. In modernity, myths are not present as already formed, but are established by artists. But since they still give form to a shared, living knowledge, they are not invented by artists. In order for a modern myth to deserve its name, it must resonate with the collective consciousness of its time. If expressed through a play, it must be 'understandable' to the audience (Schmitt 1999: 37, 47–51).[7] Clearly, 'understandability' is not meant to indicate a simplistic plot. What is implied, rather, is that a play may secretly conspire with its audience. A secret knowledge, shared by audience, playwright and actors, constitutes the collective ground on which the myth breeds. Finally, a surprising inconsistency emerges. Whereas 'play' generally serves to diminish tragedy, the play *Hamlet* intensifies the element of tragedy – not in spite of, but due to its sophisticated, multilevel-structure, integrating a play within the play (Schmitt 1999: 42–6).

These conceptualizations may appear enigmatic. Let me unravel what I find to be their implicit meaning, step by step. First, what is the tragic core of *Hamlet*? And what kind of collective knowledge is manifested through the play? On the basis of Schmitt's explicit analysis of *Hamlet*, the answers could be as follows: The historical tragedy at issue is the state of paralysis in which England was caught around the year 1600; and the collective knowledge at issue concerns the possible illegitimacy of the coming ruler and his schizophrenic religious condition. However, Schmitt makes clear that *Hamlet* did not just move its audience tragically in its time. Hamlet still means something profound to us today. Indeed, *Hamlet* constitutes *the* myth of European modernity, as Schmitt sees it (1999: 54–5).

Arguably, these statements become meaningful only in the light of Schmitt's general narrative of European modernity, summarized in part I. I have already argued that we need to grasp the historical conditions mentioned in the Hamlet-essay beyond their immediate reference. At stake is more than the interregnum period around 1600. At stake are the possibilities of monarchic rule and legitimacy after the breakdown of the old European order. Or even more generally: At stake is the possibility of legitimate rule, at all, in the modern era to come.

I suggest that the historical tragedy Schmitt implicitly refers to is the tragedy of modern political theology, the historical development towards ever more immanent gods which proved to increase polarization and demonization rather than to function as principles of peace. Relatedly, the collective knowledge at issue may be grasped as the insight – emerging in the baroque period, in the midst of civil war and religious persecutions – that political authority as such is questionable. As unfolded in part I, when political authority finally, after a century of religious wars, had found a new foundation, it came at a price. A certain indubitability had been lost forever. A potential suspicion of illegitimacy would lurk underneath any apparent stability of rule. On this basis, the collective knowledge emerging in the baroque era may be seen as encapsulating modern knowledge as such.

In essence: the fundamental myth of modernity, encapsulated in Shakespeare's *Hamlet*, concerns the problematic foundations of modern political theology. The impotent sovereign figure (the prince cheated of his throne, but unable to speak and act for his right) may be seen as the quintessential expression of the dubious foundation of modern political authority. From this perspective, *Hamlet* could be seen as nothing but a meta-reflection on modern political theology – or an aesthetic image of the same. I shall argue, however, that Schmitt's remarks on 'play' introduce a whole new element, namely performativity. Accordingly, we cannot just grasp *Hamlet* as a meta-reflection or an image.

Schmitt's remarks on 'play' are marked by severe inconsistencies. He struggles to uphold his earlier view: that 'play' stands in contrast to 'political existence', 'seriousness' and 'real tragedy'. Simultaneously, he holds that the play *Hamlet* – exactly as a play, a complex aesthetic structure – works to intensify the 'real historical tragedy' at issue. Moreover, we learn that public life of the baroque era operated as brutal theatre; the play of *Hamlet* was performed within an already theatricalized society while enhancing the theatrical nature of the same (Schmitt 1999: 42–6).

If we accept the new understanding of 'play' which emerges in Schmitt's essay (and ignore his struggle to unite it with his earlier view), we may understand the relationship between the myth of *Hamlet* and 'play' as follows: The myth of *Hamlet* breeds on living collective knowledge, concerning the questionable nature of political authority. This knowledge is essentially *played out* – not just by the actors on stage, but by the society as a whole. Through this playing, the tragedy (the logic of secularization set in motion by the blow against transcendent foundations) is itself intensified.

This element of performativity is what in my opinion opens a new terrain, different from political theology. I suggest we call it 'political mythology'. Just like political theology, political mythology would concern modern social-political life in view of the loss of transcendent foundations. But whereas political-theological life would consist in the search for immanent gods capable of replacing the lost foundation, political-mythological life would consist in *performing the loss* – hereby intensifying rather than modifying it.

But what would such a playing society look like, a society *performing the loss*?

Rebellious play and 'poison in the ear': Developing a conceptualization of political mythology

Schmitt's cursory entrance into the terrains of 'play' is undoubtedly inspired by Benjamin's 1925 study *Ursprung des Deutschen Trauerspiels*. His remarks on the already theatrical nature of baroque society, and on the possibility of the playwright to enhance this play-nature of society through the establishment of yet another play, can be seen as constituting the very first (but then quickly interrupted) steps of an analysis of a fundamentally 'playing' society. Such an analysis is carried out most sophisticatedly by Benjamin who finds the 'playing' or 'theatrical' element of baroque society to be routed in experiences of a profaned human existence.

Schmitt praises Benjamin's work. Especially, he highlights Benjamin's insight that Shakespeare binds 'the elementary' and 'the allegorical' together as mutually dependent foundations of baroque existence (Schmitt 1999: 62). Strikingly, however, 'the allegorical' figures nowhere else in Schmitt's essay. I shall argue that 'allegorical existence', as unfolded by Benjamin, offers a key to a possible conceptualization of a society continuously performing the loss of transcendent foundations. It should be noted that the following interpretation of the characteristics of 'allegorical existence' is knowingly selective and cannot do justice to Benjamin's masterpiece.

Baroque allegories, according to Benjamin, appear as fragments in a ruined, disconnected world. They may be gathered and combined in ever new arbitrary constellations. Anything can mean anything, disrupting any possibility of coherence. Accordingly, baroque art is characterized by equivocacy, opulence of meaning, imposing figuration – but likewise by bodily decay, decease and death, catastrophic nature. The 'creaturial' and the 'allegorical' are brought together in endless processes of voluptuous meaning-creation – such as corpse-poetry and cruelty-drama – by which the profaned world is somehow saved from utter profanity although still bound for death (Benjamin 1974c: 350–61, 381–4, 390–3).

Perishable, historical existence in a soulless, god-forsaken world is conceived to be the inevitable condition of human life – a condition which, once realized, opens for an enormous freedom no less than melancholy. The continuous allegorical effort is an expression of both: the endless journey of unlimited creation and the attempt to save the profaned world, destitute of meaning, by calling it by ever new names (Benjamin 1974c: 361, 397–404).

Crucially, Benjamin holds that allegorical existence still depends on a Christian horizon. The profaned world of the baroque era is exactly a fallen world; it presupposes the dynamic process of *continuously falling* from the grace of God. On this journey further and further down, towards the empty abyss, anything seems possible. But were the abyss ever to be reached, the endless signifying game would be over. Allegorical existence depends on continuously sinning against God (Benjamin 1974c: 390, 404–9). That is, the knowledge of profaned creaturial existence is what inaugurates the *need* for allegorical playing: Only through allegory may reality mean anything. But the very idea that reality *ought* to mean anything springs from the lost divine world – which, accordingly, continuously is present as absent in the plays of signification. Without this presence of absence, play would die.

Benjamin's analysis of allegorical existence concerns primarily baroque art. But he indicates that the experience of profaned, God-forsaken existence belonged to broader societal horizons at the time. It is worth noting that crucial features of his analysis of disintegrated baroque existence re-emerged in his analyses of nineteenth- and twentieth-century consumer fetishism, voyeurism and nihilism (Benjamin 1974a: 509–690; 1974b: 691–704).

I find the characteristics of allegorical existence displayed by Benjamin (here just crystallized in a brief sketch) to encapsulate exactly the characteristics of a life form that responds to the loss of a transcendent foundation by *playing that loss*, again and again. 'Playing' would then mean not just repeating the loss as a melancholic gesture, but utilizing the enormous human freedom gained by the loss in order to create ever new, shameless meaning-constellations while remaining attached to the idea of rebelling against God.

On this basis, a 'playing society' could be characterized as a society playing limitlessly and shamelessly with signification – building new connections, breaking up others, twisting meaning formations so as to make them ambiguous or driving them to the point of absurdity through jokes, vulgarity or horror images. No beliefs would be stable. Obviously, some degree of disrespect of authorities would be necessary for a society to be able to 'play' like that. It would need to be a fallen society. Not in the radical sense of a society lacking belief in God and the Monarch – but in the sense of a society understanding itself as distant from God and being aware that Monarchs are not infallible. Indeed, it would be a society that would enjoy its own sinfulness – its continuous rebellion against that distant God who had forsaken earthly life.

This would be a quite different response to the modern condition of loss than that proposed by political theology. Instead of seeking new gods for the sake of temporary stability and belief, the playing society would unfold as an unregulated world of free signification, shattered into pieces, a pile of ruins.

The collective knowledge Schmitt refers to as the basis of the *Hamlet*-myth was in part II identified as knowledge of the fundamentally unfounded nature of political authority. Such knowledge would obviously be implied in the more radical collective knowledge Benjamin refers to: that nothing living carries any meaning in itself.

In order to complete my conceptualization of political mythology I shall rely on a particular aspect of Lacan's *Hamlet*-analysis which may serve to qualify even further the kind of knowledge penetrating 'the playing society'. According to Lacan, Hamlet is the modern Oedipus. Oedipus lacked knowledge, but was capable of acting. Hamlet, by contrast, possesses knowledge but is unable to act. What he knows is not just that his father has been murdered by Claudius. The ghost has given Hamlet an even more horrifying knowledge. Lacan refers to this knowledge as 'the poison in the ear': You cannot trust anything; whatever you hear is a potential lie. Hamlet's father was murdered by such 'poison in the ear' (literally, Claudius poured deadly poison into his ear). This 'poison in the ear' is transmitted to Hamlet from the ghost – leading Hamlet into the most fiery signification plays, his insanity-performances. Everything he does from then on is staged; only through art can he move again, as Lacan points out (2019).

I find this knowledge-definition to constitute an exceedingly fruitful qualification of the knowledge underpinning the 'playing society'. Certainly, as Benjamin points out, humans are driven into 'playing' in order to compensate for what they know: that nothing is meaningful in itself. What we learn from Lacan is, however, that we are always already inscribed within webs of signification which are not just expressions of empty shells; they are invested with desire, including evil will. This creates not only a state of nihilistic melancholy, but also a state of potential paralysis. In order to move again, the only option is to take part, oneself, in the game: 'playing', oneself, this fundamental knowledge that everything could be a lie.

Building on these insights of Lacan and Benjamin, 'political mythology' foregrounds a life form responding to the loss of transcendent foundations by *playing* that loss, in the following senses:

- utilizing the enormous freedom unleashed through the loss; if nothing can be trusted, then everything could mean anything; and

- understanding this freedom as continuous rebellion against the lost order of truth.

In essence, the freedom of play is not entirely free; it depends on the idea of uproar against an absent father God.

On this basis, political mythology concerns 'myth' in two ways. Firstly, political-mythological existence depends on a basic myth encapsulating the modern knowledge that nothing – and especially not the legitimacy of political authority – can be trusted. The concept 'myth' highlights that this modern knowledge cannot itself claim to rely on a universal foundation. It is belief. Moreover, it is belief incapable of freeing itself from religion. It is driven by rebellion against religion. Secondly, the rebellious freedom constituting political-mythological existence unfolds through explosive meaning-creation – unlimited by any standard of truth. In that sense, it is not just nihilism, but a productive force of numerous, ever new, but short-lived mythic creations.

Given these qualifications, let me summarize the contrast between political mythology and political theology according to the four characteristics of the latter mentioned in part I:

1. Political mythology implies the production of numerous short-lived, broken and disconnected mythic elements, not immanent gods capable of founding political order for a certain period.
2. Political mythology relates to fragmental societies, not societies characterized by clear groups.
3. Political mythology builds on play – which, in its own way, is deadly serious.
4. Political mythology does not seek to mirror, constructively, the lost transcendent foundation, but to rebel against it.

Conclusion

According to the conceptualizations developed in this chapter, political theology and political mythology articulate two different responses to the same condition of modernity: the loss of transcendent foundations of social-political order. Through this loss, vast possibilities of human meaning-creation have come into sight, at the price of political instability and ontological vertigo.

The political-theological response consists in the taming of significatory freedom while bringing it into the service of political order. Immanent gods, functioning as legitimation principles for political regimes or groups, may enable stability and trust – for a period at least. Immanent gods may, however, also feed social polarization while providing opposing groups with powerful logics of self-justification.

Political mythology, on the other hand, urges full exploitation of the significatory freedom gained by the loss. This freedom takes the form of continuous rebellion and is driven by a constant suspicion inhabiting the ear, whispering: 'I believe nothing, everything is possible.' The consequence is social disintegration: a multiplicity of 'parallel worlds' witnessing an explosion of ambiguous meaning, codes and signs or rambling narratives.

I suggest we may detect both of these responses in contemporary publics – while observing that they each give rise to their own form of 'explosiveness'. Immanent gods are identifiable not just as foundations of established democratic rule, but also of various social movements. Even when characterized by internal heterogeneity, contemporary movements still largely display unifying ideas invested with belief and desire – ideas which belong to the human terrain, but which function, nonetheless, as ultimate principles of justification. Such ideas need not be unambiguous in order to serve their integrative role (Christianity served social-political integration on the basis of great ambiguities). Take 'black power', 'female power', 'equality', 'collective creativity', 'the nation', 'the world as we know it' or 'natural life' as possible candidates of contemporary immanent gods. Their explosive potential lies, first and foremost, in the power of belief as such – by which the possibility of battling established norms or hierarchies comes into sight at all. But self-blindness and the demonization of others constitute an explosive tendency as well – a tendency which is inherent in any belief, but which is, following Schmitt, especially acute when the object of belief resides in the human domain.

Social movements may also be expressions of 'the poison in the ear' – fundamental suspicion against every officially claimed truth – while demonstrating vast internal fragmentation. It is, however, in internet fora devoted to unlimited 'free speech' that I find the most striking manifestations of political mythology today. Suspicions and conspiracy theories thrive, and largely not through identifiable groups, but through extremely dynamic networks and search patterns. Groups, identities and common narratives may certainly develop, but even when they do, they form part of an unfathomable multiplicity of parallel worlds of dynamic myth-creation. Endless, centreless threads of fiery commentary, and unpredictable dynamics of imitation and acclamation work as explosive enforcement – as well as transformation – mechanisms. Finally, the internet is a utopia for 'players' – not just in the sense of 'gamers', but in the sense of people diving into the thrilling mysteries of a labyrinthic world inhabited by secret profiles, masks, coded messages and newly invented signs.

I opened this chapter with a reflection on Hughes Mearns' poem, 'Antigonish' to indicate that a peculiar 'present absence' operates within the explosive dynamics of contemporary publics. Grasped from the perspective of political theology, the 'present absence' would be the lost transcendent God functioning as model for immanent gods recurrently emerging in polarized modern terrains. From the perspective of political mythology, the 'present absence' would be the lost transcendent God functioning as a force of demonic revolt – of defiant, wilful freedom saying 'I believe nothing, everything is possible'.

Notes

1 The poem is available at: https://poets.org/poem/antigonish-i-met-man-who-wasnt-there

2   This is obviously not the original meaning of the poem, inspired by reports of a haunted house in Antigonish, Nova Scotia. See (Colombo 1984: 25–6).
3   The concept 'sovereignty' may, in Schmitt's works, refer to a historically specific legal concept of the modern state; power characteristics identifiable in various historical manifestations; or metaphysical features of power. This chapter relies primarily on the first-mentioned understanding – while considering that sovereignty was introduced as a core principle of monarchy in the sixteenth century (during the religious wars), but refined as a principle of a neutralized state much later.
4   These are mainly my own formulations. I find the issue of dubitability essentially implied in Schmitt's 'decisionism'.
5   Carrying this denial in its title: *Politische Theologie II: Die Legende von der Erledigung jeder Politischen Theologie*.
6   A rarely discussed text by Schmitt. The English translation (from 2009) entails, however, an excellent introduction and afterword, by Jennifer Rust and Julia Reinhard Lupton, and David Pan, respectively. Noteworthy is, moreover, Stephanie Frank's interesting interpretation (2010), who finds, like me, that Schmitt's Hamlet-essay opens a space which potentially deviates from political theology. Her interpretation is quite different from mine, though, building on 'the space of tragedy' and 'inverted representation', rather than on 'myth' and 'play'.
7   This definition of myth differs significantly from Schmitt's earlier definitions (1988b: 9–18; 1961: 88–9), which emphasized the artificial nature of myths.

References

Benjamin, W. (1974a), 'Charles Baudelaire: Ein Lyriker im Zeitalter des Hochkapitalismus', *Gesammelte Schriften*, I (2): 509–690.
Benjamin, W. (1974b), 'Über den Begriff der Geschichte', *Gesammelte Schriften*, I (2): 691–704.
Benjamin, W. (1974c), 'Ursprung des deutschen Trauerspiels', *Gesammelte Schriften*, I (1): 203–430.
Bodin, J. (1986), *Six livres de la République*, Paris: Fayard.
Colombo, J. R. (1984), *Canadian Literary Landmarks*, Toronto: Dundurn Press.
Frank, S. (2010), 'Re-imagining the Public Sphere: Malebranche, Schmitt's Hamlet, and the Lost Theater of Sovereignty', *Telos*, 153: 70–93.
Lacan, J. (2019), *Desire and Its Interpretation*, Cambridge: Polity Press.
Pan, D. (2009), 'Afterword', in C. Schmitt, *Hamlet or Hecuba: The Intrusion of the Time into the Play*, trans. D. Pan and J. Rust, New York: Telos Press.
Rust, J. and J. R. Lupton (2009), 'Introduction', in C. Schmitt, *Hamlet or Hecuba: The Intrusion of the Time into the Play*, trans. D. Pan and J. Rust, New York: Telos Press.
Schmitt, C. (1921), *Die Diktatur: Von den Anfängen des modernen Souveränitätsgedankens bis zum proletarischen Klassenkampf*, München und Leipzig: Duncker und Humblot.
Schmitt, C. (1925), *Politische Romantik*, München und Leipzig: Duncker und Humblot.
Schmitt, C. (1950a), *Donoso Cortes in gesamteuropäischer Interpretation: Vier Aufsätze*, Köln: Greven Verlag.
Schmitt, C. (1950b), *Ex Captivate Salus: Erfahrungen der Zeit 1945–47*, Köln: Greven Verlag.

Schmitt, C. (1961), *Die geistesgeschichtliche Lage des heutigen Parlamentarismus*, Berlin: Duncker und Humblot.
Schmitt, C. (1963a), *Der Begriff des Politischen*, Berlin: Duncker und Humblot.
Schmitt, C. (1963b), 'Das Zeitalter der Neutralisierungen und Entpolitisierungen', in *Der Begriff des Politischen*, 79–95, Berlin: Duncker und Humblot.
Schmitt, C. (1973a), 'Das Problem der Legalität', in *Verfassungsrechtliche Aufsätze aus den Jahren 1924–54*, 441–51, Berlin: Duncker und Humblot.
Schmitt, C. (1973b), 'Der Zugang zum Machthaber, ein zentrales verfassungsrechtliches Problem', in *Verfassungsrechtliche Aufsätze aus den Jahren 1924–54*, 430–9, Berlin: Duncker und Humblot.
Schmitt, C. (1979), *Die Tyrannei der Werte*, ed. Sepp Schulz, Hamburg: Lutherisches Verlagshaus.
Schmitt, C. (1988a), 'Der Begriff der modernen Demokratie in seinem Verhältnis zum Staatsbegriff', in *Positionen und Begriffe in Kampf mit Weimar – Genfer – Versailles; 1923–39*, 19–25, Berlin: Duncker und Humblot.
Schmitt, C. (1988b), 'Die Politische Theorie des Mythos', in *Positionen und Begriffe in Kampf mit Weimar – Genfer – Versailles; 1923–39*, 9–18, Berlin: Duncker und Humblot.
Schmitt, C. (1988c), *Die Wendung zum diskriminierenden Kriegsbegriff*, Berlin: Duncker und Humblot.
Schmitt, C. (1988d), 'Staatsethik und pluralistischer Staat', in *Positionen und Begriffe in Kampf mit Weimar – Genfer – Versailles; 1923–39*, 133–45, Berlin: Duncker und Humblot.
Schmitt, C. (1988e), 'Völkerrechtliche Formen des modernen Imperialismus', in *Positionen und Begriffe in Kampf mit Weimar – Genfer – Versailles; 1923–39*, 162–82, Berlin: Duncker und Humblot.
Schmitt, C. (1994), *Gespräche über die Macht und den Zugang zum Machthaber: Gespräch über den neuen Raum*, Berlin: Akademie Verlag.
Schmitt, C. (1995a), *Der Leviathan in der Staatslehre des Thomas Hobbes: Sinn und Fehlschlag eines politischen Symbols*, Stuttgart: Klett-Cotta.
Schmitt, C. (1995b), 'Der Staat als Mechanismus bei Hobbes und Descartes', in Günther Maschke (ed.), *Staat, Großraum, Nomos: Arbeiten aus den Jahren 1916–69*, 139–47, Berlin: Duncker und Humblot.
Schmitt, C. (1995c), 'Die vollendete Reformation', in *Der Leviathan in der Staatslehre des Thomas Hobbes: Sinn und Fehlschlag eines politischen Symbols*, 137–78, Stuttgart: Klett-Cotta.
Schmitt, C. (1996a), *Politische Theologie: Vier Kapitel zur Lehre von der Souveränität*, Berlin: Duncker und Humblot.
Schmitt, C. (1996b), *Politische Theologie II: Die Legende von der Erledigung jeder politischen Theologie*, Berlin: Duncker und Humblot.
Schmitt, C. (1997), *Der Nomos der Erde im Völkerrecht des Jus Publicum Europaeum*, Berlin: Duncker und Humblot.
Schmitt, C. (1999), *Hamlet oder Hecuba: Der Einbruch der Zeit in das Spiel*, Stuttgart: Klett-Cotta.

Part 4

BEYOND THE EUROPEAN GAZE

Chapter 10

TOWARDS A POLITICAL THEOLOGY OF POST-COLONIALITY[1]

Kwok Pui-lan

In 2019, the protests against an anti-extradition bill in Hong Kong captured the world's attention, as millions took to the streets in the former British colony, and many people took part in rallies in cities around the globe to support their struggle. Towards the end of that year, a mysterious disease broke out in the city of Wuhan, the capital of Hebei Province in the People's Republic of China. Soon, the novel coronavirus began to spread in Europe, the United States, and other parts of the world, with many people ending up in intensive care units and dying from the disease. In early spring of 2020, President Donald Trump tried to downplay the seriousness of the pandemic. Later, he used the term 'the Chinese virus' to refer to the coronavirus, despite calls from global health officials to avoid labels associating the disease with a particular nation or group of people. Trump's references to the coronavirus as 'Chinese virus' and 'Kung Flu' intensified the tensions that already existed between China and the United States as a result of a trade war and other competition between them.

As I looked for theological resources to help make sense of the changing geopolitical situations in Asia Pacific, I found a dearth of material. The majority of books on politics and theology focus on Europe, the United States, or the North Atlantic, and there are few resources on Asia Pacific, though the twenty-first century has been dubbed the Pacific Century (Kang 2014; Kim and Joh 2016; and Tran 2010). While China loomed large in world politics and foreign policy debates, many theologians acted as if they were living in a time capsule, sealed off from the changing world politics around them. When I looked at recent publications in the field of political theology, I found that most remained steeped in a Eurocentric mindset and had not caught up with the current moment.

Postcolonial theology can contribute to broadening our political imagination by challenging Eurocentric biases in the conceptualization of political theology as a field of study, which has so far not taken seriously political questions from the majority world. Instead of a Eurocentric genealogy of political theology that often begins with Carl Schmitt's *Political Theology* (2005), I argue for transnational and multicultural origins and genealogies, using developments in Asia as an example. Schmitt is not only read in Western academia, but in Asia as well. I discuss what is known as the 'Schmitt fever' in China to underscore the need to assess the

German jurist's work cross-culturally. In the final section, I outline a postcolonial and comparative theology of post-coloniality.

Whither political theology?

Schmitt penned his *Political Theology* during a time of political crisis after the First World War. He saw the legitimacy of the Weimar Republic being undermined by atheism, capitalism and political radicalism and argued that these social and political currents denied a place for transcendence in modern society which had been provided for by religion. From Schmitt, scholars have traced the development of political theology within theological discourse through Johann Baptist Metz, to Jürgen Moltmann and Dorothee Sölle after the Second World War, before moving on to the present theological turn in political discourse on both sides of the North Atlantic.

Such a (white) genealogy of modern political theology traces its origin to Europe as it grappled with the political crises of the two world wars. This genealogy foregrounds the works of European and Euro-American theologians, placing their reflections on politics at the centre of inquiry. Two introductory texts on political theology written from different viewpoints illustrate this bias. Elizabeth Philips' *Political Theology: A Guide for the Perplexed* (2012) is a text based on the traditional theological approach. The book offers a Eurocentric development of political theology, citing Schmitt, Augustine, Calvin, Yoder and Hauerwas, before discussing topics such as the church and the political, the politics of Jesus, violence and peace, and liberalism and democracy. Although she discusses oppression and liberation, she does not treat liberation theology adequately and mentions women theologians from the Global South only in passing. The audience she has in mind are primarily white students living in Western democratic countries.

In contrast to Philips, British political theorist Saul Newman offers an introductory text that we can call a 'secular' political theology. His book *Political Theology: A Critical Introduction* (2019) follows the convention of beginning with Schmitt, before moving on to central figures such as Bakunin, Stirner, Freud, Hobbes, Benjamin, Foucault and Agamben. Newman's various chapters explore sovereignty, psychology, economy, spirituality and the politics of the profane. He does not assume any belief in God, nor does he dwell on theology, for he argues that 'political theology is not so much a problem of religion in modern societies as a problem of *power*' (Newman 2019: 19, author's emphasis). On the surface, Newman's secular approach is very different from Philips' book. However, though they cite different registers of thinkers, they both draw primarily from Western sources, especially canonical figures in their respective fields.

If an introductory text by a single author is limited by the author's horizon, multi-authored companion volumes on political theology do not fare better. Both *The Cambridge Companion to Christian Political Theology* (2015) and the second edition of the *Wiley Blackwell Companion to Political Theology* (2019) are preoccupied with European and Euro-American theologians' works and contributions to the field. They have not paid sufficient attention to political theologies from Africa, Asia, the Middle East and Latin America, and the issues discussed do not touch on many political concerns from the majority world.

To combat Eurocentric biases, we have to reject the notion of a single, originating moment, or a singular tradition, of political theology. Instead, I propose a transnational and multicultural articulation of the origins and genealogies of political theology. Edward Said has taught us to read histories contrapuntally and to see histories as intertwined and overlapped (1994: 18). Around the time when Schmitt was writing *Political Theology*, a different kind of political crisis emerged on the horizon in China. On 4 May 1919, students in Beijing took to the streets to protest the transfer, to Japan, of Germany's rights over China's Shandong peninsula at the Paris Peace Conference after the First World War, even though China had entered the war on the side of the Allied powers. Germany had previously obtained the right to build a naval base in Qingdao in 1898 and occupied territories in Shandong to extend its military power in the Pacific. After the protests in Beijing, a mass movement swept through the country, denouncing Western imperialism and demanding democracy alongside radical cultural reforms.

The year 2019 marked the centenary of the May 4 movement. As we look back over the past hundred years, we find that political theology can be traced to different genealogies. A largely white and male genealogy traces its modern origin to Schmitt and is concerned about religion and the state, secularism and the post-secular world, church and politics, and liberalism and democracy. The other genealogy deprovincializes the Eurocentric approach by placing political theology in the struggles against colonialism, neo-colonialism, dictatorship, authoritarianism, militarized violence and religious and ethnic strife in the majority world. In China, Schmitt's contemporary Wu Yaozong (1893–1979) advocated in the 1930s that only a social revolution would save China and transform the world. He urged other Christians to embrace a revolutionary Christianity because, for him, Christianity should not only attend to people's spiritual lives, but should also care for their social condition. He wrote, 'A true revival of the Church will come only when it has awakened to its social task and begins to tackle it fearlessly and sacrificially' (Wu 1934: 10). Chastising the exploitation of European capitalistic powers, Wu was increasingly attracted to socialism and saw China's only way out via a social revolution (1936: 212). His appeal to Marxist critique and his criticism of idealist Christianity anticipated liberation theology that came decades later.

After the Second World War, many countries in Africa and Asia regained their political independence. This transfer of power did not usher in peace and stability, but often led to dictatorships, military coups and concentrations of power among national elites. Amid Asian revolutions and transformations, Indian theologian M. M. Thomas wrote *Christian Participation in Nation-Building* (1960) and *The Christian Response to the Asian Revolution* (1996). Similar to progressive Indian scholars at the time, Thomas challenged Western imperialism and argued that the Gospel should not be equated with Western culture. The Asian Revolution showed that the Gospel transcends all cultures since God is at work in people's histories. His understanding of Jesus was anti-colonial, for he contrasted the messianism of a conquering king with the crucified servant Christ. Jesus is seen as the model of new humanity, bringing renewal and fulfilment of all humanity (Clarke 2007: 430).

In the 1970s and 1980s, different political theologies were developed in Asia, including Korean *minjung* theology in response to Park Chung-Hee's dictatorship. *Minjung* is the Korean word for 'the masses' or 'people'. Korean theologians argued that Jesus identified with the *minjung* and not with the political elites or religious leaders of his time. In Taiwan, Homeland Theology was developed to address its increasing isolation after China was admitted to the United Nations. Taiwanese theologians argued that Taiwan belongs to the people of Taiwan and not to successive colonizers or the Chinese Nationalist government that came to the island after 1949. During the Marcos era, theologians in the Philippines developed a Theology of Struggle to articulate Filipinos' demand for democracy, identity and peoplehood. Interpreted through the suffering Filipinos, Christ was seen as a liberator, who was in solidarity with the people's struggles (Fernandez 1994). In India, Dalit theology was developed to address the dehumanization of about 200 million people, who were treated as societal outcasts and were previously labelled as 'untouchables' (Nirmal 1992: 297–310).

As these examples show, the context for political theology in Asia is postcolonial and deimperial (Chen 2010). This reality stands in sharp contrast to the postmodern and growing populist and nationalistic political climate of the North Atlantic. Political theologies in Africa, Latin America, the Middle East, and other parts of the world have their own beginnings, pioneers, and developments because of their diversity of histories and political struggles. Political theology does not have one beginning, but many diverse origins and multicultural genealogies. Theological reflections arising from anti-colonial struggles and postcolonial realities must be included in the scope and historical memory of political theology. These reflections have a broad understanding of politics and address political situations very different from those defined by Western liberal democracy. As an interdisciplinary project, political theology can learn much from the insights of postcolonial studies, subaltern studies, critical race theory and transnational and global studies. A contrapuntal and comparative reading of different political theologies enables us to grasp overlapping struggles in the past, decipher the dense politico-theological connection of the present and envision a better future.

Schmitt fever in China

Carl Schmitt's work has drawn the attention of diverse philosophers and political theorists, such as Hannah Arendt, Walter Benjamin, Jacques Derrida, Jürgen Habermas, Antonio Negri and Slavoj Žižek, among others. In China, since Schmitt's major works were translated into the Chinese language in the 2000s, his ideas have sparked much discussion in the philosophy, political science and law departments of the universities – a phenomenon that has been dubbed the 'Schmitt fever'. A discussion of the reception of Schmitt in China enables us to understand how political theories and ideas have been appropriated in a different context for diverse purposes.

Schmitt's work was introduced to China as early as the 1930s by Xu Daolin, who came from a Chinese elite family and pursued doctoral studies in legal theory in Berlin under the direction of Rudolf Smend, a long-time friend of Schmitt. In 1931, upon Smend's referral, Xu met with Schmitt several times and the two had the opportunity to discuss China (Mitchell 2020: 192). Xu's research focused on the nature and forms of constitutional changes, and he built on the works of Smend and Schmitt on constitutional law. After his return to China in 1932, Xu became a high-level adviser in Chiang Kai-Shek's government and published essays on legal and political issues. At a time when China faced divisions by warlords from inside and pressures from outside, Xu was influenced by Schmitt's decisionist account of sovereignty and favoured a strong state with authority (Mitchell 2020: 196). With the rise of Nazism in the 1930s, German state theory was discussed in China in the context of the debate over dictatorship. Some were inspired by Schmitt, the theorist of the Führer dictatorship, and wanted China to follow Germany's example to become a dictatorial government under Chiang's leadership (Schmitt 2014). They promoted Schmitt's ideas of decisionism and the friend–enemy relationship (Schmitt 1976). Others were critical of Schmitt's work and warned against the development of fascism and ethnocentric nationalism. They espoused a kind of nationalism based on Confucian values of benevolence and virtue, and the liberal ideals of freedom and equality (Mitchell 2020: 204–12).

Schmitt was not mentioned much during the Cold War era as Chinese politics and rhetoric followed the Marxist party-line. Interest in Schmitt slowly revived in the 1980s and 1990s, when China adopted reform and liberalization policies. During the 2000s, Schmitt's works were translated into Chinese and a 'Schmitt fever' developed at a time when intellectuals debated the future of Chinese political structure amid rapid economic development. Liu Xiaofeng, a professor of cultural and political theory in Beijing, became a chief proponent of Schmitt's thought. Liu studied theology with Swiss theologian Heinrich Ott and received his PhD from the University of Basel. He considers himself a cultural Christian (in the Chinese context this means a believer who does not have church affiliation) and he is a forerunner of Sino-Christian theology. In his study of Chinese and Western political thought, Liu cautions against cultural universalism and does not think the Anglo-American style of law-based liberalism would be translatable to the Chinese context (Mitchell 2020: 234). He turns to Schmitt, who had criticized liberalism in his own time. As a Catholic, Schmitt famously argued that 'all significant concepts of the modern theory of the state are secularized theological concepts' (2005: 36). Schmitt believed that only a transcendent dimension could constitute the basis of political legitimacy. Secularism and the separation of the church and the state emptied political legitimacy of its essence. Similar to Schmitt, Liu regards the crisis of legitimacy as a fundamental problem of modernity, and he follows Schmitt's distinction between friend and enemy in the political sphere. As Zhou Lian, professor of philosophy at Renmin University in Beijing, notes, 'For Liu and Schmitt, politics identifies the essence and existence of a community.

Political sovereignty is an existential question, since it concerns the resolution of an existential conflict' (2009: 131). Zhou cautions that by emphasizing a transcendental dimension, this neo-conservative school discards history and experience and adopts a dangerous 'either/or' attitude in political decision-making (2009: 131).

Since President Xi Jinping came to power, a group of Chinese scholars has gained attention because they advocate an expansive view of state authority and support the use of heavy-handed measures to maintain national stability. This group of scholars is called the 'Statists'. Schmitt appeals to them because Schmitt supported a strong German nation by arguing that the sovereign has the power to make exceptions to the rule of law while also protecting the country from foreign enemies. Citing Schmitt, Chen Duanhong, law professor at Peking University, argues that when the stability and security of the country is at stake, state leaders have the right to suspend constitutional norms, especially provisions for civil rights. During debates on the imposition of the national security law in Hong Kong in 2020, several scholars argued that protests in Hong Kong have posed grave danger to Hong Kong's stability and prosperity. On their account, the state has the right to use whatever means necessary to bring back law and order and protect Hong Kong from infiltration by foreign forces (Chang 2020).

However, the 'liberalists' in China do not share the views of the 'Statists', and are critical of Schmitt's theories about politics and state. Some claim that Schmitt's political theories contain dangerous elements of fascism, and that he was Hitler's 'Crown Jurist'. Others argue that Schmitt tended to overemphasize extraordinary politics during emergency situations while failing to maintain a balance between extraordinary politics and daily politics, which operate according to formal laws and procedures. Some Chinese scholars are particularly averse to Schmitt's political philosophy because they find dangerous parallels in Mao Zedong's thought, particularly in his sharp distinction between friend and foe. During the revolutionary period, Mao told his cadres to join forces with friends to form a united front to attack their enemies. After the Communists took over China, the government spurred successive campaigns against landlords, the bourgeoisie, anti-revolutionaries, deviant party members and others who were labelled enemies of the people. During the Cultural Revolution (1966–76), the state completely controlled the whole society by intruding into people's private lives and reforming people's thoughts so as to eradicate the influence of enemy classes. Schmitt's idea that the sovereign can suspend constitutional order in a state of exception is deeply concerning because it reminds Chinese liberals of Mao's suspension of constitutional law during the Cultural Revolution (Zheng 2012: 32–5).

Working in a communist country that promotes atheism, scholars in China do not dwell on Schmitt's Catholic background or on his argument that the sovereign's power to suspend juridical order is akin to God's sovereignty over the universe. From a comparative perspective, we can ask, 'Are there religious underpinnings in Chinese understandings of sovereignty and the power of the state?' In Chinese tradition, people revere *Tian* (Heaven). The emperor was called *Tianzi* (the Son of Heaven) and ruled China with autocratic power. China's centuries-long monarchy was abolished only in 1911, when the last imperial dynasty was overthrown. But democracy was not developed. After the Chinese Communist Party rose to power, it mounted vigorous campaigns to purge traditional folk beliefs and what it saw as superstitions. Yet, Communism functioned almost like a state religion. During the Cultural Revolution, Mao incited personal hero worship of himself, reminiscent of a religious cult in fervour. After turmoil and disturbance, Deng Xiaoping led the country towards reform and liberalization, to restore stability. Over the past several decades, the state saw its legitimacy as dependent not on any transcendent force, but on materialist things, such as the increase of income and the growth of China's GDP. The state whips up strong nationalistic fervour whenever it is criticized from the outside, especially during the Sino-American trade wars.

A postcolonial and comparative political theology

Even though colonialism and globalization have brought different religious traditions into close proximity with one another, most books on political theology focus on Christianity alone and seldom include other traditions. A comparative approach is needed because religious difference plays a critical role in colonialism, postcolonial nation-building and globalization. A postcolonial stance goes beyond the liberal recognition of diversity and religious pluralism because that recognition does not pay sufficient attention to power asymmetry and cultural hegemony rooted in colonialism. A postcolonial and comparative political theology opens Christian political theology to wisdom from other traditions and learns from complex interactions between religion and politics in diverse colonial and postcolonial situations.

The work of John Thatamanil is important because he has challenged the ways Asian 'religions' have been studied under colonial influences. Like others before him, Thatamanil argues that 'religion' has been constructed as a universal concept imposed by the West, based on the understanding of Christianity, onto other cultures and traditions (King 1999: 35–61; Locklin and Nicholson 2010: 477–9). He points out that most of the traditions that have been labelled 'Hinduism', 'Buddhism', 'Confucianism' and 'Sikhism' have 'no conceptual analogue to "religion" prior to modernity' (Thatamanil 2020: 109). The global discourse of world religions, he says, emerges 'precisely at the moment when Western colonialism and globalization brought traditions into ever greater proximity' (Thatamanil 2020: 111). Thatamanil argues that different traditions are not self-enclosed religious systems, which can be nicely fitted into the different boxes of 'world religions', but have existed alongside each other and interacted in numerous ways. Religious identity, he surmises, is not pure or singular, but 'hybrid and polyphonic' (Thatamanil 2011: 252). He further notes that there is a power differential in the study of religion because Asian religious traditions are mined for data for Western theory, while they are not allowed to furnish conceptual resources for theoretical work, such as in philosophy of religion or theology. He writes, 'Asian religious traditions are to be thought *about*. They are not what we think *with*' (Thatamanil 2020: 121). He points out that Christian theology has hitherto remained quite insular and oblivious to claims of other religious traditions, except in the subfields of theology of religions and the newer comparative theology. Comparative theologians are self-conscious of being rooted in the Christian tradition and yet open to the wisdom of other traditions.

A postcolonial comparative political theology can use insights from other traditions to think *with* some of the categories and ideas that are important in the field. I will illustrate this by discussing the debate on secularism, Carl Schmitt's notion of sovereignty and Foucault's concept of governmentality.

Secularism is an important topic in postcolonial politics because Western liberalism has assumed that the separation between the religious and the secular is important for the development of modern democracy. As Peter van der Veer has noted, 'notions of progress, liberty, tolerance, democracy, civil society, and the public sphere converge in an all-embracing notion of secularity' (2001: 14). This leads to the view that the politicization of religion, whether it is in the Islamic states or in Christian fundamentalism, is against reason and liberty. People respond to the rise of so-called political Islam, the fatwa against Salman Rushdie, the terrorist attacks of 11 September 2001, in the United States, and subsequent attacks in Europe, with scorn and condemnation. The distinction religious/secular has impacted political discourse about immigration in the United States and Europe, and, for some, strong religious influences in the immigrant populations are symptomatic of the 'backwardness' of these communities. Thus, secularism deserves to be a serious topic of scrutiny in postcolonial critique.

Postcolonial critics and their allies have different positions on secularism. Edward Said was a staunch supporter of secularism and has cast a long shadow in the field. He criticized both the ideology of Zionism (Said 2000: 114–68) and the politics of the Islamic countries, as well as the Palestinian Liberation Organization. From his vantage point as a Palestinian American, religion has caused too much bloodshed and innumerable massacres (Robbins 2013: 249–52). Spivak is also a secularist and is equally suspicious of the so-called great religions of the world. She writes, 'the history of their greatness is too deeply imbricated in the narrative of the ebb and flow of power' (Spivak 1999: 382–3). But anthropologist Talal Asad has argued that diverse cultures and societies have understood 'the secular' differently by pushing back against Western liberal ideology of secularism. Asad uses a multi-pronged approach to study 'the secular', investigating its relation not only to religion but also to modernity, democracy, nation state and civilization. He shows that historical and political factors have caused shifting understandings of secularism in the modern West and Middle East. The production of 'secularism' as a Western political project developed at a certain period, so secularism's supposed connection to rationality or modernity should neither be taken for granted nor universalized for all societies (Asad 2003). As ideas and frameworks of governance have their own contexts, a Western model cannot be taken as normative for other societies.

The discussion of religious/secular can benefit from thinking *with* the cultural and religious traditions in China, especially with regard to the Confucian tradition. Wilfred Cantwell Smith observes that the named 'religions', such as 'Buddhism', 'Hindooism', 'Taouism' and 'Confucianism', were formulated no earlier than the nineteenth century (1962: 60–1). But Westerners have been fascinated with Confucius and his teachings for some time. Enlightenment philosophers, such as Voltaire, Rousseau, Montesquieu, Comte, Leibniz and so forth, mentioned Confucius in their emerging social, political and theological criticisms against the old political order and the church. Confucius would symbolize different things for these thinkers, reflecting European debates about self, society and the sacred during the inception of the nation state. As Lionel Jensen says, in the late eighteenth century, during a time of 'conflict between the *anciens* and the *modernes*, the image of the Chinese ancient helped shape the self-image of the [Western] modern' (1997: 8). It was later, in the nineteenth century, when the comparative study of religion was instituted at Oxford as a new field, during the heyday of British colonialism, that Max Müller and his colleague James Legge constructed 'Confucianism' as a world religion among other religions like Buddhism, Islam, Hinduism and so on (Sun 2013: 45–76).

Even though the Confucian tradition has had pervasive influences in Chinese culture, it was not construed as a religion, but more as moral philosophy. The Chinese did not have an equivalent of the modern concept of 'religion' and followed the Japanese way of translating the term 'religion' as *zongjiao*, which originally meant the teachings of a particular sect (Sun 2013: 23–4). In the early twentieth century, when the last imperial dynasty was overthrown, and the republic was formed, some Chinese intellectuals proposed having a national religion to strengthen the national and cultural identity of China on the world stage. The scholar Kang Youwei proposed having the Confucian tradition as a state religion. In his encounters with the West, Kang noted that Western countries had Christianity as the foundation of their civilization and argued that the Confucian tradition could be a force in the reform and modernization of China (Sun 2013: 21–2). His attempt was unsuccessful and was considered reactionary by other radical reformers. The conversation about whether Confucianism is a religion has not died in China; instead, it has changed with the vicissitudes of Chinese politics and the government's attitudes about religion. In the late 1970s, a prominent scholar Ren Jiyu suggested that Confucianism should be considered a religion, like Buddhism and Daoism, and that the religious components of Confucianism have been harmful to the long history of China. But in the 2000s, with liberalization, some scholars have argued for a more positive view of Confucianism as a religion in order to criticize and contest the traditional Marxist treatment of religion (Sun 2013: 77–93).

Thinking *with* the Confucian tradition shows that the religious/secular controversy has been tied to a more institutionalized understanding of religion (membership, priesthood, structure and organization). Chinese religious life is more diffuse than in some other religious contexts since religious activities are performed in the family and other settings. Thus, the boundary of the religious/secular, or sacred/profane, is not so clear-cut and defined. The abovementioned discussion also shows that both in the West and in China, the debate on religious/

secular changed over time depending on social, political and cultural factors. While there has been pressure to conform to Western notions of modernity, as defined by secularism and the separation between the church and state, other constructions of religious/secular suggest other ways of constructing global modernities that are not confined to one, single model.

Another concept that is key to political theology is sovereignty. Carl Schmitt famously wrote, 'Sovereign is he who decides on the exception' (2005: 5). The sovereign power consists in the ability to declare the exception and suspend constitutional right. He argues that the political is based on the distinction between friend and enemy – that is, who is in the body and who is out of the body (Schmitt 1976). His understanding of the political and sovereignty is very different from liberal thought. Classical liberalism assumes the autonomy of self-sufficient individuals and conflicts as faulty social arrangements that need to be resolved to bring about prosperity and peace. Schmitt believes in the primacy of conflict, and that the most basic instinct of human beings as political persons is to differentiate between friend and adversary. Classical liberalism regards sovereignty as given to individuals who can build legitimate political institutions by themselves. Schmitt treats sovereignty as ushered in by an arbitrary self-founding act by a leader or a nation (Lilla 2010).

Schmitt's decisionist account of a sovereign, analogous to a transcendent God who stands outside the universe, can hardly find a parallel in traditions such as Buddhism and Daoism, which do not presume such a transcendent being. A more productive comparison to think *with* would be Islam, a member of the Abrahamic tradition. Shāh Muḥammad Ismāʿīl (1779–1831), a South Asian Muslim reformer in the early nineteenth century, offers a Muslim political theology with a notion of sovereignty very different from Schmitt's. Ismāʿīl wrote a Persian text *Manṣab-i Imāmat* (Station of Leadership) during a time of crisis of sovereignty, when South India transitioned gradually from Mughal to British rule. According to SherAli Tareen, this text shows 'a vision of Muslim political thought and understanding of sovereignty that exceeds and subverts the modern privileging of a territorial conception of the nation-state as the centerpiece of politics' (2020: 105). For Ismāʿīl, sovereign power has less to do with defending physical borders and more to do with the maintenance of public markers of Muslim identity, especially in the public performance of everyday religious life.

Ismāʿīl offers a theory or framework of an ideal form of political orders and leaders. He contrasts two different forms of politics: salvational politics and imperial politics. Salvational politics is based on the principle of abundant love and its goal is to strive for moral reform and the elevation of salvational prospects for a community. Imperial politics is for the personal gains and desires of the ruler and neglects the responsibilities of shepherding the moral lives of one's subjects. Ismāʿīl, in contrast to Schmitt, does not see imperial sovereignty as a mirror of divine sovereignty. The ideal ruler, for Ismāʿīl, is one who fears God, respects the boundaries of sharīʿa and controls his egoistic desires. It is the responsibility of the ruler to lead his people to submit to divine law and to follow the prophets' teachings. Ismāʿīl attacks the aristocratic practices and extravagances of the

Mughal elite as well as popular superstitions, such as the veneration of the saints. Similar to Schmitt, Ismāʿīl sees the human propensity to deviate from the path of the prophets and the demands of the law. Therefore, Ismāʿīl's political theology emphasizes the integration of political power and dominance with religious piety and salvation. He advocates that political leaders should model everyday performance of religious life in a way that preserves the sovereignty of divine law (Tareen 2020: 124). Schmitt distinguishes between friend and enemy. For Ismāʿīl, the ruler could become the enemy when he becomes arrogant and immersed in earthly pursuits, thereby showing brazen contempt for divine sovereignty. In this situation, rebellion against the king to remove him is called for. Ismāʿīl does not think the monarch has absolute power and offers an understanding of sovereignty based less on juridical power than on piety and faith displayed by the ruler and his ability to maintain public markers of Muslim religious identity and life.

The third concept of political theology I want to explore briefly from a comparative perspective is governmentality. Michel Foucault uses 'governmentality' to refer to the practices of governing and the techniques of power used to manage populations and control the conduct of people. Instead of focusing on centralized sovereign rule, as Schmitt did, Foucault is more interested in the 'diffuse and decentered techniques of governance' (Singh 2018: 15) such as schooling, policing and other measures adapted to preserve or control the body politic. Foucault suggests that the Christian pastorate formed the basis of modern governmentality (2007: 147–8). As God takes care of his flock as their shepherd, the pastor has the responsibility to care for and watch over the lives of members of the congregation. Foucault's historical study and his genealogical method have yielded astute analyses of modern statecraft and details about the exercise of power, but he has been criticized as Eurocentric and silent on colonialism. Critics challenge whether his analyses of Western governmental reason and techniques of power are equally applicable to a colonial context. The adaptation of Western mechanisms of governance in the colonies was not easy and was often met with suspicion and resistance. Peter Pels observes that there were complex negotiations and struggles between colonial and Western frameworks, as well as selective adoption, which gave rise to 'alternative governmentalities' (1997: 177).

The issue Foucault raises of the relationship between religion and governmentality in a Eurocentric framework – the model of a pastor overseeing a congregation – can be studied comparatively outside the Western context. Patrice Ladwig has studied how the monks and monasteries in Theravāda Buddhism have played certain roles in establishing religious and monastic governmentality in Southeast Asia (2021). He argues that the boundary between religious and secular is much more porous and permeable in Laos or Thailand. For instance, monasticism is much more widespread in Southeast Asia than in the Christian West, and boys and men can be ordained temporarily, staying a short time in the monasteries. The Buddhist monk once served as 'peasant intellectual' and taught children reading and writing before the arrival of the state school system. Temples were the only places where education was offered before the colonial era. The French built the colonial school system by extending the networks of

Buddhist monasteries. Furthermore, the monasteries continue to play important roles in the community for social and political cohesion. Recognizing the crucial roles Buddhism plays in Laos and Cambodia, the colonial government patronized Buddhism through helping to build temples and monasteries, print books, and provide higher education for monks. But it also regulated religious organizations, including the recruitment of leaders, the duties of monks and novices, the travel of monks and the construction and renovation of religious buildings (Ladwig 2019). The French also adapted Buddhist state rituals in Laos, which were formerly used to symbolize the nobility's alliance to the Laotian kings, to the new context of the king and his vassals pledging loyalty to the French in a form of 'ritual government' (Ladwig 2019: 15). Whereas in the Western context, Foucault argues that the government has assumed the pastoral functions that the church used to perform, in the colonial context, the French worked through existing religious institutions and rituals to bolster its legitimacy and governmentality. Thus, Ladwig concludes: 'in Laos and Cambodia Buddhism was crucial for establishing an "alternative governmentality" beyond the religious-secular divide' (2021: 6).

To conclude, a political theology of post-coloniality is an interdisciplinary project that pays attention to political and social theories emerging out of anti-colonial protests, nation formation after political independence and social movements against the exploitations of economic globalization and neo-colonialism. It challenges Western political theorists and theologians when they overlook the close connections between modernity and coloniality and fail to acknowledge the darker side of modernity. Modern Western political ideas did not emerge in a vacuum but were developed in societies whose political economy and social institutions benefited from colonialism. Postcolonial politics *is* global politics because colonial legacy and imperialistic administration continue to shape our world today, from responses to the Covid-19 pandemic, to the worldwide refugee crisis, to climate change. A political theology of post-coloniality needs to be transnational and interreligious, committed to thinking *with* people of other religious traditions to build solidarity and alliances across boundaries for our common future. Given the resurgent interest in the connection between religion and politics across disciplines, it is vital for post-coloniality to pose this critique of the continued centring of Western modernity in *both* politics and the study of religion and theology. Even postmodern theories and discourse reflect this preoccupation of Western modernity. By reading Western modernity not as a teleological promise and by challenging the edifice of modern theology that justifies empire, the postcolonial turn in political theology would open up spaces for incipient theology and the emerging public.

Note

1 This chapter is adapted from different sections in Kwok (2021). A version of the chapter was presented as the Bartlett Lecture at Yale Divinity School.

References

Asad, T. (2003), *Formations of the Secular: Christianity, Islam, Modernity*, Stanford, CA: Stanford University Press.

Chang, C. (2020), 'The Nazi Inspiring China's Communists: A Decades-old Legal Argument Used by Hitler Has Found Support in Beijing', *The Atlantic*, 1 December. Available online: https://www.theatlantic.com/international/archive/2020/12/nazi-china-communists-carl-schmitt/617237/

Chen, K. H. (2010), *Asia as Method: Toward Deimperialization*, Durham, NC: Duke University Press.

Clarke, S. (2007), 'M. M. Thomas', in Kwok P. L., D. H. Compier, and J. Rieger (eds), *Empire and the Christian Tradition*, 423–37, Minneapolis, MN: Fortress Press.

Fernandez, E. S. (1994), *Toward a Theology of Struggle*, Maryknoll, NY: Orbis Books.

Foucault, M. (2007), *Security, Territory, Population: Lectures at the College de France, 1977–78*, ed. M. Senellart and A. I. Davidson, New York: Palgrave Macmillan.

Jensen, L. M. (1997), *Manufacturing Confucianism: Chinese Tradition and Universal Civilization*, Durham, NC: Duke University Press.

Kang, N. S. (2014), *Diasporic Feminist Theology: Asia and Theopoetic Imagination*, Minneapolis, MN: Fortress Press.

Kim, N. and W. A. Joh, eds (2016), *Critical Theology against U.S. Militarism in Asia: Decolonization and Deimperialization*, New York: Palgrave Macmillan.

King, R. (1999), *Orientalism and Religion: Post-Colonial Theory, India, and 'The Mythic East'*, London: Routledge.

Kwok, P. L. (2021), *Postcolonial Politics and Theology: Unraveling Empire for a Global World*. Louisville, KY: Westminster John Knox Press.

Ladwig, P. (2019), 'The Religious Foundations of Colonial Governmentality: Buddhism and Colonial Rule in Laos and French Indochina (1893–1953)', paper presented at the conference on 'De-provincializing Political Theology: Postcolonial and Comparative Approaches' at Ludwig Maximilian University of Munich, Germany, 26–27 October.

Ladwig, P. (2021), 'Thinking with Foucault Beyond Christianity and the Secular: Notes on Religious Governmentality and Buddhist Monasticism', *Political Theology*, January: 1–8. Available online: https://doi.org/10.1080/1462317X.2020.1866809

Lilla, M. (2010), 'Reading Strauss in Beijing', *The New Republic*, 17 December. Available online: https://newrepublic.com/article/79747/reading-leo-strauss-in-beijing-china-marx

Locklin, R. B. and H. Nicholson (2010), 'The Return of Comparative Theology', *Journal of the American Academy of Religion*, 78 (2): 477–514.

Mitchell, R. M. (2020), 'Chinese Receptions of Carl Schmitt Since 1929', *Penn State Journal of Law & International Affairs*, 8 (1): 182–263.

Newman, S. (2019), *Political Theology: A Critical Introduction*, Cambridge: Polity Press.

Nirmal, A. P. (1992), 'Toward a Christian Dalit Theology', *Asia Journal of Theology*, 6 (2): 297–310.

Pels, P. (1997), 'The Anthropology of Colonialism: Culture, History and the Emergence of Western Governmentality', *Annual Review of Anthropology*, 26 (1): 163–83.

Philips, E. (2012), *Political Theology: A Guide for the Perplexed*, London: T. & T. Clark International.

Robbins, B. (2013), 'Is the Postcolonial Also Postsecular?', *Boundary 2*, 40 (1): 245–62.

Said, E. W. (1994), *Culture and Imperialism*, New York: Knopf.

Said, E. W. (2000), 'Zionism from the Standpoint of Its Victims', in M. Bayoumi and A. Rubin (eds), *The Edward Said Reader*, 114–68, New York: Vintage Books.
Schmitt, C. (1976), *The Concept of the Political*, trans. G. Schwab, New Brunswick, NJ: Rutgers University Press.
Schmitt, C. (2005), *Political Theology: Four Chapters on the Concept of Sovereignty*, trans. G. Schwab, Cambridge, MA: MIT Press.
Schmitt, C. (2014), *Dictatorship: From the Origin of Modern Concept of Sovereignty to Proletarian Class Struggle*, trans. M. Hoelzl and G. Ward, Malden, MA: Polity Press.
Singh, D. (2018), *Divine Currency: The Theological Power of Money in the West*, Stanford, CA: Stanford University Press.
Smith, W. C. (1962), *The Meaning and End of Religion: A Revolutionary Approach to the Religious Traditions of Mankind*, New York: Macmillan.
Spivak, G. C. (1999), *A Critique of Postcolonial Reason: Toward a History of the Vanishing Present*, Cambridge, MA: Harvard University Press.
Sun, A. (2013), *Confucianism as a World Religion: Contested Histories and Contemporary Realities*, Princeton, NJ: Princeton University Press.
Tareen, S. (2020), 'Muslim Political Theology Before and After Empire: Shāh Muslim d Ismāʿīl's Station of Leadership (*Manā ʿīl's Stati*)', *Political Theology*, 21 (1–2): 105–25.
Thatamanil, J. (2011), 'Comparative Theology after "Religion"', in S. D. Moore and M. Rivera (eds), *Planetary Loves: Spivak, Postcoloniality, and Theology*, 238–57, New York: Fordham University Press.
Thatamanil, J. (2020), *Circling the Elephant: A Comparative Theology of Religious Diversity*, New York: Fordham University Press.
Thomas, M. M. (1960), *Christian Participation in Nation-Building*, Bangalore: National Christian Council of India.
Thomas, M. M. (1996), *The Christian Response to the Asian Revolution*, London: SCM Press.
Tran, J. (2010), *The Vietnam War and Theologies of Memory: Time and Eternity in the Far Country*, Malden, MA: Wiley-Blackwell.
van der Veer, P. (2001), *Imperial Encounters: Religion and Modernity in India and Britain*, Princeton, NJ: Princeton University Press.
Wu, Y. T. (1934), 'China's Challenges to Christianity', *Chinese Recorder*, 65: 7–11.
Wu, Y. T. (1936), 'Christianity and China's Reconstruction', *Chinese Recorder*, 67: 208–15.
Zheng, Q. (2012), 'Carl Schmitt in China', *Telos*, 160 (Fall): 29–52.
Zhou, L. (2009), 'The Most Fashionable and the Most Relevant: A Review of Contemporary Chinese Political Philosophy', *Diogenes*, 221: 128–37.

Chapter 11

POLITICAL THEOLOGY AND UNCERTAINTY IN INTERNATIONAL RELATIONS

William Bain

This chapter discusses uncertainty in international relations, with the aim of moving beyond Carl Schmitt's conceptualization of political theology to explore the limits of theological analogies. Uncertainty is a ubiquitous attribute of international relations; arbitrary power and the fear that it arouses is perhaps the most prominent source of uncertainty. Institutions are widely seen as the answer to the problem of arbitrary power. The balance of power, international law, issue-specific regimes and other arrangements are thought to mitigate uncertainty and enable regular social intercourse. Uncertainty is in this respect a problem to overcome, if not completely, then to the greatest extent possible. It is from this point of departure that the so-called paradigm debates in international relations theory take shape. Realists emphasize uncertainty arising from the ambiguous intentions of statecraft; liberals accumulate information to dissipate uncertainty and promote cooperation; and constructivists look to intersubjective interaction to resolve uncertainty into shared identities and understandings (Rathbun 2007). The objective of this chapter is to show that uncertainty in international relations runs much deeper than the usual impediments to cooperation that arise from the absence of centralized authority. To bring this to light I eschew a position within the inter-paradigm debates for one located in political theology. With the insight afforded by political theology I want to argue that, at a foundational level, uncertainty born of arbitrary power is built into international relations. Uncertainty is, in other words, a consequence of a fragmented world that is intelligible in multiple interpretive keys.

I begin by elucidating political theology as a type of historical inquiry. Political theology so understood involves something quite different from justifying politics in terms of revelation. Inquiry of this type focuses on uncovering and analysing a theological inheritance that still resonates in contemporary international relations. Next, I investigate the politics of the exception – that is, extraordinary action that contravenes the established legal order – as it emerged in theology and then migrated to politics and law. The point of interest here is a recurring analogy between God and human rulers. Popes and kings imitate God in exercising power insofar as they can act apart from the established legal order, just as God can transgress the ordinary course of nature to perform a miracle. I then explore the limits of this analogy. I argue that the divine–human analogy breaks down when the sources of authority are radically plural. Then it becomes exceedingly difficult to distinguish righteous action from arbitrary power. What appears to some as justified action will appear to others as a self-serving apology for power. This, I argue in the final section, leads to an abiding uncertainty that arises from incommensurable principles of interpretation. There is no reliable way to resolve conflict between principles without recourse to a transcendent point of reference that tells us what human beings should be or do. All that is left is an ad hoc assertion of subjective preference in pursuit of a favourable policy outcome. Uncertainty of this kind cannot be overcome, no matter how hard we might try, because it is the underlying condition of modern international relations.

Faith and history

Political theology involves the analysis of politics in the context of God's nature and attributes, and his relation to the created world. Thus, theological ideas and concepts are used to comment on sources of authority, exercising power, constructing political institutions and other related questions. Augustine, for example, asserts that the power to grant kingdoms, pagan no less than Christian, belongs to God alone (1998: 228). Theology and politics are similarly mingled in the early modern theory of the divine right of kings, enough so that the now familiar distinction between church and state obscures the critical analogy between divine authority and human authority (Figgis 1922: 11). Of course, analogies of this sort are as old as political thought itself: as with God, so too with kings and popes. Such analogies bring the Bible, ecclesiastical and political thought, jurisprudence and literature together in a shared language of correspondence. Not only do human rulers derive their power from God, but they also exercise it in a manner that resembles God's government of the universe (Kahn 2009; Oakley 2006: ch. 5). The correspondence of divine and human is intelligible in quintessentially modern texts that are widely seen – problematically to be sure – as making a decisive break with divine authority. Thomas Hobbes's political philosophy is a particularly apposite example in this instance. Transfixed by the perils of the state of nature and the move to civil society, most readers neglect what Hobbes says on the first page of *Leviathan*. There he says human beings can make a commonwealth as God made the universe: 'the *Pacts* and *Covenants*, by which the parts of this Body Politique were at first made, set together, and united, resemble that *Fiat*, or the *Let us make man*, pronounced by God in the Creation' (Hobbes 2012/vol. 2: 16, emphasis in original).

But discerning what political theology contributes to our understanding of politics, extant and potential, is often met with suspicion, if not outright hostility. Suspicion follows from the deeply internalized assumption that secular politics is the inevitable outcome of modernization (Berger 1990: ch. 5). Therefore, allowing theological discourse to intrude into politics is regressive and, for some, imprudent because it is liable to stir passions and inflame grievances. Mark Lilla warns against the complacency of assuming that secular politics will persist without effort. Severing the link between theology and politics – the Great Separation as he calls it – is a noble experiment rather than a historical inevitability. Political theology threatens this separation because it is a 'primordial' form of thought that yokes a biblical politics to the promise of redemption on earth (Lilla 2007: 4, 58). And when redemption is the prize, the modest but workable goals of coexistence and civility will always appear as second-best compared to attaining ultimate truth. Herein lies the danger: subsuming political life to a theological vision runs the grave risk of creating a giant prison. For Lilla, those who mingle politics and theology are destined, like the sorcerer's apprentice, to be 'swept away by spiritual forces beyond their control' (2007: 308). Suspicion of political theology gives way to hostility given its close association with Carl Schmitt. His membership in the Nazi Party and full-throated defence of the regime's policies provide powerful incentives to discount political theology as regressive and dangerous. Critics, unwilling to detach Schmitt's thought from his action, draw a straight line from extra-legal action – the miracle in jurisprudence – and Hitler seizing absolute power in 1933.

Indiscriminate usage complicates any assessment of political theology and its contribution. Conflating distinct understandings elides important differences in identity and purpose. To dispel confusion, it is useful to distinguish faith and history. Political theology viewed from the standpoint of faith holds out divine revelation as the ultimate ground of politics. Romans 13:1 is the best-known source of authority for this understanding: 'Let every soul be subject unto the higher powers. For there is no power but of God: the powers that be are ordained by God.' But this position does not lead to an uncompromising fideism. Questions such as 'Who shall rule?' and 'Why should I obey?' can be addressed from more than one perspective. Philosophers, orators and historians all have something to contribute, but revelation is the final arbiter of knowledge furnished by reason, rhetoric, usage and custom. Thus, Augustine maintains that when we practise philosophy according to God, human wisdom and divine revelation disclose a harmonious relationship that is mediated by Scripture (1998: 325–9). In contrast, political theology viewed from the standpoint of history comprehends political ideas in the context of theological antecedents. This contributes to greater self-understanding in a world where God is no longer at the centre of human thought and action. Cast in this mode, political theology recovers what is concealed from sight: a theological inheritance that persists in a secular world, even among those who self-consciously disavow faith. Political theology conceived along these lines has an important role in de-centring myths that ratify founding moments like the purported secularization of international relations by the Peace of Westphalia. It also corrects dubious interpretations of canonical figures and deepens understanding of cardinal concepts, such as anarchy, balance of power and international law (Bain 2020: chs 7–8).

For better or worse, Schmitt provides what is perhaps the iconic account of this historical understanding of political theology. He writes in the essay

Political Theology: '[a]ll significant concepts of the modern theory of the state are secularized theological concepts' (Schmitt 1985: 36). By this he means two things: First, political concepts – sovereignty above all else – originated in the domain of theology and subsequently migrated to the domain of politics and law. Second, and essential to making sense of this historical development, theological ideas and political ideas bear a structural resemblance that conditions the possibilities of political life. There is, then, a continuous thread that joins theology, metaphysics and politics in a comprehensive world view: '[t]he metaphysical image that a definite epoch forges of the world has the same structure as what the world immediately understands to be appropriate as a form of its political organization' (Schmitt 1985: 46). Taken together, historical development and structural resemblance provide the basis of a recurring analogy between the divine and the human. For example, the all-powerful God portrayed in the book of Job is the model for Hobbes's commonwealth, which he describes as a '*Mortall God*, to which wee owe under the *Immortall God*, our peace and defence' (2012/vol. 2: 260). In this respect, political theology provides a history of our intellectual culture by explaining, for example, how we came to imagine ourselves as inhabiting a world composed of sovereign states or one ordered according to the principle of anarchy. Inquiry of this kind involves something quite different from justifying this image of international relations – or any other political arrangement for that matter – in terms of revealed truth. It is one step removed from the business of theological justification in that it focuses on describing, analysing and understanding the theological character of our political vocabulary.

Nothing is more salient in this regard than the decisionist politics of sovereignty and exceptional action that transgresses the established international legal order. Here, normal political life stands in tension with what is sometimes required to preserve or restore normal politics. Divine omnipotence is the model for this type of action. As Schmitt explains, '[t]he exception in jurisprudence is analogous to the miracle in theology' (1985: 36). Human rulers can contravene the law to remedy injustice, just as God divided the waters to the Red Sea, contrary to the ordinary course of nature, to save the children of Israel from the Pharaoh's pursuing army (Exod. 14:13–31). Some of the most contentious issues in international relations are intelligible in the politics of the exception. Such action elicits objections precisely because it cannot be codified or regulated (Schmitt 1985: 6, 12–13). The 'ticking bomb' scenario is but one case in point. Contravening the absolute prohibition of torture to secure the safety of the people marks the moment at which law dissolves into power. This, of course, sits uneasily with a liberal international order that seeks to regularize power by subjecting it to rules of law. I want to interrogate the theological antecedents of the exception for what it suggests about international relations. My aim in doing so is to provide a better history of a practice that is condemned more often than theorized. Indeed, there is no equivalent in international relations scholarship of what Giorgio Agamben's *The State of Exception* (2005) is in political theory. But, more than that, I want to show that political theology discloses a practical dimension that illuminates the thoroughgoing uncertainty of contemporary international relations. To relate past and present I shall explore the character of divine power and the way in which it tracks on to political power.

Two kinds of power

In a letter to Eustochium, laying out requirements for a properly chaste life, Jerome (c. 347–420) suggests: 'although God can do all things, He cannot raise up a virgin after she has fallen. He has power, indeed, to free her from the penalty, but He has no power to crown one who has been corrupted' (Jerome 1963: 138). This proposition serves as the foil for a centuries-long debate about the nature and extent of God's power. The immediate implication is that God possesses the power to determine and order but that, once established, he cannot alter or transgress what he has established. God can, in the act of creation, will that the heavenly bodies move in a circular motion, but he cannot, at a later point in time, will that they move in a rectilinear motion. What is more, God is incapable of making more than one world or making a better world than the one he created. To some commentators this view impermissibly infringed God's freedom. Peter Damian, responding to Jerome nearly seven centuries later, defends God's freedom to perform opposites, arguing: 'whatever God was able [to do], he is also able [to do] it, because his present never turns into the past, his today does not change into tomorrow or into any alteration of time' (1996: 301). God, being eternal, transcends the category of time; he is neither before nor after time, but beyond time. Divine activity is coeternal with God, which means he possesses the capacity to do all things. Consequently, it cannot be true that God is incapable of doing what he chooses not to do (Damian 1996: 298, 302). Peter Damian believed that he had done enough to put an end to this debate, but speculation about God's freedom continued well into the modern period, when secular sensibilities are thought to have loosened the grip of mediaeval religiosity.

The politics of the exception in contemporary international relations develops out of this debate. Mediaeval theologians theorized divine freedom by distinguishing *potentia dei absoluta* from *potentia dei ordinata*, or God's absolute power and ordained or ordinary power (Oakley 1999). They invoked this distinction to vindicate God's freedom while affirming the regularity of created order – natural, salvific and moral. The point was to sustain the claim that God does not act out of necessity, thus created order can, in principle, be other than it presently is (Oakley 1999: 282). It is important to note, before proceeding further, that the *potentia* distinction can be interpreted in two ways. According to the so-called classical interpretation, *potentia absoluta* refers to God's power considered in itself, without regard for what he has, in fact, established *de potentia ordinate* (Oakley 1999: 287; Courtenay 1974: 39). Aquinas illustrates this understanding when, citing the case of Jerome's fallen virgin, he says God cannot do what manifestly implies a contradiction. He can take away her corruption, but he cannot remove the fact that she was once corrupted. This does not mean that God is subject to the order he established; possibilities that fall outside the scope of ordinate power remain within the scope of absolute power (Aquinas 2006/vol. 5: 171). As William Courtenay explains, these powers constitute a dialectic that affirms God's freedom and the contingency of the created order. Absolute power refers to 'the total possibilities *initially* open to God, some of which were realized by creating the established order; the unrealized possibilities are now only hypothetically possible' (Courtenay 1974: 39, emphasis in original). Equating absolute power with what is hypothetically possible does not, therefore, refer to one of two ways that God can act or might act, one ordinary and the other miraculous (Courtenay 1974: 39–40; Oakley 1999: 297).

The juristic interpretation of the *potentia* distinction makes room for what the classical interpretation excludes, namely a mode of divine action by which God can contravene the ordinary course of created order. The focus here is on an active power, rather than a statement of logical possibility, which is modelled on a biblical God of power and might (Oakley 1999: 330). John Duns Scotus laid the foundation for this interpretation when he asserted that when the law and what the law prescribes are in the power of an agent it is possible, actually rather than hypothetically, for that agent to order things differently than they are at present. Thus, God can act apart from what he freely chose to establish *de potentia ordinata*. By his absolute power he can suspend the existing order, or he can establish a different order altogether. Significantly, what is true of God is true of any free agent. Duns Scotus says that with 'any free agent that can act both in accordance with the dictate of correct law and outside or contrary to such a law, one must distinguish between ordered [ordained] and absolute power' (2017: 95–6). He makes good on the parallel between divine power and royal power when he says that, like God, kings prescribe general laws according to which they act ordinately (Duns Scotus 2017: 97). With this analogy the *potentia* distinction is redefined, inaugurating a fertile period of intellectual development that spilled over the walls of theology into the domain of politics. And this, in turn, shaped early modern thinking about sovereignty, bridging what is normally kept apart: a mediaeval inheritance that is habitually thought to have been superseded by the achievements of modernity.

This inheritance remains largely hidden because theorists of international relations typically look in the wrong places. They take little notice of thought that conceives the mediaeval church as a political community over which a monarch presides (Kantorowicz 1981: 206). It is through this portal that the juristic understanding of absolute power passed into political discourse. For example, the canon lawyer Hostiensis argues that in extraordinary situations, the pope can do by his absolute power what cannot be done by his ordained power (Oakley 1999: 282–3). Likewise, the theologian Giles of Rome says fullness of power entails the ability to do directly what is otherwise done indirectly through a secondary cause. The pope can act as a primary cause, like God, because he is 'free to use his power to act beyond these laws and beyond the usual course' (Giles 2004: 369). We find something similar in James I's defence of royal prerogative. Kings imitate God in exercising power; they 'haue power to exalt low things, and abase high things' (James I 1918: 308). The language of absolute power is similarly intelligible in the writings of those who are credited with paving the way for modern secular politics. Hugo Grotius asserts that miracles signify God's resolution to act 'out of the ordinary Course of Nature', the law of which is by his appointment and in his power (Grotius 2012: 44–5). Hobbes, also speaking of miracles, distinguishes what is done by natural means, through an order of secondary causes, and what is done directly 'by the immediate hand of God' (Hobbes 2012/vol. 3: 682). And John Locke maintains that God can alter the ordinary course of natural things by overturning established principles of knowledge; or he can annihilate the existing order and create something else (Locke 1954: 259; King 1829: 123–4; Oakley 1997: 647–8).

An observation and a question follow this exploration of divine power and the way in which it presents in a political context. The observation is that it illustrates what I understand as political theology operating in a historical mode. It elucidates the *potentia* distinction that mediaeval theologians used to theorize divine power and explains its migration from theology to politics, ecclesiastical and secular. It recovers a way of thinking about power that is embedded in early modern political thought but has been lost or simply ignored because it does not fit the dominant secular narrative. And it highlights the structural resemblance between the juristic interpretation of the *potentia* distinction and the modern politics of the exception that evokes interest and consternation among theorists of international relations (Agamben 2005; Huysman 2006). In this respect, divine omnipotence provides a model for extraordinary action in human affairs. But we are left to ask – and here the question becomes apparent – what exactly does this exploration of mediaeval and early modern thought contribute to understanding the exception in the present? Does political theology offer anything more than a statement to the effect that the modern exception has roots in mediaeval theology? Or does political theology look forward as well as backward in casting light on current problems? There should be no doubt that political theology offers a better history of the theological origins of modern political concepts. That granted, I want to claim more than a better history that locates the exception in esoteric speculation about fallen virgins. Political theology contributes to understanding the present by illuminating the limits of theological analogies. I want to argue that the analogy between divine action and human action breaks down at a certain point, which effaces the line between rightful freedom and arbitrary power.

Power, restraint and faith

Exercising power inevitably invites conflicting interpretations. What one sees as righteous action, another sees as an unconscionable transgression of settled law. This much is evident in the discourse of humanitarian intervention, nuclear non-proliferation, counterterrorism and so much else. The Israeli air strike on the Osirak nuclear reactor in 1981 is one example that I submit in place of many. Invoking the inherent right of self-defence enshrined in Article 51 of the United Nations Charter, Israel justified the attack as 'an elementary act of self-preservation' (UNSC 1981a: 8). Japan condemned the same event as an 'outrageous action' and

China called it a 'barbarous crime of aggression' (UNSC 1981b: 8–9). Even the United States, Israel's closest ally, criticized the attack as being inimical to regional peace and security (UNSC 1981c: 3–4). Of course, states and the persons who represent them do not always adhere to rules and norms that they voluntarily accept. This is so, as Schmitt observes, because general rules are situational in the circumstances; hence, the politics of the exception cannot be subsumed to the constraints of law, no matter how hard one might try (1985: 13). But accepting the extra-legal character of the exception does not forsake all manner of restraint. The discourse of extraordinary action in mediaeval and early modern usage is tempered by considerations of common welfare or the public good. For example, papal power might be 'without limit of number, weight, and measure', but the use of absolute power must not be indiscriminate; it is conditional insofar as it is justified by reasonable cause and is consistent with the spiritual mission of the church. This conditionality extends to occasional intervention in temporal affairs, in 'special circumstances', when they impinge on spiritual concerns (Giles 2004: 307, 321, 361–71).

The power to perform the equivalent of a miracle in politics must be interpreted against the backdrop of God's self-imposed promise to uphold what he freely chose to establish. That is to say, God's promise is the bulwark that protects the regularity of order from the intrusion of unconstrained and, therefore, unpredictable power. So, while God can contravene what he willed into existence by performing a miracle, he can also bind himself to govern the universe according to what is ordinarily the case (Oakley 1984: 62, 84, 112). Moreover, human beings can repose confidence in God's promise because of his undefilable nature: to say God is God is also to say God is good. God neither jokes nor deceives when he promises, thus there is no danger that he will suddenly overturn created order, plunging all of humankind in a permanent state of uncertainty. Again, the parallel with human rulers is easy to discern. In a speech given in the Star Chamber, James I declared his intention to uphold the established order of the commonwealth, resolving 'to renew my promise and Oath made at my Coronation concerning Iustice, and the promise therein for maintenance of the Law of the Land' (1994: 208). God's government and the rewards he offers as an incentive for observing his laws preserves the intelligibility and integrity of this declaration. James observes in this regard: 'I haue only GOD to answere to, and to expect punishment at his hands, if I offend' (1994: 211). It is this modicum of restraint – the prospect of God's punishment – that demarcates the limits of human power. God's immutable goodness guarantees the reliability of created order, and politics, insofar as the activity of ruling must be consistent with what God has ordained.

But confidence in promises given by human rulers quickly dissipates when this guarantee is no longer believable and when the sources of authority are radically plural. It is useful to recall at this point that political theology experienced a revival in the early twentieth century in response to the historicist claim that meaning arises from standards of judgement, reasoning and value that are immanent in history (Kahn 2012: 236). Unsurprisingly, historicism nourished a cultural relativism that called into question universal and, indeed, trans-historical principles of evaluation. For example, nineteenth-century thinkers interpreted the meaning of progress in terms of social adaptation, rooted in Darwinian science, which supported an optimistic account of progress and human perfectibility (Bury 1932: ch. 19; Passmore 2000: ch. 12). In time, however, optimism gave way to pessimism following the human and material destruction wrought by the First World War. That the ostensible meaning of history could be harnessed to aggressive nationalism and doctrines of racial superiority laid bare a crisis of confidence in Western civilization itself. Triumphal stories about a progressive march from barbarism to civilization fell to the side as the war provided a sobering reminder of the barbarism lurking not far beneath the surface of what the self-proclaimed custodians of enlightenment portrayed as the apex of human development (Kahn 2011: 23–6; Hall 2019: 173–8). The British international relations scholar Martin Wight channelled this anxiety when he remarked that belief in progress – expressed as self-determination, social justice, democracy and so forth – had proven to be an ephemeral substitute for the bedrock once provided by natural law. But, with the path of progress blocked and a return to natural law unlikely, he feared that the abyss of nihilism might be the only plausible path forward (Wight 2005: 44; Bain 2014: 943–60; Hall 2006: ch. 6).

Political theology, its advocates believed, held out an interpretative key that could fix meaning and draw civilization back from the edge of the abyss. Yet doubt remains. In the aftermath of another calamitous world war Hans Morgenthau suggested that '[t]he state has become indeed a "mortal God," and for an age that believes no longer in an immortal God, the state becomes the only God there is' (1945: 15). This passage, while illuminating, is only partially correct. The abiding uncertainty of modern international relations can be attributed to the absence of a transcendent good or final cause that guides human conduct to an end that indicates what human beings should do and be. But, as Morgenthau readily concedes, God's goodness and the reliability of his promise are no longer available to guarantee the integrity of international political order or to restrain these mortal gods. Universal human rights provide the most compelling rejoinder to the cultural relativism of historicism, and with it, the unfettered freedom of the modern state in a world that no longer believes in an immortal God. Human rights invest human relations with a purpose and unifying goal that it otherwise lacks. But is it enough? The French philosopher Jacques Maritain intimated an uncomfortable answer when he said, shortly after the adoption of the Universal Declaration of Human Rights, that we agree on human rights on the condition that no one asks us why (1950: 9). The worry here is that in a purely constructed world there is little room for anything that is truly universal, much less eternal. This includes principles that are meant to impose limits on the exercise of power because, in a world where everything is made and nothing is discovered, they too are contingent artefacts of human decision.

But Morgenthau exaggerates when he says the modern state is all there is, loosed from all restraint in a world that no longer believes in God. Political theology, as a mode of historical inquiry, draws attention to theological concepts and analogies that invest the state, and its relations with other states, with meaning it otherwise lacks. This should temper the conceit of hagiographic narratives of secularization that banish God from the cathedral of international relations; it underscores, as well, the extent to which theology shapes the way in which theorists of international relations interpret their subject. The so-called resurgence of religion provides a powerful, and at times violent, reminder – if any was needed – that God is not yet dead to all men and women. But taking the claims of political theology seriously does not lead to the concomitant conclusion that nihilism is the alternative to God. Belief in God is only one of several possible ways of ascribing meaning and justifying what human beings make and do (Taylor 2007: 3). In addition to God, rational autonomy, human dignity and common humanity, or perhaps economic justice or environmental protection, can be invoked to ascribe meaning in international relations and to keep the ignorance and violence of barbarism at bay. Here, the student of political theology sits alongside the Kantian moralist and the human rights activist, with each trying to make sense of the world in their own distinctive way. The international realm conceived along these lines is a self-sufficient order that can be understood and explained on its own terms, albeit from the standpoint of more than one interpretive key.

Faith is important in this context, even for those who assiduously disavow belief in God. The believer reposes confidence in the authority of divine revelation and conclusions of reason that derive from theologically acceptable premises. What is less well understood is that the non-believer, while insisting that unverifiable gods and spirits have no place in scholarly inquiry, also reposes confidence in unverifiable premises. Faith in this context does not refer to belief in a transcendent entity, such as the personal God of Christianity or the gods of Greek and Norse mythology. Yet, what Jews, Christians and Muslims hold by faith is not altogether different from what the social scientist assumes. To explain relationships between observed phenomena the social scientist relies on assumptions to generate testable hypotheses. Indeed, the activity of science itself rests on ideas that cannot be derived from or proved by scientific inquiry. The scientist assumes the orderliness of the universe before setting off to investigate it, otherwise the universe is inaccessible to scientific knowledge (Torrance 1981: 26–7). In this respect, belief in God is not unlike belief in rational autonomy, human dignity or some other fundamental postulate. They rest on an unevident decision – a stipulation of will – in the quest for knowledge (Strauss 1997: 29). That is to say, these ideas are presupposed for the purpose of explanation; and explanation is possible only so far as those who grant them believe they are useful. Thus, the problem is not one of tension between faith and reason or the fact that God's existence cannot be demonstrated; it arises from incommensurable postulates that are asserted and then sustained by belief in what is asserted.

The malaise of uncertainty

In conditions of plural belief and rationality, the politics of the exception is likely to resemble justified action to some and an apology for power to others.

Unlike the theological original and its political cognates, extraordinary action in contemporary international relations founders on the shoals of subjective preference masquerading as universal truth. What processes under the banner of 'illegal but legitimate', the righteous vindication of self-determination, democracy and human rights in Kosovo, is also portrayed as an ideologically motivated breach of the UN Charter (IICK 2000: 4; Koskenniemi 2002: 161–2). So, given multiple keys of interpretation, how does one distinguish exceptional action for the benefit of the community – however that might be conceived – from capricious power? God's goodness mediates what constitutes reasonable cause for extraordinary action only for those that share that premise. Likewise, rational autonomy will yield a plausible justification only for those who accept that premise. But there is no common standard that can be called upon to resolve conflicts between premises, much less tell us that one is better than another. In posing this question I do not mean to suggest that mediaeval theologians always agreed on such matters. The difference between then and now is that they argued over *the* truth, while today we argue over multiple truths that cannot be reconciled no matter how much effort and imagination we exert. There is, then, little alternative apart from simply choosing between postulates; we assert a preference for one among many and attribute to it a transcendent character that is used to confer legitimacy on a favoured position.

Political theology brings to light the implications of this choice. Uncovering the theological ground of the exception draws attention to its structure and meaning in contemporary politics and international relations. This, after all, is the basis of Schmitt's influential claim that the exception in politics is analogous to the miracle in theology. But political theology offers more than an account of forerunners and antecedents that explains how 'we' came to find ourselves 'here'. A genealogy, no matter how thorough, is unlikely to appeal to theorists who are consumed by the fury of the present. Pointing out that the exception in politics can be traced to mediaeval debates about God's omnipotence is, to the practically minded theorist, 'about as interesting and important as learning that English works have their origin in old Norse' (Kahn 2011: 3). If political theology is to offer anything more than 'just history', it must show that theological ideas continue to exert a logic that structures how we know and explain the world. An important part of this task is to show that international relations might not be secular in the way it is typically thought to be. But focusing too intently on the persistence of theological ideas in modern thought might unhelpfully direct attention away from how inherited ideas, analogies and metaphors have changed over time. Here, political theology assumes a diagnostic role that uncovers incoherence and contradiction in accepted ways of thinking. It shows, for example, that the politics of the exception in contemporary international relations is a problematic copy of the theological original.

The exception was deployed in mediaeval theology to reconcile God's freedom with the regular order of nature. It provided the basis of certainty by aligning what is revealed in Scripture with ordinary lived experience, that fire warms and the sun rises in the east. As such, the universe, though utterly dependent on the divine will, discloses a reliable pattern of order in which human beings can have confidence. In politics, both papal and regal, the exception refers to discretionary action that is justified by common benefit. However, the laws of God and the laws of nature constrain this power of derogation such that popes and kings should act in accordance with the established political and legal order. But subtract God from this picture and certainty dissolves into uncertainty. There is no settled way of resolving conflicts between fundamental values. Where belief in God is one possibility among many it is left to the theorist to resolve plurality into unity; and that might involve God, or it might not. Conflicts between universal rights and cultural diversity, or the sanctity of the human person and the security of the community, are resolved on an ad hoc basis, typically by balancing competing interests. The superiority of one value is asserted at *this* particular time and for *this* particular purpose, albeit disguised and then projected as universal. The point here, as Kahn puts it, is that '[e]verything is relative, until it is not' (2011: 118). In bringing this to the surface, political theology diagnoses the malaise of modern international relations. The exception cannot help but look like an apology for power in a fragmented world that can be interpreted with reference to multiple postulates. Uncertainty rather than nihilism is the result. However, this uncertainty is not a problem that can be solved; it is the underlying condition of modern international relations.

References

Agamben, G. (2005), *The State of Exception*, Chicago, IL: University of Chicago Press.

Aquinas, T. (2006), *Summa Theologiae*, vol. 5, ed. T. Gilby, Cambridge: Cambridge University Press.

Augustine (1998), *The City of God Against the Pagans*, ed. and trans. R. W. Dyson, Cambridge: Cambridge University Press.

Bain, W. (2014), 'Rival Traditions of Natural Law: Martin Wight and the Theory of International Society', *International History Review*, 36 (5): 943–60.

Bain, W. (2020), *Political Theology of International Order*, Oxford: Oxford University Press.

Berger, P. (1990), *The Sacred Canopy: Elements of a Sociological Theory of Religion*, New York: Anchor Books.

Bury, J. B. (1932), *The Idea of Progress: An Inquiry Into Its Growth and Origin*, New York: Dover Publications.

Courtenay, W. (1974), 'Nominalism and Late Medieval Religion', in C. Trinkaus and H. Oberman (eds), *The Pursuit of Holiness in Late Medieval and Renaissance Religion*, 26–59, Leiden: E. J. Brill.

Duns Scotus, J. (2017), *John Duns Scotus: Selected Writings on Ethics*, ed. and trans. T. Williams, Oxford: Oxford University Press.

Figgis, J. N. (1922), *The Divine Right of Kings*, 2nd edn, Cambridge: Cambridge University Press.

Giles of Rome (2004), *On Ecclesiastical Power*, ed. and trans. R. W. Dyson, New York: Columbia University Press.

Grotius, H. (2012), *The Truth of the Christian Religion*, ed. M. R. Antognazza, Indianapolis: Liberty Fund.
Hall, I. (2006), *The International Thought of Martin Wight*, Basingstoke: Palgrave.
Hall, I. (2019), 'The English School's Histories and International Relations', in B. Schmidt and N. Guilhot (eds), *Historiographical Investigations in International Relations*, 171–202, Basingstoke: Palgrave Macmillan.
Hobbes, T. (2012), *Leviathan*, 3 vols., ed. N. Malcolm, Oxford: Clarendon Press.
Huysmans, J. (2006), 'International Politics of Exception: Competing Visions of International Political Order Between Law and Politics', *Alternatives: Global, Local, Political*, 31 (2): 135–65.
IICK. (2000), *Kosovo Report: Conflict, International Response, Lessons Learned*, Oxford: Oxford University Press.
James, I. (1918), *The Political Works of James I*, Cambridge, MA: Harvard University Press.
James, I. (1994), *Political Writings*, ed. J. Sommerville, Cambridge: Cambridge University Press.
Jerome (1963), 'Letter 22', in *The Letters of St Jerome*, vol. 1., trans. C. C. Mierow, New York: Newman Press.
Kahn, P. (2011), *Political Theology: Four New Chapters on the Concept of Sovereignty*, New York: Columbia University Press.
Kahn, V. (2009), 'Political Theology and Fiction in *The King's Two Bodies*', *Representations*, 106 (1): 77–101.
Kahn, V. (2012), 'Political Theology and Liberal Culture: Strauss, Schmitt, Spinoza, and Arendt', in G. Hammill, J. R. Lupton and E. Balibar (eds), *Political Theology and Early Modernity*, 23–43, Oxford: Oxford University Press.
Kantorowicz, E. (1981), *The King's Two Bodies: A Study in Mediaeval Political Theology*, Princeton, NJ: Princeton University Press.
King, P. (ed.) (1829), *The Life of John Locke*, London: Henry Colburn.
Koskenniemi, M. (2002), '"The Lady Doth Protest Too Much": Kosovo, and the Turn to Ethics in International Law', *Modern Law Review*, 65 (2): 159–75.
Lilla, M. (2007), *The Stillborn God: Religion, Politics, and the Modern West*, New York: Alfred A. Knopf.
Locke, J. (1954), *Essays on the Law of Nature*, trans. W. von Leyden, Oxford: Clarendon Press.
Maritain, J. (1950), 'Introduction', in Unesco (ed.), *Human Rights: Comments and Interpretations*, 9–17 London: Allan Wingate.
Morgenthau, H. (1945), 'The Evil of Politics and the Ethics of Evil', *Ethics*, 56 (1): 1–18.
Oakley, F. (1984), *Omnipotence, Covenant, and Order: An Excursion in the History of Ideas from Abelard to Leibniz*, Ithaca: Cornell University Press.
Oakley, F. (1997), 'Locke, Natural Law and God—Again', *History of Political Thought*, 18 (4): 624–51.
Oakley, F. (1999), *Politics and Eternity: Studies in the History of Medieval and Early-Modern Political Thought*, Leiden: Brill.
Oakley, F. (2006), *Kingship: The Politics of Enchantment*, Oxford: Blackwell Publishing.
Passmore, J. (2000), *The Perfectibility of Man*, 3rd edn, Indianapolis: Liberty Fund.
Peter Damian (1996), 'Letter on Divine Omnipotence', in A. Schoedinger (ed.), *Readings in Medieval Philosophy*, 296–303, Oxford: Oxford University Press.
Rathbun, B. (2007), 'Uncertain About Uncertainty: Understanding the Multiple Meanings of a Crucial Concept in International Relations Theory', *International Studies Quarterly*, 51 (3): 533–57.

Schmitt, C. (1985), *Political Theology: Four Chapters on the Concept of Sovereignty*, trans. G. Schwab, Chicago, IL: University of Chicago Press.
Strauss, L. (1997), *Spinoza's Critique of Religion*, trans. E. M. Sinclair, Chicago, IL: University of Chicago Press.
Taylor, C. (2007), *A Secular Age*, Cambridge, MA: Harvard University Press.
Torrance, T. (1981), *Divine and Contingent Order*, Oxford: Oxford University Press.
UNSC. (1981a), Security Council Official Records, 2280th Meeting, 12 June 1981, S/PV.2280.
UNSC. (1981b), Security Council Official Records, 2282th Meeting, 15 June 1981, S/PV.2282.
UNSC. (1981c), Security Council Official Records, 2288th Meeting, 19 June 1981, S/PV.2288.
Wight, M. (2005), *Four Seminal Thinkers in International Theory*, ed. G. Wight and B. Porter, Oxford: Oxford University Press.

CODA TO PART 4:

ASIA AND THE POLITICAL THEOLOGY TURN
REVISITING AND OVERCOMING SCHMITT IN THE CENTENARY

Milinda Banerjee

The political context for the political theology turn

In recent years, there has been a remarkable surge in scholarship that uses optics of political theology to analyse Asian history and society across the colonial and postcolonial epochs. Or, at least, that is the argument this short chapter advances as a point of provocation – urging a broad reflection that coincides with the centenary of Carl Schmitt's publication of *Political Theology*. During the Cold War, for both the political right and the political left, (ostensibly) secular ideologies of modernity and progress were hegemonic. The global political and cultural landscape has transformed dramatically since then. I would argue that these changes have precipitated the rise of political theology as an academic category in Asian studies. The (so-called) 'War on Terror'; the explosion of various forms of radical religious politics across Asia (and the Americas, Europe and Africa); the rise of majoritarian strongman nationalisms, often explicitly or implicitly organized through the grammar of 'one leader, one (dominant) religion, one nation': these, I suggest, provide the obvious backdrop for this rise in scholarship on political theology (Banerjee, 2018b). Such processes have nourished a growing incredulity towards secular-modernist grand narratives of progress, and created an opening for perspectives of political theology which had not existed earlier in scholarship on Asia.

For reasons of space and argumentative cohesion, this chapter focuses on South Asia and West Asia. Caesarist political theologies celebrating sacred monarchs are especially ascendant in public culture and popular imagination in these regions: from Bollywood movies in Narendra Modi's India to television epics in Recep Tayyip Erdoğan's Turkey. The latter have even been at the centre of dramatic conflicts, in a landscape where Saudi Arabia's Crown Prince Mohammed Bin Salman accused Erdoğan of attempting to resurrect an Ottoman Caliphate (Bhutto 2019).

Defining political theology for Asian studies

Political theology is understood here in two intersecting ways. First, a body of scholarship that draws, even if critically, upon the classic European theoretical canon of political theology, self-consciously named as such: from the age of Carl Schmitt (1985) and Ernst Kantorowicz (1957), to, more recently, Giorgio Agamben (2011). Second, any scholarship which examines how political forms and theological forms nourish and saturate each other: for example, in constructing models of sovereignty, political economy, revolution and much more.

The theological should be understood capaciously here: not just in terms of the monotheistic God, but also in terms of deities as well as sacral law. In Hindu and Buddhist Asia, the monism of sacral law (*dharma*) often anchors political unification and monistic sovereignty. The unity of *dharma* anchors the ideological unity of the nation state. Admittedly, the divine as being also often plays a vital role here, with periodic tendencies towards monotheistization of the pantheon.

Political theology as academic category in South and West Asian studies

The first monograph to offer a comprehensive intellectual history of modern Indian political and social thought, with political theology as the central prism and explicitly drawing upon the European theoretical canon, was published in 2018 (Banerjee 2018a). In that same year, a doctoral dissertation on the origins of political theology in colonial India was defended (Mou Banerjee 2018), and a journal special section on 'Political Theology in India' was published (Devji Mukhopadhyay and Giri 2018). The trinity of Schmitt, Kantorowicz and Agamben reappear in a recent edited volume on South Asian sovereignty (Gilmartin, Price and Ruud 2019). Schmitt and political theology have also entered the field of early modern Indian history (Simmons 2020). This rise in political-theological scholarship is to be expected at a time when muscular and Caesarist Hindu nationalism is forging ahead in India, with political theism saturating public rhetoric, above all, that of Prime Minister Narendra Modi. One must, however, also take into account more emancipatory struggles, such as the upsurge of Dalit/lower-caste politics and theology in India: this has inspired a new monograph on subaltern public and political theology (Patrick 2020; see also Kumar 2015).

Meanwhile, in the field of Islamic intellectual history, the term 'political theology' appeared in the title of a doctoral dissertation already in 2013; the thesis referenced Schmitt in detail while discussing Iranian political thought. Given the paradigmatic importance of the Iranian Revolution in the contemporary world, this focus appears as no surprise (Sadeghi-Boroujerdi 2013). The term 'political theology' was also discussed and debated in a major edited volume on Islamic thought published in 2017 (Devji and Kazmi 2017). More recently, a monograph published in 2019 also draws upon Schmitt and the lens of political theology (March 2019). The rise of polities like the Islamic State have obviously intensified focus on this paradigm (Goldberg 2018). In case of both South and West Asia, questions of empire and colonialism also form an important backdrop (Strathern 2019).

Political theology discussions in Asian languages

In tandem with the theologization of actual politics, the conceptual framework of 'political theology' is entering Asian linguistic spaces. The term has been translated into Arabic as *al-kalām al-siyāsī (Sachedina 2009)*. It has been translated in Persian as *ilāhīyāt-i siyāsī*.[1] In the Bengali language press – one of the oldest and numerically biggest in the non-Western world – articles have appeared in mainstream newspapers and journals, exploring the relation between theology (*ishvaratattva*) and the political (Banerjee 2016; 2015a), as well as on political spirituality (*rajnaitik adhyatmikata*) (Samaddar 2020). The author of the article where the latter term figures, uses it to interpret the rise of right and left populist politics across the world. He probably draws the expression from Michel Foucault's observation about 'a political spirituality' (*une spiritualité politique*) in relation to the Iranian Revolution (Foucault 1978). (For some scholars, the term 'spirituality' works better than 'political theology' in understanding the Global South; see P. Banerjee 2018.)

I have not yet detected any discussion in print using what would be a literal Bengali rendition of political theology: *rajnaitik ishvaratattva* or *rajnaitik devatattva*. However, the term *rajnaitik dharmatattva* has been used in two books: in one case, in a translation of a book by the French thinker Bernard-Henri Lévy; in another case, for a more original and elaborate discussion on West Asia and the Islamic world, which also references Agamben (Lévy 2020; Alam 2020). The use of the term *dharma*, rather than *ishvara* or *deva*, can be related to the importance of sacral-moral law in Asia, as well as to the manner in which *dharma* evades confessional specificity. Similarly, in Hindi, the term *rajnitik dharmashastra* has been used to translate Schmitt's term – in an article on American drone warfare – as well as to reference a discussion by the American political scientist Mark Lilla (Pandey 2013; cf. Lilla 2007; Winch 2017).[2] In general, more research is needed to explore discussions on political theology in multiple Asian languages. This forum may serve as an invitation towards that wider task too.

What can Asia do? Deprovincializing and subalternizing political theology

In the Schmittian genealogy, political theology has an authoritarian and elitist bent. The monotheistic European-Christian God and the monistic form of centralized state sovereignty and leadership reinforce each other in this framework. Jacques Derrida confesses about 'the unavowed political theology' of democratic sovereignty that hauntingly mirrors monarchic political theology (Derrida 2005). In a recent book authored by two anthropologists, the Schmittian vision provides a point of departure to think of world history as an incessant translation of the authority of gods and spirits into the powers of human chiefs and rulers across all continents (Graeber and Sahlins 2017).

Can a focus on Asia help subalternize political theology? After all, classic works of the Subaltern Studies collective, such as by Ranajit Guha and Gautam Bhadra, did precisely attempt that, without directly using the word 'political theology'. They demonstrated that forms of political organization constructed by peasants and other labouring classes were imbued with theological conceptions (Guha 1983; Bhadra 1994). Gayatri Chakravorty Spivak's famous question 'Can the Subaltern Speak?' resists any facile answer (1988). But the provocation retains a dialectical imperative: a call to dialogue with voices that are submerged but never wholly silenced.

Many of the works on Asia referenced earlier point to alternative ways of conceptualizing political theology: from the standpoint of the multitudes, of women, of the rural and urban poor, who, in variegated ways, claim divinity or a messianic or caliphal mantle. Recent works in anthropology, with or without using the term 'political theology', have demonstrated how subaltern claims on divinity concretely translate into horizontal political practice (Michelutti 2008; Singh 2015). In a parallel move, frameworks of cosmopolitics and political ontology – originally advanced by scholars interpreting Central and South America (Latour 2004; Blaser 2013) – have now been turned towards Asia. They have been used to analyse the counter-hegemonic politics and theologies of the 'highlanders' who inhabit the South-Southeast Asian borderlands (Wouters 2022).

From political theology to economic theology

In scholarship on Europe and North America, the field of economic theology has made its self-conscious appearance (Dean 2019; Schwarzkopf 2020). A lot more research is needed on Asian economic theologies: and especially, in line with what I have been arguing: critical economic theologies that articulate subaltern perspectives.

In our neoliberal world, capitalism produces strange bedfellows, drawing Asia into the orbit of Euro-American economic theologies. The American president Donald Trump, during a visit to India, invoked the nineteenth-century Indian reformer Vivekananda, to suggest that belief in God and the identification of divinity in everyone, facilitated commercial development in both the United States and India (ABP News 2020). This is essentially a political-economic theology of capitalism that seeks to ally neo-conservative Christian and Hindu nationalist politics. Against this 'monotheism of capital' (*punjir ekeshvaravad*) – to borrow a term deployed, in another context, by the postcolonial theorist Partha Chatterjee (2013) – we have to posit more subversive ways of visualizing the divine.

I have argued elsewhere that subaltern claims to be divine and regal are often nothing but radical claims to sovereignty that transfigure and (at least, partially) overthrow imperial and native-elite power. Subaltern political and economic theologies express forms of sociality and solidarity, as well as heterodox political economies of production and exchange, which erode structures of sovereign domination and exploitation. They sometimes imbue labour – rather than property, capital or money – with divinity and theologically articulated value. The labourer becomes the site of epiphany of the divine. He or she is recognized as the creator and foundation of value, as the real sovereign. The labouring commoner, rather than the surplus-extracting and terrorizing master, is recognized as the truly autonomous being (see Banerjee 2018a; 2015b; 2020).[3]

Subaltern political and economic theologies: Towards new worlds

Subaltern political and economic theologies should hence be recognized for what they often are in essence: manifestos for turning the world upside down. Their importance for our present world – where the logic of capitalist commodification serves as an ersatz divinity ('the invisible hand'), with relentless objectification and degradation of human and non-human multitudes – hardly needs emphasis (Banerjee and Wouters 2022). Studies on Asian political theology can serve a social function, if they continue to offer critiques of the existing order and deepen the plausibility of fundamental change: indeed, if they can draw some of the very blueprints for the spring to come.

In that sense, revisiting Carl Schmitt's *Political Theology* on the occasion of its centenary should also involve overcoming Schmitt – certainly, one of the darkest intellectual metonyms for the genocidal excesses of state and capital that Europe has unleashed on the world over the past few centuries. And this overcoming may well arise from the decolonial margins and multitudes of the planet that Schmitt's European nomos could only incompletely subjugate.

Notes

1 I am grateful to Amanda Lanzillo for help with Persian language discussions.
2 I am grateful to Philipp Sperner for drawing my attention to these two texts.
3 My dialectic here with Hegel should be transparent.

References

ABP News. (2020), 'Donald Trump Invokes Vivekananda at "Namaste Trump" Event', 24 February. Available online: news.abplive.com/videos/news/india-donald-trump-invokes-vivekananda-at-namaste-trump-event-1164706

Agamben, G. (2011), *The Kingdom and the Glory: For a Theological Genealogy of Economy and Government*, trans. L. Chiesa with M. Mandarini, Stanford, CA: Stanford University Press.

Alam, P. (2020), *Madina*, Dhaka: Adarsha.

Banerjee, M. (2015a), 'Vidushaker Nagarikatva', *Anushtup*, 50 (1): 1031–6.

Banerjee, M. (2015b), 'All This is Indeed Brahman: Rammohun Roy and a "Global" History of the Rights-Bearing Self', *Asian Review of World Histories*, 3 (1): 81–112.

Banerjee, M. (2016), 'Satya, Sakshya o Vicharer Tribhuj-Samparka', *Pratidin*, 25 June.

Banerjee, M. (2018a), *The Mortal God: Imagining the Sovereign in Colonial India*, Delhi: Cambridge University Press.

Banerjee, M. (2018b), 'Spectral Sovereigns and Divine Subalterns', *Journal of the History of Ideas Blog*, 7 November. Available online: https://jhiblog.org/2018/11/07/spectral-sovereigns-and-divine-subalterns/

Banerjee, M. (2020), 'Sovereignty as a Motor of Global Conceptual Travel: Sanskritic Equivalents of "Law" in Bengali Discursive Production', *Modern Intellectual History*, 17 (2): 487–506.

Banerjee, M. and J. Wouters (2022), *Subaltern Studies 2.0: A Manifesto for Being in the Age of the Capitalocene*, Chicago: Prickly Paradigm Press.

Banerjee, Mou (2018), 'Questions of Faith: Christianity, Conversion and the Ideological Origins of Political Theology in Colonial India, 1813–1907', PhD diss., Harvard University Press.

Banerjee, P. (2018), 'Theories from the South I: An Interview', *Borderlines*, 6 November. Available online https://www.borderlines-cssaame.org/posts/2018/11/6/theories-from-the-south-i-an-interview-with-prathama-banerjee

Bhadra, G. (1994), *Iman o Nishan: Unish Shataker Banglar Krishak Chaitanyer ek Adhyay, c. 1800–1850*, Calcutta: Subarnarekha.

Bhutto, F. (2019), 'How Turkish TV is Taking Over the World', *The Guardian*, 13 September. Available online: https://www.theguardian.com/tv-and-radio/2019/sep/13/turkish-tv-magnificent-century-dizi-taking-over-world

Blaser, M. (2013), 'Ontological Conflicts and the Stories of Peoples in Spite of Europe: Toward a Conversation on Political Ontology', *Current Anthropology*, 54 (5): 547–68.

Chatterjee, P. (2013), 'Bangali Sanskritir Vishvajanin Itihas', in Partho Chatyapadhay (ed.), *Janapratinidhi*, 68–70, Calcutta: Anushtup.

Dean, M. (2019), 'What is Economic Theology? A New Governmental-Political Paradigm', *Theory, Culture and Society*, 36 (3): 3–26.

Derrida, J. (2005), *Rogues: Two Essays on Reason*, trans. P. Brault and M. Naas, Stanford, CA: Stanford University Press.

Devji, F. and Z. Kazmi, eds (2017), *Islam after Liberalism*, Oxford: Oxford University Press.

Devji, F., P. Mukhopadhyay and S. Giri (2018), 'Special Section: Political Theology in India', *Political Theology*, 19 (8): 704–50.

Foucault, M. (1978), 'À quoi rêvent les Iraniens?', *Le Nouvel Observateur*, 727: 48–9. Available online: http://1libertaire.free.fr/MFoucault143.html; translated in https://press.uchicago.edu/Misc/Chicago/007863.html

Gilmartin, D., P. Price and A. E. Ruud, eds (2019), *South Asian Sovereignty: The Conundrum of Worldly Power*, London: Routledge.

Goldberg, O. (2018), *Faith and Politics in Iran, Israel and the Islamic State: Theologies of the Real*, Cambridge: Cambridge University Press.

Graeber, D. and M. Sahlins (2017), *On Kings*, Chicago: HAU Books.

Guha, R. (1983), *Elementary Aspects of Peasant Insurgency in Colonial India*, Delhi: Oxford University Press.

Kantorowicz, E. H. (1957), *The King's Two Bodies: A Study in Mediaeval Political Theology*, Princeton, NJ: Princeton University Press.

Kumar, A. (2015), *Radical Equality: Ambedkar, Gandhi, and the Risk of Democracy*, Stanford, CA: Stanford University Press.

Latour, B. (2004), 'Whose Cosmos, Which Cosmopolitics? Comments on the Peace Terms of Ulrich Beck', *Common Knowledge*, 10 (3): 450–62.
Lévy, B.-H. (2020), *Bangladesh Jakhan Svadhin Hachchhila*, trans. S. Bhattacharja, Dhaka: Adarsha.
Lilla, M. (2007), 'The Politics of God', *The New York Times Magazine*, 19 August. Available online: https://www.nytimes.com/2007/08/19/magazine/19Religion-t.html
March, A. F. (2019), *The Caliphate of Man: Popular Sovereignty in Modern Islamic Thought*, Cambridge, MA: Harvard University Press.
Michelutti, L. (2008), *The Vernacularisation of Democracy: Politics, Caste and Religion in India*, Delhi: Routledge.
Pandey, M. (2013), *Alochana Mein Sahamati-Asahamati*, Delhi: Vani Prakashan.
Patrick, G. (2020), *Public Theology: Indian Concerns, Perspectives, and Themes*, Minneapolis: Fortress Press.
Sachedina, A. (2009), *Islam and the Challenge of Human Rights*, New York: Oxford University Press.
Sadeghi-Boroujerdi, E. (2013), 'Disenchanting Political Theology in Post-revolutionary Iran: Reform, Religious Intellectualism and the Death of Utopia', PhD diss, Oxford University.
Samaddar, R. (2020), 'Hayto E Ek Antarbarti Adhyay', *Anandabazar Patrika*, 2 January. Available online: https://www.anandabazar.com/editorial/populism-and-the-rise-of-neo-right-wing-politics-has-become-a-new-challenge-to-the-leftists-1.1089824
Schmitt, C. (1985), *Political Theology: Four Chapters on the Concept of Sovereignty*, trans. George Schwab, Cambridge, MA: MIT Press.
Schwarzkopf, S., ed. (2020), *The Routledge Handbook of Economic Theology*, Abingdon: Routledge.
Simmons, C. (2020), *Devotional Sovereignty: Kingship and Religion in India*, New York: Oxford University Press.
Singh, B. (2015), *Poverty and the Quest for Life: Spiritual and Material Striving in Rural India*, Chicago: Chicago University Press.
Spivak, G. C. (1988), 'Can the Subaltern Speak?', in C. Nelson and L. Grossberg (eds), *Marxism and the Interpretation of Culture*, 271–313, Basingstoke: Macmillan Education.
Strathern, A. (2019), *Unearthly Powers: Religious and Political Change in World History*, Cambridge: Cambridge University Press.
Winch, T. (2017), 'The Political Theology of US Drone Warfare', *Counterpunch*, 22 June. Available online: https://www.counterpunch.org/2017/06/22/the-political-theology-of-us-drone-warfare/
Wouters, J. J. P., ed. (2022), *Exploring Vernacular Politics in Northeast India: Democracy, Ethnicity and Indigeneity*, Delhi: Oxford University Press.

INDEX

Abrahamic religions 38–9, 88, 166–7, 180
absolute power
   conditional use of 178
   of God 175–7
   of monarch 167
   of state 45–6
acclamations 7, 17–18, 35–6, 42, 72 n.16
   confessions and 23–5
   as ritual of truth 63–4, 68–71
   as social institution 21
Adam, A. 72 n.15
Adam Kadmon ('great man') 81
affirmative biopolitics 79
Agamben, G.
   on analogy 19
   on Benjamin's influences on Schmitt 77, 89 n.4
   critique of economic theology 15, 18
   on exception 114
   in Indian political thought 186
   'logic of sovereignty' 115–18
alèthurgie 23–4, 63, 70–1
allegorical existence 140, 147–50
alternative governmentalities 167–8
anarchism
   Bakunin's 47–8, 78–80, 90 n.12
   Russian anarchism 141
   social anarchism 77–8
anti-confessional conduct 99–102
'Antigonish' (Mearns) 139, 151
anti-racist politics, confession in 6, 21–4
anti-Roman affect 102
anti-Semitism 3–4
Aquinas, T. 175–6
Arabic, *al-kalām al-siyāsī* 187
Arabic Aristotelianism 82, 87
arbitrary power 171–2
Arendt, H. 1
Aroney, N. 71 n.3
Asad, T. 164

Asian political theology 159–60, 185–9
Asian religions 163–6
assertory oath 71 n.2
Assmann, J.
   critique of political monotheism 31, 38–42
   on political theology 6, 13–15, 17
atheism
   in Christianity 80–3, 87
   democracy and 77–80, 88
   political 7, 46, 52–5
Atheism in Christianity (Bloch) 80–3
Augustine, St. 83, 172, 173
auratic representation, violent tendencies of 37–42
Ausnahmezustand. *See* exception
Austin, J. 71 n.2
authoritarian democracy 36–7
authoritarianism 45–6
authority
   anarchist opposition to 47–8
   of Church 33–5
   of God 38–41
   revelation and 173
   of sovereign 116
   of state 35–7, 51–2, 71 n.3, 162
autocracy, and acclamations 68–70
Averroes 82
Avicenna 82

Bakunin, M.
   anarchism of 78–80, 90 n.12
   appropriation from 6, 14–15, 46–8, 89 n.5
   critique of religion 15, 46–7, 53–5
   Schmitt's characterization of 56 n.7
Balibar, É. 4
Balke, F. 113
baroque art 148
Bauer, B. 119
Bellah, R. 25–6, 95, 96, 105

Bengali language, *rajnaitik ishvaratattva*
    or *rajnaitik devatattva* 187
Benito Cereno (Melville) 3–4
Benjamin, W.
    on allegorical existence 140, 147–50
    on exception 117–18
    influences of 77, 89 n.4
    as 'Left' thinker 15
Benveniste, E. 64, 71 nn.4–5
Bhadra, G. 188
Bloch, E., on atheism and
    messianism 77, 80–4, 86–9
Blumenberg, H. 2, 18, 137 n.5
Bodin, J. 51–2, 56 n.12
Bolshevism 66, 68
Boniface VIII, Pope 52
Borborites 100, 102
bourgeois society 132–3
Buddhism 166
    monasticism in 167–8

Cambodia 168
*The Cambridge Companion to Christian
    Political Theology* 158–9
capitalism 188
Carpocrates/Carpocratians 100, 102
Catholic Church/Catholicism. *See also*
    Christianity
    acclamations 18
    as charismatic organization 69,
        73 n.19
    internal strife and persecution
        in 37–8, 40
    popular unity through symbolic
        rituals 34–6, 39
    and Protestantism conflicts 144–5
    representation in 33–5, 41,
        66–7
    unity in the body of Christ 31
charisma 20, 25–6, 69, 73 n.19
charismatic sects 100
Chen, D. 162
China
    political theology in 159
    religion in 164–6
    'Schmitt fever' in 157–8, 160–3
Christian historicity 129–32
Christianity
    atheism and 80–3, 87

confessional practices in 22, 70
Kingdom of God 91 n.24
pastorate 167–8
political theology's focus on 163–4
secular in 18–19
church. *See also* Catholic Church/
    Catholicism
    religious idea of 99–100
    as sacred site 98
    and sect distinction 24–5, 34–5,
        37–8
    social and political forms of 20–1
    'visibility' of 82–5
civil religion
    LGBTQ+ as 95–9, 105–6
    in US 25–6
climate change 112
collective effervescence 98
collective knowledge 145–7, 149
collective memorialization 97–9
collective power 53–4, 140
colonialism 167–8
commemorative marches 97–8
commonwealth 172, 174
comparative political theology 163–8
complexio oppositorum 34–5, 40
conceptual political theology 16–17,
    19–21
confession 73 n.20
    anti-confessional conduct 99–102
    anti-racist politics and 6, 21–4
    as ritual of veridiction 70–1
Confucianism 164–6
constitution 65
*A Contribution to the Critique of Hegel's
    Philosophy of Right* (Marx) 14
Covid-19 crisis 117, 157
creation 81–2
crisis 111
    in Catholic Church history 38
    Koselleck's conception of 7, 118–21
    Marxist understanding of 123 n.14
    Roitman's conception of 118
    sovereignty and 7, 111–13, 121–2
crisis sovereignty 113–18, 121–2
critique 119
Critique and Crisis (Koselleck) 118–19
Cultural Revolution (China) 162–3
culture wars 80

Dalit theology 160, 186
Damian, P. 175
death 87–8
decision 1, 51, 56 n.9, 78–80, 94, 130, 161, 166, 174
    crisis as 116, 118–21
democracy 7, 30
    acclamations and 68–9, 72 n.16
    atheism and 77–80
    authoritarian democracy 36–7
    legitimacy of 76–80, 88–9
    messianism and 77, 85–8
Deng Xiaoping 163
Derrida, J.
    democracy and messianism in 77, 85–9
    on intelligible matter 82
    on political theology 187
dharma 186, 187
Dialogue on New Space 134–5
DiAngelo, R. 23
dictatorship 90 n.10, 161
    antithesis between anarchism and 79, 90 n.12
    legitimacy of 78–9
    sovereign dictatorship 89 n.6
Diodorius, S. 14
direct representation, and acclamations 68–70
divine freedom 175–6
divine-human analogy 171–2, 174
divine omnipotence 174, 177, 181
divine power, nature and extent of 175–7
divine promise 178–9
divine revelation 85–7, 173
divine right 51, 56 n.10, 172
Donoso Cortés, J. 4, 48, 79, 90 n.10, 119
dualism 133–4
Durkheim, É. 96, 98
Dyke March 105

East/West binary 134
economic theology 15, 18, 20, 94–5
    Asian 188–9
    subaltern 189
Elizabeth I, Queen of England 144–5
end-of-history 125–6, 128–9, 135–6
England
    'British values' 103
    impotence of sovereignty in 143–7
    'island England' 133–4
epistemic anarchism 56 n.14
eternal life-force 82–3, 86–8, 91 n.30
ethical community 84
Euripides 13–14
Eurocentric biases 157–9, 167–8
European modernity
    historical-philosophical analysis of 139–43
    myth of 146
exagoreusis 22
exception (*Ausnahmezustand*) 94, 114–18, 166, 171–2
    international relations and 174–8, 180–2
exomologesis 22–4

Faderman, L. 97
faith
    Derrida's conception of 85–8
    history and 172–5, 179–80
    in a transcendent divine being 96
faithfulness 64–5
fanatic zeal 37–41
Fascism 18, 56 n.6, 66, 68, 162
Fauconnett, P. 21
Ficino, Marsilio 14
fidelity, faith as 85–6
Floyd, George 22
formulaic phrases 36
Foucault, M.
    on *alèthurgie* 23–4, 63, 70–1
    on confession 22–4, 73 n.20
    on Gnostic sects 102
    on governmentality 167–8
    on Iranian Revolution 14
    on political spirituality 187
    on truth-telling 73 n.21
freedom, rebellious 149–51
French colonialism 167–8
friend/enemy distinction 38, 40, 79–80, 126, 142, 161–2, 166, 167
Fukuyama, F. 114, 135

Gentile, G. 56 n.6
Germany 162
Giles of Rome 176
Gnostic sects 95, 100–2

God. *See also headings beginning* divine ...
  absence in oath-taking 7
  absolute authority of 38–41
  continuous sinning against 148
  existence of 84
  as illusory projection 54
  oaths and 64
  theistic and deistic conceptions
    of 56 n.9
  transcendent and omnipotent 50–2
The Gordian Knot (Jünger) 132
governmentality 167–8
great spaces (*Großräume*) 127–9, 135–6
Grotius, H. 177
Guha, R. 188
Guizot, F. 66

Habermas, J.
  critique of Schmitt 4
  democracy and messianism in 77,
    80–1, 87–8
  idea of invisible church 83–5
Hägglund, M. 83, 85, 89 n.3
Hamlet (Shakespeare) 7, 143–4
  impotent sovereign figure in 145–7
  Lacan's interpretation of knowledge
    in 140, 149–50
  plot structure and historical
    conditions 144–5
Hegel, G. W. F. 126, 127, 132–3
Heidegger, M. 123 n.8
Herrero, M. 18–19
Hindu nationalism 186
historical conditions 144–5, 185–6
historical materialism, and
    messianism 77
historicism 7, 178–9
history
  Christian conception of 129–30
  critique of one-sidedness in 16–17
  faith and 172–5, 179–80
  role in post-war political theology 7,
    125–6
History of Sexuality (Foucault) 102
Hitler, Adolf 72 n.11
Hobbes, T. 51–2, 72 n.8, 116, 127, 141,
    172, 174, 177
homeland theology 160
(social) homogeneity 30–2, 36, 66, 68

homology 19
Hong Kong protests 162
Hostiensis 176
Hudson, John Paul 98
'humanity' 141–2
human reason 141

idealism 47–8
Identitarian movement 104
immanence, and democracy 7, 76–80,
    88–9
immanent aggression 7, 95
immanent gods 140–3, 146
imperial politics 166–7
impotence and omnipotence of
    sovereign 112–13, 118, 122,
    143–7
Indian political thought 159–60, 166,
    185, 186
Industrial Revolution 133–4
institutional political theology 20–1,
    24–6
insurrectionary movements 38
intelligible matter (*khora*) 82, 86–7
international relations
  exception and 174–7
  uncertainty in 8, 171, 178–82
invisible church 82–5
Iranian political thought 186–7
Iranian Revolution 14, 186, 187
Islam 166
Ismāʿīl, Shāh Muḥammad 166
Israel 177–8

James VI and I, King of Scotland and
    England 144–5, 178
Jerome 175
Jesus
  as anti-colonial 159–60
  'Son of Man' and 'Son of God' 81–2,
    91 n.30
Jones, Cleve 98
'Judaism in Jurisprudence' conference 3
Jünger, E. 132
juramentum assertorium 63
juramentum promissorium 63
Justice in Policing bill (US) 21–2

Kang, Y. 165

Kant, I., doctrine of invisible church 82–5
Kantorowicz, E. 17–18, 21, 34, 69, 186
katechon 132, 135, 136
Kelsen, H. 56 n.14, 77, 78, 89 n.4, 114
knowledge, in Shakespeare's *Hamlet* 140, 149–50
Koekkoek, R. 90 n.7
Kojève, A. 125–7, 134–6
Korea 160
Koselleck, R., conception of crisis 7, 113, 116, 118–21, 123 nn.14–15
Krabbe, H. 114

Lacan, J. 139, 149–50
Lactantius 49
Ladwig, P. 167–8
land/sea binary 133–4
Laos 167–8
Lasalle, F. 65
law and legislation 32
legalism 72 n.11
legal positivism 65, 114
Lévy, B.-H. 187
LGBTQ+
    anti-confessional conduct of 101–2
    anti-Roman affect 102
    as civil religion 95–9, 105–6
    sectarian-Gnostic character of 104–5
liberal economism 65
liberalism 166
    anti-elitist diagnosis of 31–3
    Catholic representation and 34
    in China 162
    critique of 1, 125, 161
Lilla, M. 173, 187
liturgical acclamations 23
Liturgical Movement 18
liturgical unity 33–7
Liu, X. 161–2
Löwith, K. 130–2, 135, 137 nn.4–5

Mann, G. 112
Manṣab-i Imāmat (Station of Leadership) (Ismāʿīl) 166
Mao Zedong 162, 163
Maritain, J. 178
Markus, R. A. 18
Marx, K., 'opium of the people' 14
Mary, Queen of Scots 144–5

mass democracy 32, 66, 68–70
materialism 46–7, 53–5, 56 n.15
    messianic hope and 86–7
matter
    conception of 82–3
    khora 82, 86–7
Mauss, M. 21
May Fourth Movement (Beijing) 159
Mazzini, G. 47–8, 56 n.6
Meaning in History (Löwith) 130–2, 135
medical fascism 25
Mehring, R. 3
Meier, H. 89 n.5
Melandri, E. 19
Melville, H. 3–4
memory 65
messianism 7, 84–5, 88–9
    atheism and 77, 80–1
    public reason and 84–8
methodological atheism 77, 80
Millenarianism 38
minjung theology 160
minorities 32–3
miracles 177
misarchy 101
modernity 16–19
    colonialism and 168
    as crisis time 7, 113, 116–18, 121
    immanent framework of 76–7
modern state 152 n.3
    authority of 71 n.3
    profane reconceptualization of 6, 45–6, 54–5
    rituals of truth in 69–71
Modi, Narendra 37, 185, 186
monarchy
    absolute power of 167, 176–7
    authority of 51–2
    divine and human rulers analogy 171–2
    divine right 51, 56 n.10, 172
    impotence of 145–7
    monarchs as sovereigns 56 n.12
monasticism 167–8
monotheism 68, 88
    violence and 31, 38–42
Monroe doctrine 128
morality 83–4
Morgenthau, H. 179–80

Moses (Biblical figure) 14
Müller, J.-W. 37
Muslim political theology 166
myth
    historical reality and 145–7
    play and 139–40, 144–7

NAMES Project AIDS Memorial
    Quilt 98–9
natura naturans 82, 87, 90 n.6
Nazism 3–4, 42 n.1, 142, 161, 173
Newman, S. 158

oath 7, 23, 63–5, 70–1
    of alliance 72 n.6
    difference between confession
        and 71
    of office and allegiance 71 n.3
    types of 71 n.2
Öffentlichkeit. *See* public discussion
Old Testament 81
oracles 63
ordained power 176
original sin 31, 79
orthodoxy 40
Osirak nuclear reactor (Iraq), air strike
    on 177–8
Outlines of Church History (Sohm) 20

Paeschke, H. 130
parliamentarism 65–7
parrhesia 71
patristic theology 2
the people 141
performativity 146–7
permanent crisis 116
Persian, *ilāhīyāt-i siyāsī* 187
Peterson, E. 2, 20–1, 35, 47, 68, 69,
    72 n.14
Philippines 160
Philips, E. 158
Philo 85–6, 88
philosophical faith 86
Pius XI, Pope 18
Pius XII, Pope 18
playing society 139–40, 142–3, 148–50
plebiscitary democracy 36–7, 41
poison in the ear 149, 151
political atheism 7, 46, 52–5

political legitimacy, China 161–3
political liturgies 35–7, 41–2
political metaphysics 113–14
political monism 129–30
political mythology 139–40, 147–51
political power 175–7
political spirituality 187
political theology
    as academic category 1–3, 8–9
    in analytical terms 1, 15–21, 27, 94
    in Asian linguistic spaces 187
    in Asian studies 185–7
    comparative 163–8
    conception of 14–15
    development of 8, 158–9
    origins of 6, 14–15, 46–8
    relevance of 5–7, 13, 111, 121–2
    repurposed 125–6
    subalternizing 187–9
    transnational and multicultural
        origins and genealogies
        of 157–60
Political Theology: A Critical Introduction
    (Newman) 158
*Political Theology: A Guide for the
    Perplexed* (Philips) 158
'Political Theology of Mazzini'
    (Bakunin) 14, 47–8
politics
    as confession 21–4
    de-confessionalization/
        de-theologization of 17, 26
    end of 127–9, 135–6
    forms of 166–7
    relations between theology and 1–2,
        16–21, 49
politics of difference 79–80
Polybius 14
popular unity 30–4, 79. *See also* world
    unity
    Catholic Church and 34–5
    state liturgies and 35–7, 41–2
populism 6, 37–42
    notion of 30
positive anthropology 79
postcolonial theology 7–8, 157–8, 163–8
post-secularism 7, 76, 89 n.1
poverty, in bourgeois society 132–3
Powell, E. 103

power
  exercise of 167–8, 171–2, 177–80
  kinds of 175–7
present absence 139–40, 151
Pride Parades 96–7, 99
Prodi, P. 64
profane 6, 45–6, 54–5, 96
progress 179
progressive and reactionary political movements, sect-like behaviour of 24–5
pro-Life movement 103–4
promise, human *vs.* divine 178–9
promissory oath 71 n.2
proportional representation 67
The Protestant Ethic and the Spirit of Capitalism (Weber) 20
Protestantism 69
  and Catholicism conflicts 144–5
  emergence of 38
Protestant sects 34–5, 100
Proudhon, P.-J. 14, 15, 78–80
public confession 6, 21–4
public discussion 7, 32, 63–7, 70–1
public good 177–8
public liturgies 34–6, 39, 41–2
public reason, messianicity of 84–8

QAnon movement 104, 105
Querdenker protest movement 25

redemption 81–2
  through sin 100, 102
Reinach, A. 65, 72 n.9
religion
  critique of 13–15
  etymology of 49
  materialist critique of 46–7, 53–5
  notion of 96
  as 'opium of the people' 14
  religion of technicity 129–30
religion/secular distinction 164–6
religious and monastic governmentality 167–8
religious conflict 144–5
representation 33–5, 41, 83
  acclamation and 68–9
  public discussion and 66–7
  transcendence and 90 n.7

restraint 178–81
resurrection 82
reverse acclamation 23
right-wing populism 30
  violent potential of 6, 31
Roitman, J. 118, 120–1
Roth, G. 73 n.19
Rousseau, J.-J. 65, 72 n.8
Runciman, D. 121

Sabbatian sects 95, 100, 102
the sacred 96
  LGBTQ+ and 97–8
Said, E. 164
salvational politics 166–7
Salvini, Matteo 37
Saralegui, M. 90 n.7
Schmitt, C.
  critique of 4, 162, 173
  influences of 118–19
  legacy of 8
  Nazi membership 3–4, 42 n.1, 173
  reception in China 157–8, 160–3
  renewed interest in 5, 161, 185–6
Schmitt, C., works of
  'Appropriation/Distribution/Production' ['Nehmen/Teilen/Weiden'] 126–7
  Constitutional Theory 64, 65, 68, 78, 90 n.7
  The Crisis of Parliamentary Democracy 65–6, 78
  Hamlet or Hecuba 7, 143–7
  'The Historical Structure of the Contemporary World- Opposition between East and West' 132–3
  Legality and Legitimacy 78
  Nomos of the Earth 7, 17, 125, 133–4
  Political Theology (1922) 1–2, 4–6, 16, 21, 45–7, 56 n.3, 95
  Political Theology II (1970) 2, 142
  Roman Catholicism and Political Form (*Römischer Katholizismus und Politische Form*) 20, 21, 33, 47, 66, 83
  'The Tyranny of Values' 7, 95, 102–6

Volksentscheid und Volksbegehren. Ein Beitrag zur Auslegung der Weimarer Verfassung und zur Lehre von der unmittelbaren Demokratie (Schmitt)   68
Scotus, J. D.   176
sect(s)
   and church distinction   24–5, 34–5, 37–41, 99–100
   types of   100
secularism   172–3
   democracy and   76
   in postcolonial politics   164–6
secularization   16–19, 26, 46, 49–51, 56 n.11, 102, 141
   oaths and   70
self-empowerment   18
self-transformation   24–7, 102
sexuality   99–102
Singh, D.   19
signature   19
Sino-Christian theology   161
Sloterdijk, P.   6, 39
Smend, R.   161
social and economic theology   94–5
social institutions   21
sociology   16, 18
   of the sacred   96
   of sovereignty   53
Sohm, R.   69, 73 n.19
Son of God   81–2, 91 n.30
Son of Man   81–2, 91 n.30
sovereign dictatorship   89 n.6
sovereignty   45–6, 94, 143–7, 152 n.3, 161
   authority of   31–3
   classical liberal view of   166
   crisis and   7, 111–13, 118–21
   illusory projection of   54–5
   impotence of   112–13, 118, 122, 143–7
   Kelsen's notion of   56 n.14
   legitimacy of dictatorship and   78–9
   liminal concept of   114–15
   monarch as 'sovereign'   56 n.12
   origin and development of the concept of   51–2, 174
   secularized theological concept   50–1
   theological origin and structure of   45–6
space   127–9, 135–6
   of land and sea   133–4
Spinoza, B.   82, 90 nn.6-7
Spivak, G.   164, 188
Spurr, J.   71 n.3
state
   absolute power of   45–6
   emergence of modern state   16, 17
   obsolescence of   127–9, 136
   public expressions of allegiance to   36–7
   Roman state   55 n.2
   strong state   31–3
Statists   162
Stonewall Inn (New York), as sacred site   97–8
structural analogy   16–17, 19
subaltern   187–9

Taiwan   160
Taylor, C.   76
temporality of crisis   7, 121
testimonies   63
Thailand   167
Thatamanil, J.   163–4
theology and politics   1–2, 16–21, 49
theology of struggle   160
Third World   135
Thomas, M. M.   159–60
Toynbee, A.   133
tragedy, and historical reality   145–7
transcendence
   immanent ground of   82–3
   political legitimacy and   161–2
   religious conception of   49
   'religious' transcendence   76
   representation and   90 n.7
   structure of transcendence   49–52
   structure of transcendence, rejection of   53–4
transpositive model   16–17
Troeltsch, E.   34–5, 38, 99–100
Trump, Donald   25, 27, 37, 41, 157, 188
truthfulness   64–5
   courage for   71, 73 n.21
truth liturgies

in modern state   69–71
    types of   63–9
Turkey   185

uncertainty in international relations   8, 171, 178–82
United States Capitol Riots (2021)   4, 25, 104, 106
Universal human rights   179
Ursprung des Deutschen Trauerspiels (Benjamin)   147–50

value-orientation   102–7
Values Voter   104
veridiction   70–1
violence
    dissemination of   6, 38–42
    the sacred and   97–8
Vogl, J.   112

Wainwright, J.   112
Weber, M.
    account of modernity   16–17
    church and sect distinguished   24–5, 34–5
    interpretation of charisma   69, 73 n.19
    on types of sects   100
Western values   102–3
Wiley Blackwell Companion to Political Theology   158–9
Wilson, Woodrow   128
world religions   163
world unity   126–30, 134. *See also* popular unity
Wu, Y.   159

Xi, J.   162
Xu, D.   161

www.ingramcontent.com/pod-product-compliance
Lightning Source LLC
Chambersburg PA
CBHW061829300426
44115CB00013B/2311